WAY

325 NEW HOME PLANS FOR 2004

Today's Top Design Trends

HOME PLANNERS

325
NEW HOME PLANS
FOR 2004

Published by Home Planners, LLC
Wholly owned by Hanley-Wood, LLC
3275 W. Ina Road, Suite 220
Tucson, Arizona 85741

Distribution Center
29333 Lorie Lane
Wixom, Michigan 48393

President, Jayne Fenton
Vice President, Publishing, Jennifer Pearce
Vice President, General Manager, Marc Wheeler
Executive Editor, Linda Bellamy
Managing Editor, Jason D. Vaughan
Special Projects Editor, Kristin Schneidler
Associate Editors, Nate Ewell, Kathryn R. Sears
Lead Plans Associate, Morenci C. Clark
Plans Associates, Jill M. Hall, Elizabeth Landry, Nick Nieskes
Proofreaders, Douglas Jenness, Sarah Lyons
Technical Specialist, Jay C. Walsh
Lead Data Coordinator, Fran Altemose
Data Coordinators, Misty Boler, Melissa Siewert
Production Director, Sara Lisa
Production Manager, Brenda McClary

Big Designs, Inc.
President, Creative Director, Anthony D'Elia
Vice President, Business Manager, Megan D'Elia
Vice President, Design Director, Chris Bonavita
Editorial Director, John Roach
Assistant Editor, Tricia Starkey
Director of Design and Production, Stephen Reinfurt
Group Art Director, Kevin Limongelli
Photo Editor, Christine DiVuolo
Art Director, Jessica Hagenbuch
Graphic Designer, Mary Ellen Mulshine
Graphic Designer, Lindsey O'Neill-Myers
Graphic Designer, Jacque Young
Assistant Photo Editor, Mark Storch
Project Director, David Barbella
Assistant Production Manager, Rich Fuentes

Photo Credits

Front Cover: Design HPT900006 by Alan Mascord Design Associates Inc., for details see page 10.
Photo by Dan Tyrpak.

Back Cover: Design HPT900007 by Design Basics Inc., for details see page 11.
Photo by Design Basics.

10 9 8 7 6 5 4 3 2 1

Printed in the United States of America

Library of Congress Control Number: 2002115918

ISBN: 1-931131-16-3

5

11

10

325 NEW HOME PLANS FOR 2004

HOME PLANS

5	NEW DESIGN SHOWCASE
17	SUMMER HOMES & COTTAGES
57	RUSTIC GETAWAYS & RETREATS
77	FARMHOUSES & RANCHES
117	URBAN DESIGNS & TRADITIONALS
151	COLONIALS & HISTORICAL HOUSES
179	ENGLISH & PROVENCAL MANORS
219	MEDITERRANEAN & SPANISH STYLES

HOW TO ORDER

253	EVERYTHING YOU NEED TO ORDER YOUR DREAM HOME

ON THE COVER:
Design HPT900006 on page 10 features a spacious Craftsman-style home. Enjoy the rustic feel of this four-bedroom retreat, which includes modern amenities like a media room, lavish master suite, game room, wet bar, and even a wine cellar.

SEE DESIGN HPT900010 ON PAGE 13.

PHOTO BY: STEVE DIGGS

WELCOME HOME

Today's hottest designs have been compiled into this one collection, offering you 325 exciting new home plan options ranging in size from 840 to 6,000 square feet. All the plans have been created by some of America's most talented and trusted designers. And we've selected their very best designs to provide inspiration as you begin the home building journey.

To make finding your ideal plan easier, we've divided the book into eight sections. The New Design Showcase is a four-color section highlighting several of the best new plans available today, ranging in both style and size. Summer Homes & Cottages features a mix of seaside bungalows and larger cottage-style homes. Meanwhile, Rustic Getaways & Retreats incorporates mostly Craftsman-style home plans, but it includes country cottages, traditional, and contemporary plans, too. And Farmhouses & Ranches presents the latest designs of these more typical American homes—perfect for any region.

Interested in the city life? Then Urban Designs & Traditionals should be your starting point. Colonials & Historical Houses combines the classic look of the past with the comforts of the 21st century. English & Provencal Manors also lends new twists to Old World style, providing homeowners with the best of both worlds. And finally, Mediterranean & Spanish Styles highlights residences ideal for warmer climates.

Once you find a plan you like and are ready to order, see the user-friendly instructions on page 244; this section offers helpful tips, a price schedule, and more. After choosing your ideal home plan, consider a deck or landscape set, which will undoubtedly complement your new home. See page 253 or call toll-free 1-800-521-6797 to order today.

FOR MORE DETAILED INFORMATION, PLEASE CHECK THE FLOOR PLANS CAREFULLY.

plan # HPT900001

- **STYLE:** TRADITIONAL
- **FIRST FLOOR:** 4,208 SQ. FT.
- **SECOND FLOOR:** 1,352 SQ. FT.
- **TOTAL:** 5,560 SQ. FT.
- **BEDROOMS:** 4
- **BATHROOMS:** 4½ + ½
- **WIDTH:** 94'-0"
- **DEPTH:** 68'-0"
- **FOUNDATION:** CRAWLSPACE, SLAB

SEARCH ONLINE @ EPLANS.COM

Two-story pilasters create a sense of the Old South on the facade of this modern update of the classic Adam style. The foyer opens through an archway, announcing the breathtaking circular staircase. The formal dining room is situated on the right while the private library is found to the left. The grand family room is crowned with a sloped ceiling. The angled, galley kitchen adjoins the breakfast nook while the butler is pantry facilitates service to the dining room. The master suite finds privacy on the left with an elegant sitting area defined with pillars. Two bedroom suites, each with a walk-in closet, share the second floor with the game room.

FIRST FLOOR

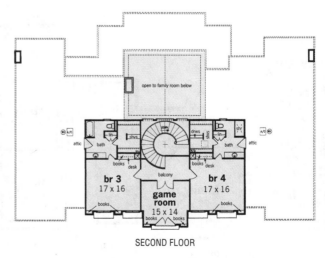

SECOND FLOOR

PHOTO BY SHANNON SHERIDAN

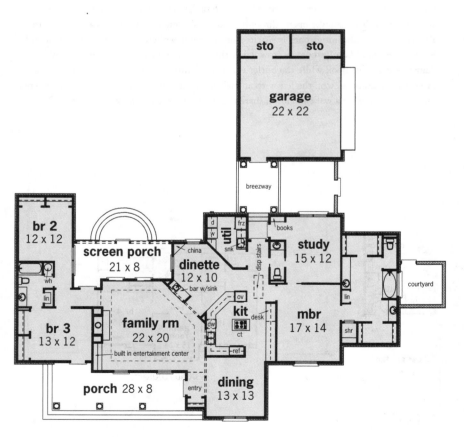

plan # HPT900002

- **STYLE: FRENCH COUNTRY**
- **SQUARE FOOTAGE: 2,503**
- **BEDROOMS: 3**
- **BATHROOMS: 2½**
- **WIDTH: 81'-0"**
- **DEPTH: 84'-0"**
- **FOUNDATION: SLAB**

SEARCH ONLINE @ EPLANS.COM

Pillars, a covered porch and plenty of window views lend a classic feel to this lovely country cottage. Inside, the entry room has a roomy closet and an interior entry door to eliminate drafts. The light-filled L-shaped kitchen lies conveniently near the entrance. A large room adjacent to the kitchen serves as a dining, living and viewing area. A fireplace adds warmth to the entire living space. A master suite boasts a walk-in closet and full bath. On the second floor, a second bedroom and full bath provide privacy to guests or family.

FOR MORE DETAILED INFORMATION, PLEASE CHECK THE FLOOR PLANS CAREFULLY.

plan # HPT900003

- STYLE: TRADITIONAL
- FIRST FLOOR: 2,709 SQ. FT.
- SECOND FLOOR: 788 SQ. FT.
- TOTAL: 3,497 SQ. FT.
- BONUS SPACE: 383 SQ. FT.
- BEDROOMS: 4
- BATHROOMS: 3
- WIDTH: 82'-10"
- DEPTH: 52'-5"
- FOUNDATION: CRAWLSPACE, SLAB

SEARCH ONLINE @ EPLANS.COM

Arched windows and a stucco and brick facade present historic grace that is rarely seen in new homes today. Inside, the entry yields to a study with French doors, and a two-story dining room with high rounded windows. The family room is stunning, with a soaring ceiling and two-story windows. A warming fireplace is inviting, and built-in cabinetry adds convenience and style. The gourmet island kitchen easily serves the breakfast nook and dining room. The master suite enjoys privacy and quiet, with no rooms directly above and a romantic bath with a corner whirlpool tub. A second first-floor bedroom makes a great guest room. Two upstairs bedrooms share a balcony overlook to the family area below, and access a future game room.

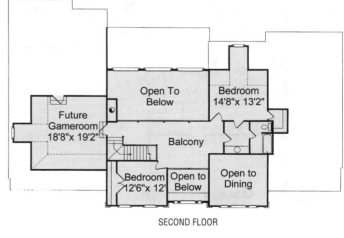

SECOND FLOOR

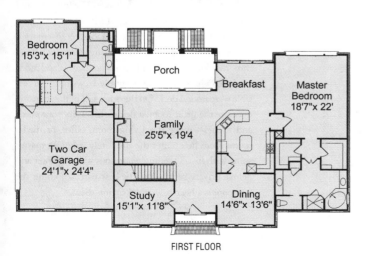

FIRST FLOOR

PHOTO BY: DESIGN BASICS, INC.

plan # HPT900004

- **STYLE:** TRADITIONAL
- **SQUARE FOOTAGE:** 2,114
- **BEDROOMS:** 1
- **BATHROOMS:** 1½
- **WIDTH:** 70'-0"
- **DEPTH:** 69'-4"

SEARCH ONLINE @ EPLANS.COM

As you can see from the facade, this plan is all about angles. Hipped rooflines and quoins bring historic good looks to the up-to-date layout inside. The front covered porch leads to a gallery foyer, which opens through a door to the great room. This spacious room enjoys a corner fireplace and access to the eating area, which flows into the kitchen. The kitchen's angled island adds intrigue, while its windows supply views of the accessible wraparound deck. On the other side of the staircase, opposite the great room, a flex room awaits your needs and wishes—make it a living room, office, or media room. From here, enter the absolutely stunning master suite, with its tray ceiling, enormous walk-in closet and deluxe private bath. And the best part: adjoining the bedroom is a hearth-warmed sitting room.

plan# HPT900005

- STYLE: CRAFTSMAN
- MAIN LEVEL: 2,602 SQ. FT.
- LOWER LEVEL: 2,440 SQ. FT.
- TOTAL: 5,042 SQ. FT.
- BEDROOMS: 4
- BATHROOMS: 4½ + ½
- WIDTH: 88'-0"
- DEPTH: 50'-0"
- FOUNDATION: BASEMENT

SEARCH ONLINE @ EPLANS.COM

This rustic Craftsman home combines an earthy stone and siding facade with a luxurious floor plan for a wonderful home that will please everyone. The great room greets family and friends with a stone hearth and French doors to the rear deck. With an enormous walk-in pantry and a butler's pantry with a wine niche off the dining room, the vaulted kitchen is ready for entertaining. In the master bedroom, a vaulted ceiling and French doors add simple elegance; the bath pampers with a spa tub and block-glass encased shower. Downstairs—or take the elevator—the games room is the center of attention with a wine cellar, wet bar, fireplace and media center. Three bedroom suites complete this level.

MAIN LEVEL

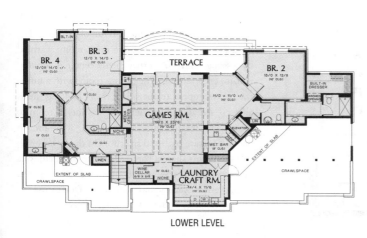

LOWER LEVEL

MAIN LEVEL

LOWER LEVEL

plan# HPT900006

- **STYLE: CRAFTSMAN**
- **MAIN LEVEL: 2,172 SQ. FT.**
- **LOWER LEVEL: 1,813 SQ. FT.**
- **TOTAL: 3,985 SQ. FT.**
- **BEDROOMS: 4**
- **BATHROOMS: 3½**
- **WIDTH: 75'-0"**
- **DEPTH: 49'-0"**
- **FOUNDATION: BASEMENT**

SEARCH ONLINE @ EPLANS.COM

With the Craftsman stylings of a mountain lodge, this rustic four-bedroom home is full of surprises. The foyer opens to the right to the great room, warmed by a stone hearth. A corner media center is convenient for entertaining. The dining room, with a furniture alcove, opens to the side terrace, inviting meals alfresco. An angled kitchen provides lots of room to move. The master suite is expansive, with French doors, a private bath and spa tub. On the lower level, two bedrooms share a bath, while the third enjoys a private suite. The games room includes a fireplace, media center, wet bar and wine cellar. Don't miss the storage capacity and work area in the garage.

plan# HPT900007

- **STYLE:** TRADITIONAL
- **FIRST FLOOR:** 1,004 SQ. FT.
- **SECOND FLOOR:** 843 SQ. FT.
- **TOTAL:** 1,847 SQ. FT.
- **BEDROOMS:** 3
- **BATHROOMS:** 2½
- **WIDTH:** 44'-4"
- **DEPTH:** 57'-8"

SEARCH ONLINE @ EPLANS.COM

This home recreates the traditional floor plan into a fresh arrangement of living space. The entry foyer leads to a flex room—make it a study, a living room, or whatever you wish—that shares a see-through fireplace with the eating area. This area accesses the side property and flows right into the island kitchen, complete with a recycling center and a door to the three-season porch in back. Tucked behind the staircase is a spacious gathering room, which you can make formal or casual. A powder room and utility area join forces for convenience while the double garage features a hobby area. The second floor is home to two family bedrooms that share a full bath and a tray-ceilinged master suite with its own roomy private bath. Storage options abound with unfinished space on the second floor and an attic above.

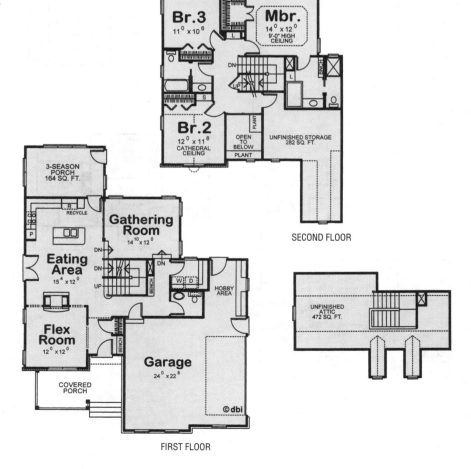

SECOND FLOOR

FIRST FLOOR

PHOTO COURTESY OF: ISLANDS OF BEAFORT, BEAFORT, SC

SECOND FLOOR

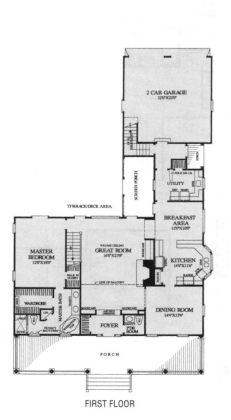

FIRST FLOOR

plan # HPT900008

- STYLE: COUNTRY COTTAGE
- FIRST FLOOR: 1,704 SQ. FT.
- SECOND FLOOR: 734 SQ. FT.
- TOTAL: 2,438 SQ. FT.
- BONUS SPACE: 479 SQ. FT.
- BEDROOMS: 3
- BATHROOMS: 4½
- WIDTH: 50'-0"
- DEPTH: 82'-6"
- FOUNDATION: CRAWLSPACE

SEARCH ONLINE @ EPLANS.COM

Elegant country—that's one way to describe this attractive three-bedroom home. Inside, comfort is evidently the theme, with the formal dining room flowing into the U-shaped kitchen and casual dining taking place in the sunny breakfast area. The spacious, vaulted great room offers a fireplace and built-ins. The first-floor master suite is complete with a walk-in closet, a whirlpool tub and a separate shower. Upstairs, the sleeping quarters include two family bedrooms with private baths and walk-in closets.

plan# **HPT900010**

- **STYLE:** FARMHOUSE
- **FIRST FLOOR:** 1,927 SQ. FT.
- **SECOND FLOOR:** 879 SQ. FT.
- **TOTAL:** 2,806 SQ. FT.
- **BONUS SPACE:** 459 SQ. FT.
- **BEDROOMS:** 4
- **BATHROOMS:** 3½
- **WIDTH:** 71'-0"
- **DEPTH:** 53'-0"
- **FOUNDATION:** CRAWLSPACE

SEARCH ONLINE @ EPLANS.COM

This charming Southern plantation home packs quite a punch in 2,800 square feet! The elegant foyer is flanked by the formal dining room and the living room. To the rear, the family room enjoys a fireplace and expansive view of the outdoors. An archway leads to the breakfast area and on to the island kitchen. The luxurious master suite is tucked away for privacy behind the two-car garage. Three additional bedrooms rest on the second floor where they share two full baths. Space above the garage is available for future development.

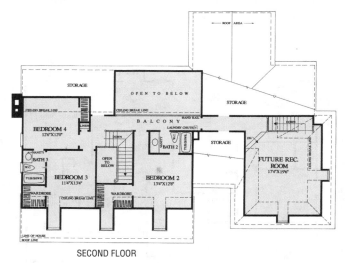

SECOND FLOOR

FIRST FLOOR

plan # HPT900014

- **STYLE: TRADITIONAL**
- **FIRST FLOOR: 1,967 SQ. FT.**
- **SECOND FLOOR: 891 SQ. FT.**
- **TOTAL: 2,858 SQ. FT.**
- **BEDROOMS: 5**
- **BATHROOMS: 4**
- **WIDTH: 60'-10"**
- **DEPTH: 55'-0"**
- **FOUNDATION: BASEMENT, CRAWLSPACE**

SEARCH ONLINE @ EPLANS.COM

This is a grand family home—the kind that will be loved and kept by generations. Gracious window detailing adds a custom look to the traditional brick-and-siding facade. Inside, the heart of the home is the enormous vaulted family room, featuring a fireplace and views to the rear property. To the left, the kitchen's space goes on and on, with a sunny bayed breakfast room and a hearth-warmed keeping room both adjacent to it. A guest suite with a walk-in closet is secluded to the side. Taking up the entire right wing of the first floor is the master suite, with all the deluxe amenities—bayed sitting area, tray ceiling, and elegant private bath. The second floor is home to three more bedrooms and two baths.

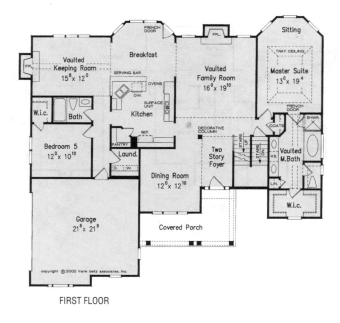

FIRST FLOOR

SECOND FLOOR

© 2001 Donald A. Gardner, Inc.

plan # HPT900012

- STYLE: TRADITIONAL
- FIRST FLOOR: 2,511 SQ. FT.
- SECOND FLOOR: 1,062 SQ. FT.
- TOTAL: 3,573 SQ. FT.
- BONUS SPACE: 465 SQ. FT.
- BEDROOMS: 4
- BATHROOMS: 3½
- WIDTH: 84'-11"
- DEPTH: 55'-11"

SEARCH ONLINE @ EPLANS.COM

An abundance of windows and an attractive brick facade enhance the exterior of this traditional two-story home. Inside, a study and formal dining room flank either side of the two-story foyer. Fireplaces warm both the great room and first-floor master suite. The suite also provides a separate sitting room, two walk-in closets and a private bath. The island kitchen extends into the breakfast room. The second floor features three additional family bedrooms, two baths and a bonus room fit for a home office.

SECOND FLOOR

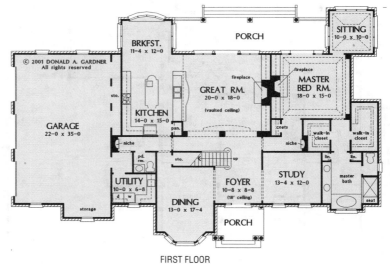

FIRST FLOOR

© The Sater Design Collection, Inc.

In true colonial style, this stately brick manor features large, bright windows, impressive columns and stucco accents. Three entrances—a grand main portico, a side "friends'" porch and a mudroom—cater to any occasion, welcoming family and guests. Encased in twin bay windows, a study and dining room enjoy elegant ceiling treatments. The two-story grand room is warmed by abundant sunlight and a fireplace framed by built-ins. The large family kitchen is joined by a bayed breakfast nook and an all-weather outdoor kitchen. In the master suite, a stepped ceiling and bay window embellish the bedroom; the bath has a walk-in shower and a corner whirlpool tub. Three upstairs bedrooms have private baths—Bedroom 2 and the guest suite offer private decks.

plan# HPT900016

- ■ STYLE: COLONIAL
- ■ FIRST FLOOR: 2,232 SQ. FT.
- ■ SECOND FLOOR: 1,269 SQ. FT.
- ■ TOTAL: 3,501 SQ. FT.
- ■ BEDROOMS: 4
- ■ BATHROOMS: 4½
- ■ WIDTH: 63'-9"
- ■ DEPTH: 80'-0"
- ■ FOUNDATION: SLAB

SEARCH ONLINE @ EPLANS.COM

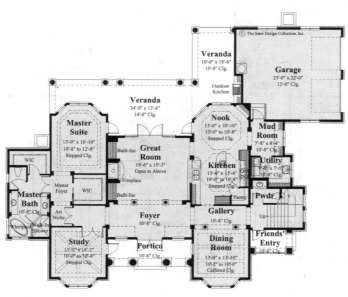

FIRST FLOOR

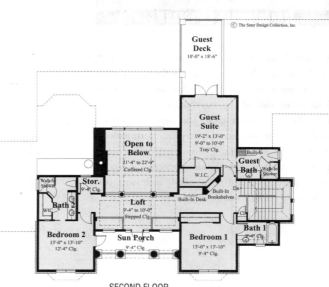

SECOND FLOOR

© 2002 Donald A. Gardner, Inc.

plan# HPT900009

- STYLE: TRADITIONAL
- FIRST FLOOR: 1,687 SQ. FT.
- SECOND FLOOR: 807 SQ. FT.
- TOTAL: 2,494 SQ. FT.
- BEDROOMS: 4
- BATHROOMS: 2½
- WIDTH: 52'-8"
- DEPTH: 67'-0"

SEARCH ONLINE @ EPLANS.COM

This glorious farmhouse was designed with the best of family living in mind. The beautiful wraparound porch is accented with stone and columns, and varying window detail adds a custom look to the facade. Inside, a soaring two-story foyer opens to a gallery hall that opens to the great room through columns. A fireplace, built-ins and rear-porch access make this room perfect for entertaining or just hanging out. The swanky master suite takes up the entire left wing of the plan with its enormous private bath and double closets. To the right of the plan, the spacious kitchen is bookended by a formal dining room at the front and a cozy breakfast nook to the rear. A utility room opens to the garage. Upstairs, three bedrooms share a bath as well as attic storage. A balcony looks down into the foyer and great room.

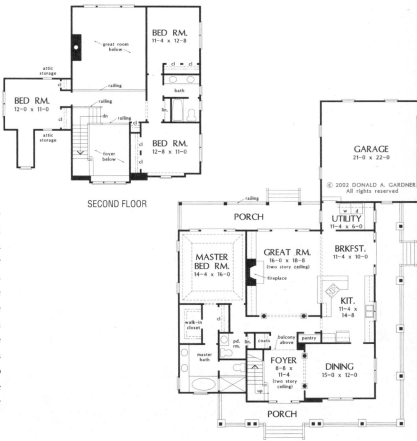

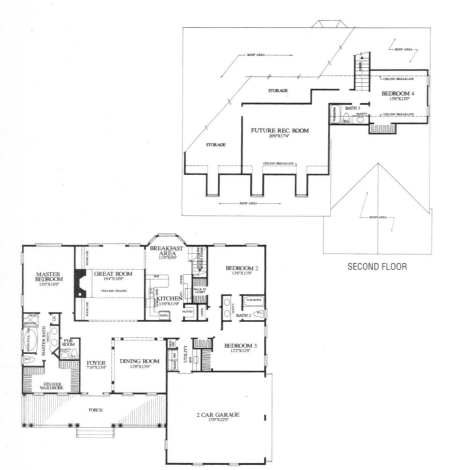

SECOND FLOOR

FIRST FLOOR

plan# HPT900018

- STYLE: COUNTRY COTTAGE
- FIRST FLOOR: 1,981 SQ. FT.
- SECOND FLOOR: 291 SQ. FT.
- TOTAL: 2,272 SQ. FT.
- BONUS SPACE: 412 SQ. FT.
- BEDROOMS: 4
- BATHROOMS: 3½
- WIDTH: 58'-0"
- DEPTH: 53'-0"
- FOUNDATION: CRAWLSPACE

SEARCH ONLINE @ EPLANS.COM

With three dormers and a welcoming front door accented by sidelights and a sunburst, this country cottage is sure to please. The dining room, immediately to the right from the foyer, is defined by decorative columns. In the great room, a volume ceiling heightens the space and showcases a fireplace and built-in bookshelves. The kitchen has plenty of workspace and flows into the bayed breakfast nook. A considerate split-bedroom design places the plush master suite to the far left and two family bedrooms to the far right. A fourth bedroom and future space upstairs allow room to grow.

plan# HPT900015

- **STYLE: COTTAGE**
- **FIRST FLOOR: 918 SQ. FT.**
- **SECOND FLOOR: 532 SQ. FT.**
- **TOTAL: 1,450 SQ. FT.**
- **BEDROOMS: 3**
- **BATHROOMS: 2**
- **WIDTH: 26'-4"**
- **DEPTH: 37'-0"**
- **FOUNDATION: BASEMENT**

SEARCH ONLINE @ EPLANS.COM

Nature enthusiasts are right at home in this engaging two-story home with expansive views and a delightful sun room. The enclosed vestibule opens to the spacious living/dining room where sunlight abounds. The adjoining, U-shaped island kitchen has access to the angular sun room for casual yet visually stimulating dining. The utility room is tucked away behind the stairs with the full bath. One bedroom is found on the first floor while two additional bedrooms share a full bath on the second floor.

SECOND FLOOR

FIRST FLOOR

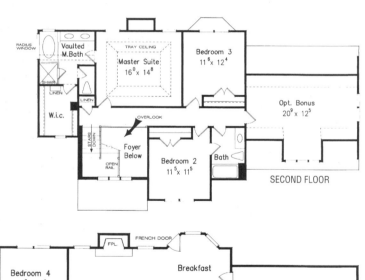

SECOND FLOOR

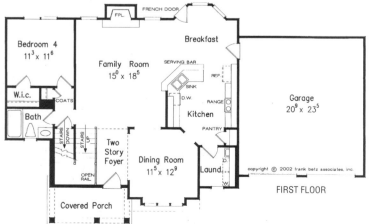

FIRST FLOOR

plan# HPT900011

- **STYLE: COUNTRY COTTAGE**
- **FIRST FLOOR: 1,119 SQ. FT.**
- **SECOND FLOOR: 910 SQ. FT.**
- **TOTAL SQUARE FEET: 2,029**
- **BONUS SPACE: 304 SQ. FT.**
- **BEDROOMS: 4**
- **BATHROOMS: 3**
- **WIDTH: 60'-0"**
- **DEPTH: 37'-6"**
- **FOUNDATION: BASEMENT, CRAWLSPACE**

SEARCH ONLINE @ EPLANS.COM

This traditional facade offers a cottage look with stone detailing and a columned porch. Enter the soaring two-story foyer for a great view of the huge hearth-warmed family room. This room opens on the right to a sunny bayed breakfast nook, adjacent to the very roomy kitchen—complete with a pantry closet and access to the laundry room. Up front is a formal dining room; in back to the left, a convenient guest suite. Upstairs, two more family or guest bedrooms reside along with bonus space and a stunning master suite. A tray ceiling ups the luxury factor, and a vaulted master bath has everything you need to feel perfectly pampered—windowed tub, walk-in closet and a twin-sink vanity.

© 2002 Donald A. Gardner, Inc.

plan# HPT900017

- **STYLE: TRADITIONAL**
- **SQUARE FOOTAGE: 2,076**
- **BONUS SPACE: 351 SQ. FT.**
- **BEDROOMS: 4**
- **BATHROOMS: 2**
- **WIDTH: 55'-4"**
- **DEPTH: 60'-6"**

SEARCH ONLINE @ EPLANS.COM

With a brick and siding exterior and beautiful box-bay windows, this home will complement any neighborhood. A fireplace and tray ceiling add a cozy element in the great room, and a window seat in the breakfast nook adds comfort and charm. The master suite is located on the far right, with dual walk-in closets and a fantastic bath. To the far left, three family bedrooms—or make one a study—all have outstanding features. Bonus space above the garage provides room to grow.

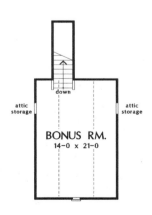

Traditional in every sense of the word, you can't go wrong with this charming country cottage. The foyer opens on the right to a columned dining room, and ahead to the family room. Here, a raised ceiling and bright radius windows expand the space and a warming fireplace lends a cozy touch. A sunny bayed breakfast nook flows into the angled kitchen for easy casual meals. Down the hall, two bedrooms share a full bath, tucked behind the two-car garage to protect the bedrooms from street noise. The master suite is indulgent, pampering homeowners with a bayed sitting area, tray ceiling, vaulted spa bath and an oversize walk-in closet. A fourth bedroom and bonus space are available to grow as your family does.

plan# HPT900019

- **STYLE:** COUNTRY COTTAGE
- **TOTAL SQUARE FOOTAGE:** 1,933
- **BONUS SPACE:** 519 SQ. FT.
- **BEDROOMS:** 3
- **BATHROOMS:** 2½
- **WIDTH:** 62'-0"
- **DEPTH:** 50'-0"
- **FOUNDATION:** BASEMENT, CRAWLSPACE

SEARCH ONLINE @ EPLANS.COM

copyright © 2002 frank betz associates, inc.

plan# HPT900020

- **STYLE:** TRADITIONAL
- **SQUARE FOOTAGE:** 1,789
- **BONUS SPACE:** 312 SQ. FT.
- **BEDROOMS:** 3
- **BATHROOMS:** 2
- **WIDTH:** 39'-0"
- **DEPTH:** 79'-4"

SEARCH ONLINE @ EPLANS.COM

Here is a narrow-lot home with a convenient front-entry garage. Columns make a statement outside and inside the home. A rear dormer above a set of French doors fills the great room with light, and the screened porch is perfectly positioned for outdoor entertaining. The bonus room can be easily accessed from the common living areas and would make a great home theater, gym, or playroom for the kids. A cathedral ceiling in the great room and vaulted ceilings in the master bedroom and dining room add visual space as well as beauty. An angled counter keeps the cook in the heart of conversation, and allows the kitchen to remain open to the great room.

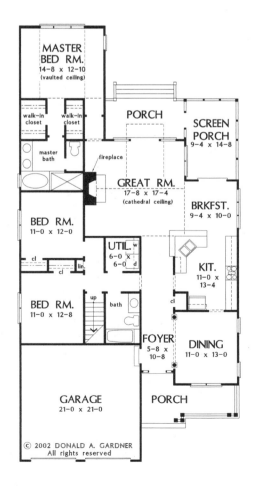

MASTER BED RM.
14-8 x 12-10
(vaulted ceiling)

walk-in closet

walk-in closet

master bath

PORCH

SCREEN PORCH
9-4 x 14-8

fireplace

GREAT RM.
17-8 x 17-4
(cathedral ceiling)

BRKFST.
9-4 x 10-0

BED RM.
11-0 x 12-0

cl

lin.

UTIL.
6-0 x
6-0

w
d

KIT.
11-0 x 13-4

cl

BED RM.
11-0 x 12-8

up

bath

FOYER
5-8 x 10-8

DINING
11-0 x 13-0

GARAGE
21-0 x 21-0

PORCH

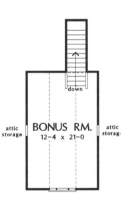

down

BONUS RM.
12-4 x 21-0

attic storage

attic storage

© 2002 Donald A. Gardner, Inc.

This home's traditional good looks will make it a stunner in any neighborhood. Inside, the well-thought floor plan offers great options for easy living. The heart of the home is the fireplace-warmed great room, which features a cathedral ceiling, built-in shelving and French-door access to the rear porch. To the left, the dining room and kitchen make a smart combo, enjoying light from the dining room's picture window and convenience from the kitchen's access to the utility room. Stairs right off the hallway lead to bonus space and attic storage. The vaulted master suite is privately secluded to the right rear of the plan, featuring double closets and a gorgeous private bath with a garden tub. Two more bedrooms—convert one into a study if you wish—share a bath up front.

plan# HPT900021

- STYLE: TRADITIONAL
- SQUARE FOOTAGE: 1,654
- BONUS SPACE: 356 SQ. FT.
- BEDROOMS: 3
- BATHROOMS: 2
- WIDTH: 60'-4"
- DEPTH: 47'-10"

SEARCH ONLINE @ EPLANS.COM

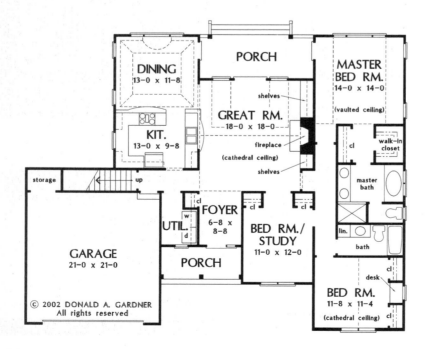

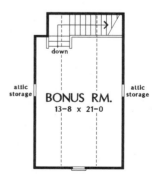

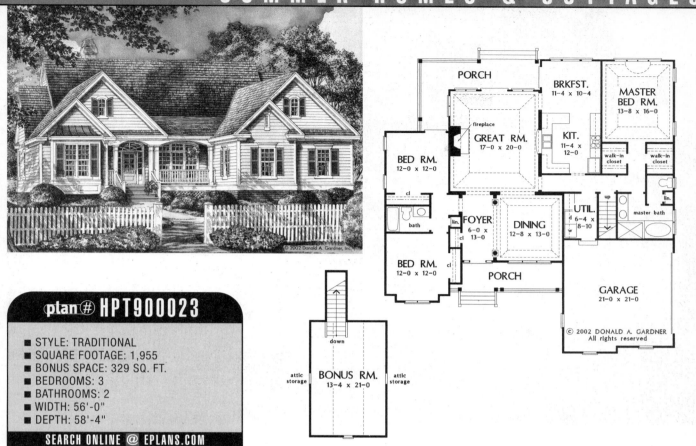

PORCH

BRKFST.
11-4 x 10-4

MASTER
BED RM.
13-8 x 16-0

fireplace

GREAT RM.
17-0 x 20-0

KIT.
11-4 x
12-0

walk-in
closet

walk-in
closet

BED RM.
12-0 x 12-0

cl

master bath

bath

lin.

FOYER
6-0 x
13-0

DINING
12-8 x 13-0

UTIL.
d 6-4 x
w 8-10

up

lin.

cl

BED RM.
12-0 x 12-0

cl

PORCH

GARAGE
21-0 x 21-0

down

attic
storage

BONUS RM.
13-4 x 21-0

attic
storage

plan# HPT900023

- STYLE: TRADITIONAL
- SQUARE FOOTAGE: 1,955
- BONUS SPACE: 329 SQ. FT.
- BEDROOMS: 3
- BATHROOMS: 2
- WIDTH: 56'-0"
- DEPTH: 58'-4"

SEARCH ONLINE @ EPLANS.COM

MASTER
BED RM.
12-0 x 14-0

walk-in
closet

BRKFST.
9-0 x 8-0

PORCH

UTIL.
5-8 x
6-4

KIT.
8-4 x
9-0

GREAT RM.
13-4 x 16-4

BED RM.
11-4 x 12-4

master
bath

d w

fireplace

cl

cl

up

(cathedral ceiling)

cl

bath

DINING
11-4 x 12-0

FOYER
5-0 x
11-0

(vaulted ceiling)

GARAGE
21-0 x 21-0

BED RM./
STUDY
11-4 x 11-8

PORCH

cl seat cl

down

attic
storage

BONUS
13-4 x 21-0

attic
storage

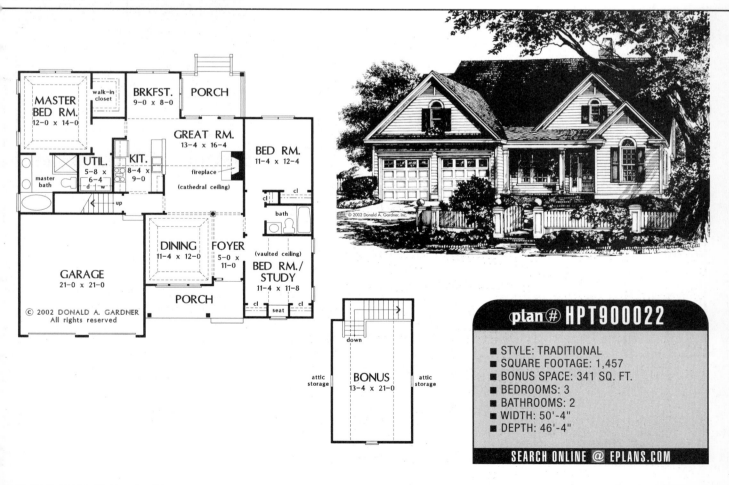

plan# HPT900022

- STYLE: TRADITIONAL
- SQUARE FOOTAGE: 1,457
- BONUS SPACE: 341 SQ. FT.
- BEDROOMS: 3
- BATHROOMS: 2
- WIDTH: 50'-4"
- DEPTH: 46'-4"

SEARCH ONLINE @ EPLANS.COM

© 2002 Donald A. Gardner, Inc.

plan# HPT900024

- STYLE: COUNTRY
- SQUARE FOOTAGE: 1,700
- BONUS SPACE: 333 SQ. FT.
- BEDROOMS: 3
- BATHROOMS: 2
- WIDTH: 49'-0"
- DEPTH: 65'-4"

SEARCH ONLINE @ EPLANS.COM

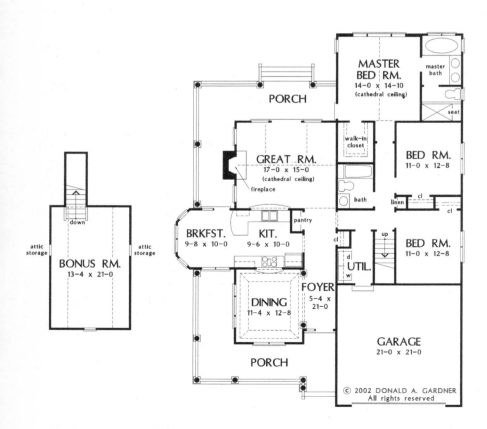

This homespun traditional plan has a porch that goes on and on—and that's accessible from nearly every room in the house. Columns and fanlight windows dress up the facade, while the interior offers a unique layout that's perfect for family living. The hearth-warmed great room is amplified by a cathedral ceiling, and it views the porch at the side and rear. The spacious kitchen, complete with pantry, opens to a bay-windowed breakfast nook that has a door to the porch. Three bedrooms make up the right wing's sleeping quarters, including two that share a full bath and access to the utility room. The deluxe master suite at the rear boasts a picture window, walk-in closet, elegant bath and porch access. Upstairs, bonus space can become whatever kind of room you wish.

plan ⊕ HPT900025

- STYLE: SOUTHERN COLONIAL
- FIRST FLOOR: 1,883 SQ. FT.
- SECOND FLOOR: 803 SQ. FT.
- TOTAL: 2,686 SQ. FT.
- BONUS SPACE: 489 SQ. FT.
- BEDROOMS: 3
- BATHROOMS: 3½
- WIDTH: 63'-0"
- DEPTH: 81'-10"
- FOUNDATION: CRAWLSPACE

SEARCH ONLINE @ EPLANS.COM

Where creeks converge and marsh grasses sway in gentle breezes, this is a classical low country home. Steep rooflines, high ceilings, front and back porches plus long and low windows are typical details of these charming planters' cottages. The foyer is flanked by the formal dining room, and the living room, which opens to the family room. Here, several windows look out to the terrace and a fireplace removes the chill on a winter's night. The sunny breakfast room, which adjoins the kitchen, offers a wonderful space for casual dining. Two bedrooms, the lavish master suite and the two-car garage complete the floor plan.

SECOND FLOOR

FIRST FLOOR

plan# HPT900027

- STYLE: BUNGALOW
- SQUARE FOOTAGE: 1,927
- BEDROOMS: 3
- BATHROOMS: 2
- WIDTH: 54'-0"
- DEPTH: 55'-0"
- FOUNDATION: CRAWLSPACE

SEARCH ONLINE @ EPLANS.COM

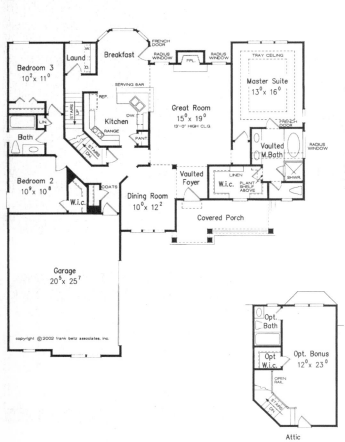

plan# HPT900026

- STYLE: COUNTRY COTTAGE
- SQUARE FOOTAGE: 1,727
- BONUS SPACE: 318 SQ. FT.
- BEDROOMS: 3
- BATHROOMS: 2
- WIDTH: 55'-0"
- DEPTH: 62'-0"
- FOUNDATION: BASEMENT, CRAWLSPACE

SEARCH ONLINE @ EPLANS.COM

TO ORDER BLUEPRINTS CALL TOLL FREE 1-800-521-6797

© 2002 Donald A. Gardner, Inc.

SECOND FLOOR

FIRST FLOOR

© 2002 DONALD A. GARDNER
All rights reserved

plan# HPT900029

- STYLE: CRAFTSMAN
- FIRST FLOOR: 1,856 SQ. FT.
- SECOND FLOOR: 610 SQ. FT.
- TOTAL: 2,466 SQ. FT.
- BONUS SPACE: 322 SQ. FT.
- BEDROOMS: 3
- BATHROOMS: 2½
- WIDTH: 59'-0"
- DEPTH: 47'-8"

SEARCH ONLINE @ EPLANS.COM

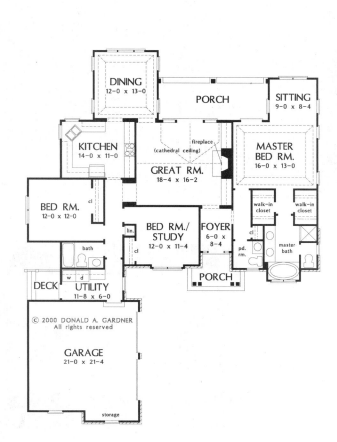

© 2000 DONALD A. GARDNER
All rights reserved

© 2000 Donald A. Gardner

plan# HPT900028

- STYLE: CRAFTSMAN
- SQUARE FOOTAGE: 1,854
- BEDROOMS: 3
- BATHROOMS: 2½
- WIDTH: 56'-0"
- DEPTH: 73'-0"

SEARCH ONLINE @ EPLANS.COM

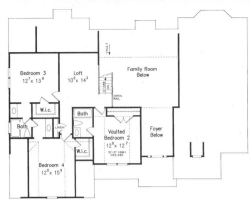

SECOND FLOOR

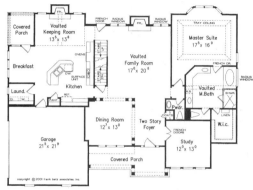

FIRST FLOOR

plan# HPT900030

- STYLE: COUNTRY COTTAGE
- FIRST FLOOR: 2,024 SQ. FT.
- SECOND FLOOR: 958 SQ. FT.
- TOTAL: 2,982 SQ. FT.
- BEDROOMS: 4
- BATHROOMS: 3½
- WIDTH: 62'-0"
- DEPTH: 50'-4"
- FOUNDATION: BASEMENT, CRAWLSPACE

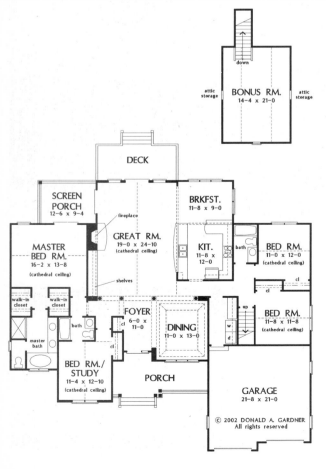

plan# HPT900031

- STYLE: TRADITIONAL
- SQUARE FOOTAGE: 2,259
- BONUS SPACE: 352 SQ. FT.
- BEDROOMS: 4
- BATHROOMS: 3
- WIDTH: 64'-10"
- DEPTH: 59'-6"

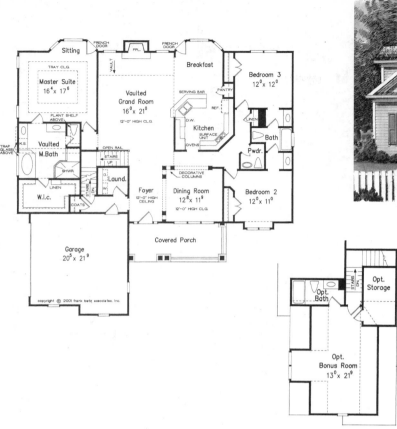

plan # HPT900032

- STYLE: CAPE COD
- SQUARE FOOTAGE: 2,148
- BONUS SPACE: 467 SQ. FT.
- BEDROOMS: 3
- BATHROOMS: 2½
- WIDTH: 58'-0"
- DEPTH: 59'-6"
- FOUNDATION: BASEMENT, CRAWLSPACE

SEARCH ONLINE @ EPLANS.COM

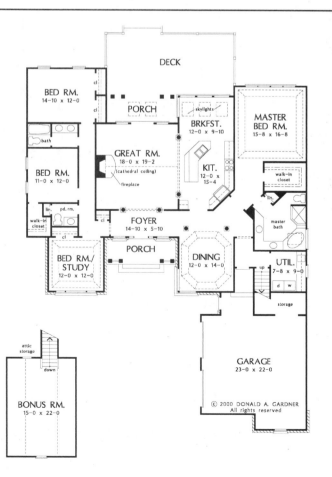

plan # HPT900033

- STYLE: TRADITIONAL
- SQUARE FOOTAGE: 2,544
- BONUS SPACE: 394 SQ. FT.
- BEDROOMS: 4
- BATHROOMS: 2½
- WIDTH: 62'-8"
- DEPTH: 82'-1"

SEARCH ONLINE @ EPLANS.COM

© 2002 Donald A. Gardner, Inc.

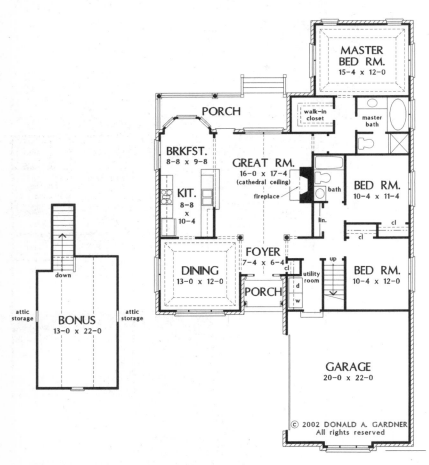

plan # HPT900034

- **STYLE: TRADITIONAL**
- **SQUARE FOOTAGE: 1,608**
- **BONUS SPACE: 328 SQ. FT.**
- **BEDROOMS: 3**
- **BATHROOMS: 2**
- **WIDTH: 42'-7"**
- **DEPTH: 72'-11"**

SEARCH ONLINE @ EPLANS.COM

This narrow-lot traditional home has a lot to offer for its modest square footage. A clerestory highlights the dormer and mimics the arches in the Palladian window and fanlight above the front door. A box bay window adds interest to the garage, while brick accents the front facade. The sleeping quarters are located on one side of the house for privacy; the master suite is located in this quiet area and features a walk-in closet, separate shower and tub. Tray ceilings highlight both the master bedroom and dining room. A bay window extends the breakfast nook, and all of the living areas have a glimpse of the great room is striking fireplace. For expansion, a bonus room is located above the garage.

plan# HPT900035

- **STYLE:** COUNTRY COTTAGE
- **SQUARE FOOTAGE:** 1,725
- **BONUS SPACE:** 256 SQ. FT.
- **BEDROOMS:** 3
- **BATHROOMS:** 2
- **WIDTH:** 58'-0"
- **DEPTH:** 54'-6"
- **FOUNDATION:** BASEMENT, CRAWLSPACE

SEARCH ONLINE @ EPLANS.COM

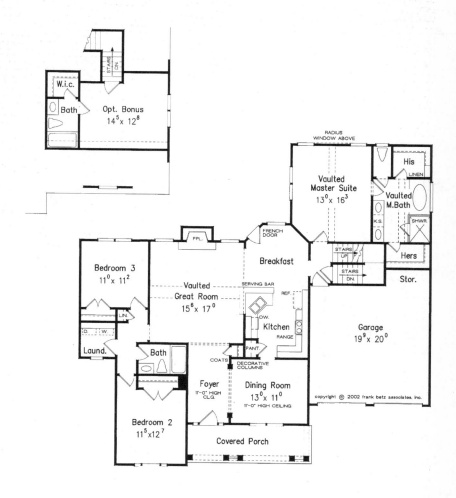

This sweet cottage showcases the best in rustic refinement. Pedimented window treatments dress up the facade, as does the columned porch. Inside, the foyer opens to a vaulted great room, complete with fireplace and views to the rear property. To the right is the spacious kitchen, bookended by a formal dining room and a sunny bayed breakfast nook featuring French-door access to the backyard. Two bedrooms share a full bath and convenient access to the laundry room on the left of the plan. Secluded behind the two-car garage is the vaulted master suite. Its private bath is also vaulted and enjoys a windowed tub, twin-sink vanity and double walk-in closets. Optional bonus space upstairs can be made into guest quarters with a full bath and walk-in closet.

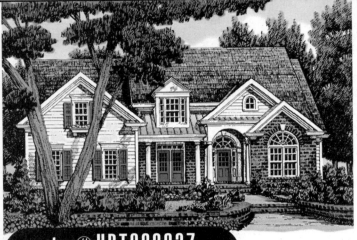

SECOND FLOOR

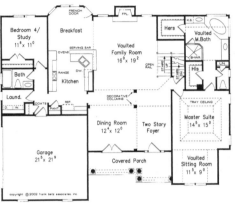

FIRST FLOOR

plan # HPT900037

- STYLE: COUNTRY COTTAGE
- FIRST FLOOR: 1,976 SQ. FT.
- SECOND FLOOR: 676 SQ. FT.
- TOTAL: 2,653 SQ. FT.
- BONUS SPACE: 314 SQ. FT.
- BEDROOMS: 4
- BATHROOMS: 3
- WIDTH: 58'-0"
- DEPTH: 50'-6"
- FOUNDATION: BASEMENT, CRAWLSPACE

SEARCH ONLINE @ EPLANS.COM

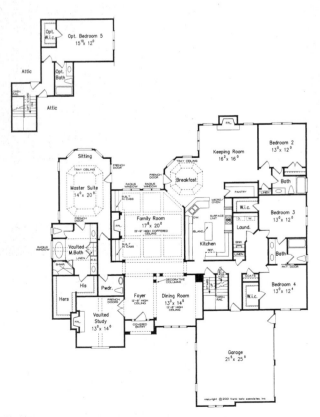

plan # HPT900036

- STYLE: COUNTRY COTTAGE
- SQUARE FOOTAGE: 3,418
- BONUS SPACE: 185 SQ. FT.
- BEDROOMS: 4
- BATHROOMS: 3½
- WIDTH: 70'-7"
- DEPTH: 81'-10"
- FOUNDATION: BASEMENT, CRAWLSPACE

SEARCH ONLINE @ EPLANS.COM

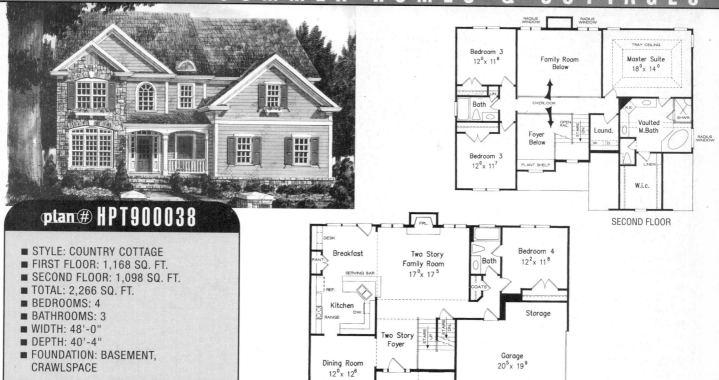

SECOND FLOOR

FIRST FLOOR

copyright © 2002 frank betz associates, inc.

plan # HPT900038

- **STYLE: COUNTRY COTTAGE**
- **FIRST FLOOR: 1,168 SQ. FT.**
- **SECOND FLOOR: 1,098 SQ. FT.**
- **TOTAL: 2,266 SQ. FT.**
- **BEDROOMS: 4**
- **BATHROOMS: 3**
- **WIDTH: 48'-0"**
- **DEPTH: 40'-4"**
- **FOUNDATION: BASEMENT, CRAWLSPACE**

SEARCH ONLINE @ EPLANS.COM

SECOND FLOOR

copyright © 2001 frank betz associates, inc.

FIRST FLOOR

plan # HPT900039

- **STYLE: COUNTRY COTTAGE**
- **FIRST FLOOR: 1,132 SQ. FT.**
- **SECOND FLOOR: 1,279 SQ. FT.**
- **TOTAL: 3,543 SQ. FT.**
- **BEDROOMS: 5**
- **BATHROOMS: 3**
- **WIDTH: 51'-0"**
- **DEPTH: 41'-4"**
- **FOUNDATION: BASEMENT, CRAWLSPACE**

SEARCH ONLINE @ EPLANS.COM

plan# HPT900041

- **STYLE:** FRENCH COUNTRY
- **FIRST FLOOR:** 1,266 SQ. FT.
- **SECOND FLOOR:** 1,192 SQ. FT.
- **TOTAL:** 2,458 SQ. FT.
- **BEDROOMS:** 4
- **BATHROOMS:** 3
- **WIDTH:** 42'-0"
- **DEPTH:** 48'-0"
- **FOUNDATION:** BASEMENT, CRAWLSPACE

SEARCH ONLINE @ EPLANS.COM

SECOND FLOOR

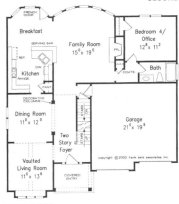

FIRST FLOOR

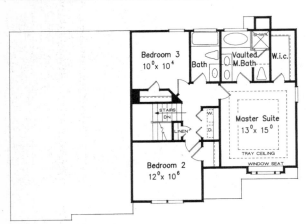

SECOND FLOOR

plan# HPT900040

- **STYLE:** COUNTRY COTTAGE
- **FIRST FLOOR:** 1,064 SQ. FT.
- **SECOND FLOOR:** 760 SQ. FT.
- **TOTAL:** 1,824 SQ. FT.
- **BEDROOMS:** 4
- **BATHROOMS:** 3
- **WIDTH:** 50'-0"
- **DEPTH:** 36'-4"
- **FOUNDATION:** BASEMENT, CRAWLSPACE

SEARCH ONLINE @ EPLANS.COM

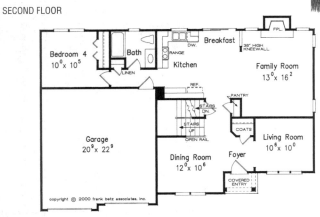

FIRST FLOOR

TO ORDER BLUEPRINTS CALL TOLL FREE 1-800-521-6797

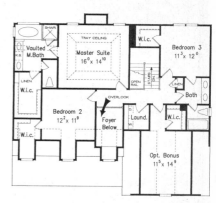

SECOND FLOOR

FIRST FLOOR

plan# HPT900042

- **STYLE: COUNTRY COTTAGE**
- **FIRST FLOOR: 1,125 SQ. FT.**
- **SECOND FLOOR: 1,062 SQ. FT.**
- **TOTAL: 2,187 SQ. FT.**
- **BONUS SPACE: 229 SQ. FT.**
- **BEDROOMS: 4**
- **BATHROOMS: 3**
- **WIDTH: 45'-0"**
- **DEPTH: 42'-4"**
- **FOUNDATION: BASEMENT, CRAWLSPACE**

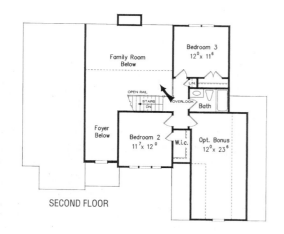

SECOND FLOOR

FIRST FLOOR

plan# HPT900043

- **STYLE: COUNTRY COTTAGE**
- **FIRST FLOOR: 1,415 SQ. FT.**
- **SECOND FLOOR: 448 SQ. FT.**
- **TOTAL: 1,863 SQ. FT.**
- **BONUS SPACE: 297 SQ. FT.**
- **BEDROOMS: 3**
- **BATHROOMS: 2½**
- **WIDTH: 53'-0"**
- **DEPTH: 45'-10"**
- **FOUNDATION: BASEMENT, CRAWLSPACE**

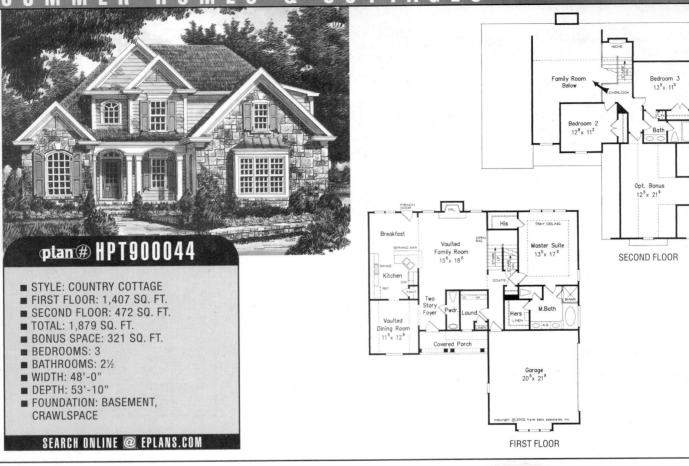

plan# HPT900044

- STYLE: COUNTRY COTTAGE
- FIRST FLOOR: 1,407 SQ. FT.
- SECOND FLOOR: 472 SQ. FT.
- TOTAL: 1,879 SQ. FT.
- BONUS SPACE: 321 SQ. FT.
- BEDROOMS: 3
- BATHROOMS: 2½
- WIDTH: 48'-0"
- DEPTH: 53'-10"
- FOUNDATION: BASEMENT, CRAWLSPACE

SEARCH ONLINE @ EPLANS.COM

SECOND FLOOR

FIRST FLOOR

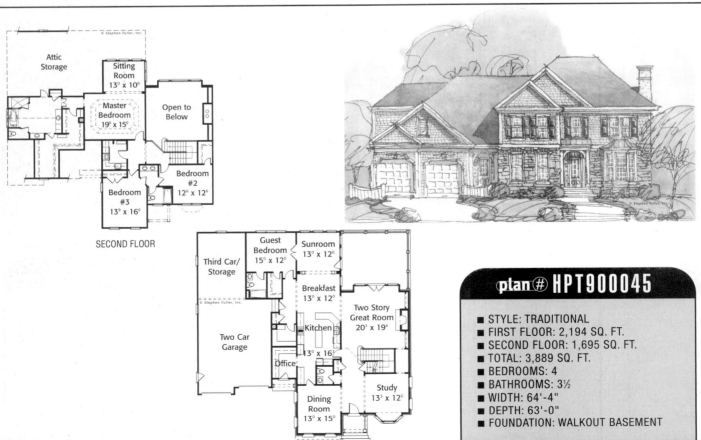

SECOND FLOOR

FIRST FLOOR

plan# HPT900045

- STYLE: TRADITIONAL
- FIRST FLOOR: 2,194 SQ. FT.
- SECOND FLOOR: 1,695 SQ. FT.
- TOTAL: 3,889 SQ. FT.
- BEDROOMS: 4
- BATHROOMS: 3½
- WIDTH: 64'-4"
- DEPTH: 63'-0"
- FOUNDATION: WALKOUT BASEMENT

SEARCH ONLINE @ EPLANS.COM

TO ORDER BLUEPRINTS CALL TOLL FREE 1-800-521-6797

plan# HPT900047

- STYLE: TRADITIONAL
- FIRST FLOOR: 1,319 SQ. FT.
- SECOND FLOOR: 1,181 SQ. FT.
- TOTAL: 2,500 SQ. FT.
- BONUS SPACE: 371 SQ. FT.
- BEDROOMS: 4
- BATHROOMS: 2½
- WIDTH: 60'-0"
- DEPTH: 42'-0"
- FOUNDATION: CRAWLSPACE

SEARCH ONLINE @ EPLANS.COM

SECOND FLOOR

FIRST FLOOR

SECOND FLOOR

FIRST FLOOR

plan# HPT900046

- STYLE: SOUTHERN COLONIAL
- FIRST FLOOR: 2,175 SQ. FT.
- SECOND FLOOR: 1,647 SQ. FT.
- TOTAL: 3,822 SQ. FT.
- BEDROOMS: 4
- BATHROOMS: 3½
- WIDTH: 64'-4"
- DEPTH: 63'-0"
- FOUNDATION: WALKOUT BASEMENT

SEARCH ONLINE @ EPLANS.COM

© Stephen Fuller, Inc.

A sweet, traditional neighborhood home with eclectic touches, this spacious plan is sure to please. The formal spaces, including the bayed living room, are located near the entry, defined by arches. The gourmet kitchen serves the dining room through a butler's pantry, and opens to a bright breakfast nook. The vaulted great room features a fireplace for those chilly nights, and a sun room for warm, lazy days. Twin bedrooms toward the front of the plan share a full bath; the master suite is tucked to the rear with a tray ceiling and a sumptuous bath. Bonus space is limited only by your imagination.

plan # HPT900048

- STYLE: TRADITIONAL
- FIRST FLOOR: 3,108 SQ. FT.
- SECOND FLOOR: 512 SQ. FT.
- TOTAL: 3,620 SQ. FT.
- BONUS SPACE: 605 SQ. FT.
- BEDROOMS: 3
- BATHROOMS: 2½
- WIDTH: 65'-0"
- DEPTH: 81'-0"
- FOUNDATION: WALKOUT BASEMENT

SEARCH ONLINE @ EPLANS.COM

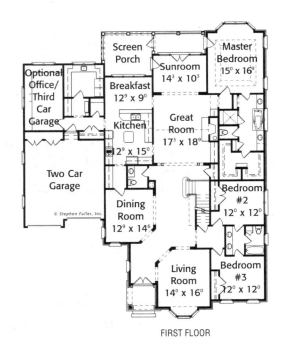

FIRST FLOOR

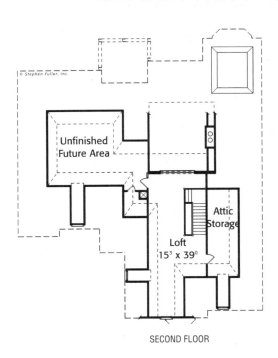

SECOND FLOOR

© Stephen Fuller, Inc.

plan# HPT900049

- STYLE: TRADITIONAL
- FIRST FLOOR: 3,081 SQ. FT.
- SECOND FLOOR: 622 SQ. FT.
- TOTAL: 3,703 SQ. FT.
- BONUS SPACE: 1,437 SQ. FT.
- BEDROOMS: 3
- BATHROOMS: 2½
- WIDTH: 65'-0"
- DEPTH: 78'-6"
- FOUNDATION: WALKOUT BASEMENT

SEARCH ONLINE @ EPLANS.COM

A brick facade with the charm of a Cape Cod cottage, this home is designed for flexibility and family living. The formal living and dining rooms flank the entry, which leads to the vaulted great room. A lateral fireplace is surrounded by built-in shelving; access to the sun room assures year-round enjoyment. The gourmet island kitchen serves a sunny breakfast nook and accesses the dining room through a butler's pantry. The master suite is tucked to the rear of the plan, with a bay window, and a fabulous bath with a spa tub. Unfinished areas upstairs allow room to grow. Don't miss the optional office/third-car garage addition.

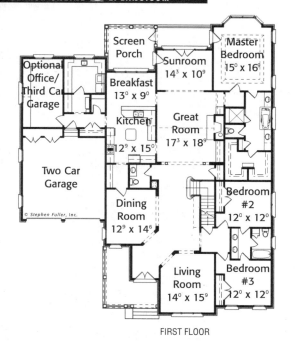

FIRST FLOOR

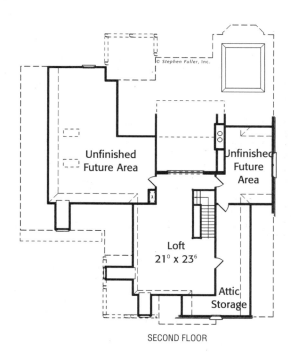

SECOND FLOOR

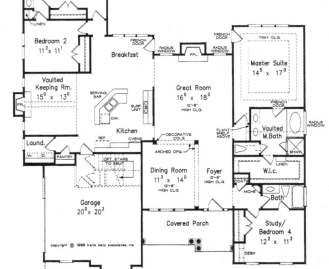

GARAGE LOCATION WITH BASEMENT

plan # HPT900050

- **STYLE:** COUNTRY COTTAGE
- **SQUARE FOOTAGE:** 2,319
- **BEDROOMS:** 4
- **BATHROOMS:** 3
- **WIDTH:** 60'-0"
- **DEPTH:** 67'-4"
- **FOUNDATION:** CRAWLSPACE

SEARCH ONLINE @ EPLANS.COM

SECOND FLOOR

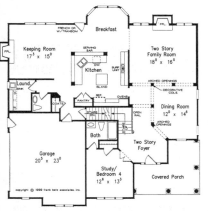

FIRST FLOOR

plan # HPT900051

- **STYLE:** COUNTRY COTTAGE
- **FIRST FLOOR:** 1,811 SQ. FT.
- **SECOND FLOOR:** 1,557 SQ. FT.
- **TOTAL:** 3,368 SQ. FT.
- **BEDROOMS:** 4
- **BATHROOMS:** 3½
- **WIDTH:** 53'-4"
- **DEPTH:** 54'-6"
- **FOUNDATION:** BASEMENT, CRAWLSPACE

SEARCH ONLINE @ EPLANS.COM

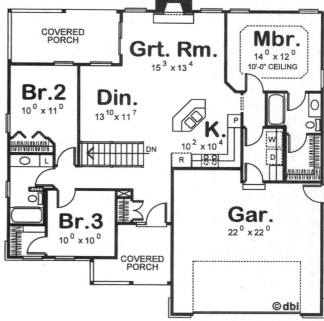

plan# HPT900053

- STYLE: TRADITIONAL
- SQUARE FOOTAGE: 1,333
- BEDROOMS: 3
- BATHROOMS: 2
- WIDTH: 47'-0"
- DEPTH: 47'-0"

SEARCH ONLINE @ EPLANS.COM

Grt. Rm.
15³ x 13⁴

Mbr.
14⁰ x 12⁰
10'-0" CEILING

COVERED PORCH

Br.2
10⁰ x 11⁰

Din.
13¹⁰ x 11⁷

K.
10² x 10⁴

Br.3
10⁰ x 10⁰

Gar.
22⁰ x 22⁰

COVERED PORCH

©dbi

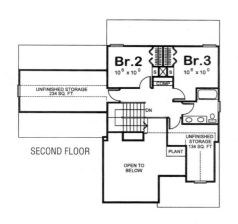

Br.2
10⁸ x 10⁰

Br.3
10⁸ x 10⁰

UNFINISHED STORAGE 234 SQ. FT.

UNFINISHED STORAGE 134 SQ. FT

OPEN TO BELOW

PLANT

SECOND FLOOR

Gar.
20⁸ x 22⁰

Din.
14⁰ x 10⁰

K.
12⁸ x 10⁰

Mbr.
12⁰ x 14⁰
9'-0" CEILING

Liv. Rm.
13⁰ x 15⁴

COVERED PORCH

©dbi

FIRST FLOOR

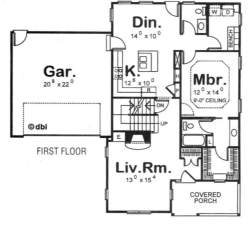

plan# HPT900052

- STYLE: TRADITIONAL
- FIRST FLOOR: 1,137 SQ. FT.
- SECOND FLOOR: 454 SQ. FT.
- TOTAL: 1,591 SQ. FT.
- BEDROOMS: 3
- BATHROOMS: 2½
- WIDTH: 48'-0"
- DEPTH: 45'-8"

SEARCH ONLINE @ EPLANS.COM

plan# HPT900054

- STYLE: TRADITIONAL
- SQUARE FOOTAGE: 1,570
- BEDROOMS: 3
- BATHROOMS: 2
- WIDTH: 49'-8"
- DEPTH: 49'-4"

SEARCH ONLINE @ EPLANS.COM

This traditional plan has it all in just a little over 1,500 square feet. The tiled foyer opens to a hearth-warmed living room that enjoys access to the wraparound front porch. Straight ahead from the foyer, past the coat closet and utility room, lies the U-shaped kitchen with its huge pantry and serving-bar counter that looks into the adjoining dining area. To the left of the plan are two bedrooms that share a full hall bath and feature plenty of closet space. The tray-ceilinged master suite is secluded on the right, behind the garage, with a huge walk-in closet and private bath.

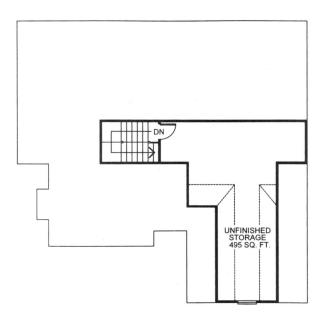

plan# HPT900055

- STYLE: COUNTRY COTTAGE
- FIRST FLOOR: 1,281 SQ. FT.
- SECOND FLOOR: 611 SQ. FT.
- TOTAL: 1,892 SQ. FT.
- BEDROOMS: 4
- BATHROOMS: 3
- WIDTH: 30'-0"
- DEPTH: 58'-6"
- FOUNDATION: SLAB

SEARCH ONLINE @ EPLANS.COM

Traditional stylings meld with the Southern feel of the nested gables and pedimented-like entry of this four-bedroom home. A corner fireplace warms the living room, which is open to the dining and kitchen area. Secluded on the right, the master suite delights with a luxurious bath that boasts a double-sink vanity and twin walk-in closets that flank the garden tub. Two family bedrooms share a full bath on the second floor while a second full bath resides next to the fourth bedroom, making a perfect guest room.

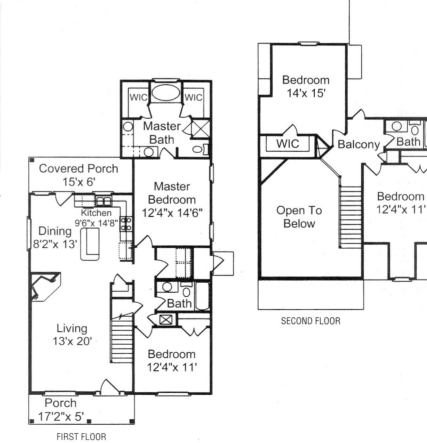

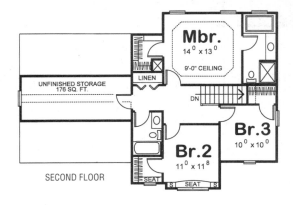

SECOND FLOOR

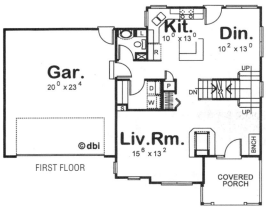

FIRST FLOOR

plan# HPT900057

- **STYLE:** TRADITIONAL
- **FIRST FLOOR:** 799 SQ. FT.
- **SECOND FLOOR:** 771 SQ. FT.
- **TOTAL:** 1,570 SQ. FT.
- **BEDROOMS:** 3
- **BATHROOMS:** 2½
- **WIDTH:** 47'-0"
- **DEPTH:** 37'-0"

SEARCH ONLINE @ EPLANS.COM

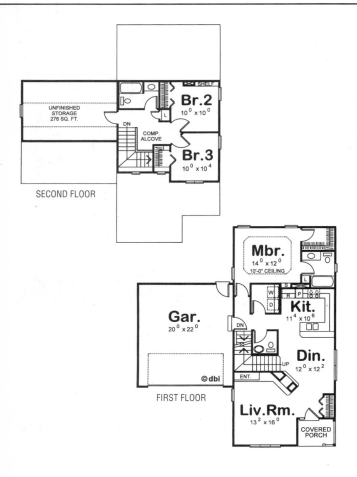

SECOND FLOOR

FIRST FLOOR

plan# HPT900056

- **STYLE:** TRADITIONAL
- **FIRST FLOOR:** 1,008 SQ. FT.
- **SECOND FLOOR:** 415 SQ. FT.
- **TOTAL:** 1,423 SQ. FT.
- **BEDROOMS:** 3
- **BATHROOMS:** 2½
- **WIDTH:** 42'-4"
- **DEPTH:** 48'-0"

SEARCH ONLINE @ EPLANS.COM

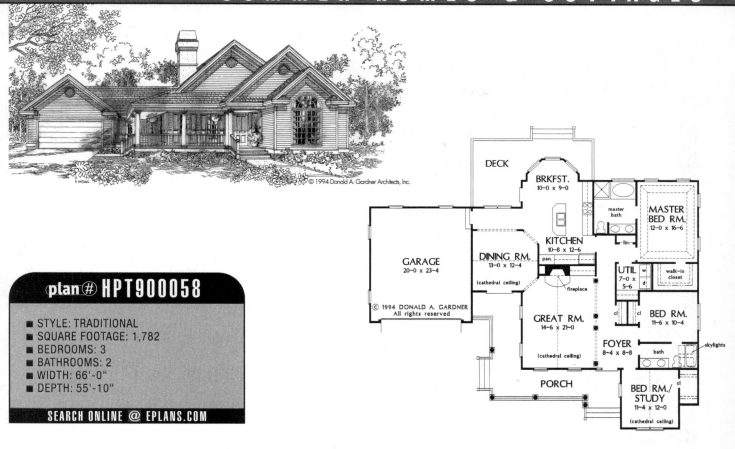

© 1994 Donald A. Gardner Architects, Inc.

plan # HPT900058

- **STYLE:** TRADITIONAL
- **SQUARE FOOTAGE:** 1,782
- **BEDROOMS:** 3
- **BATHROOMS:** 2
- **WIDTH:** 66'-0"
- **DEPTH:** 55'-10"

SEARCH ONLINE @ EPLANS.COM

DECK

BRKFST.
10-0 x 9-0

master bath

MASTER BED RM.
12-0 x 16-6

KITCHEN
10-8 x 12-6

GARAGE
20-0 x 23-4

DINING RM.
13-0 x 12-4
(cathedral ceiling)

pan.

fireplace

UTIL
7-0 x 5-6

walk-in closet

GREAT RM.
14-6 x 21-0
(cathedral ceiling)

BED RM.
11-6 x 10-4

FOYER
8-4 x 8-8

bath

skylights

PORCH

BED RM./ STUDY
11-4 x 12-0
(cathedral ceiling)

---

attic storage

BONUS RM.
13-4 x 21-0

attic storage

down

PORCH

MASTER BED RM.
14-8 x 12-0
(vaulted ceiling)

master bath

BED RM.
11-4 x 10-4

fireplace

BRKFST.
9-8 x 8-0

GREAT RM.
14-0 x 18-0
(cathedral ceiling)

KIT.
9-8 x 10-0

w
d

walk-in closet

up

storage

BED RM.
11-4 x 10-4
(10' ceiling)

bath

FOYER
9-8 x 4-0

DINING
12-0 x 10-4

GARAGE
21-0 x 21-0

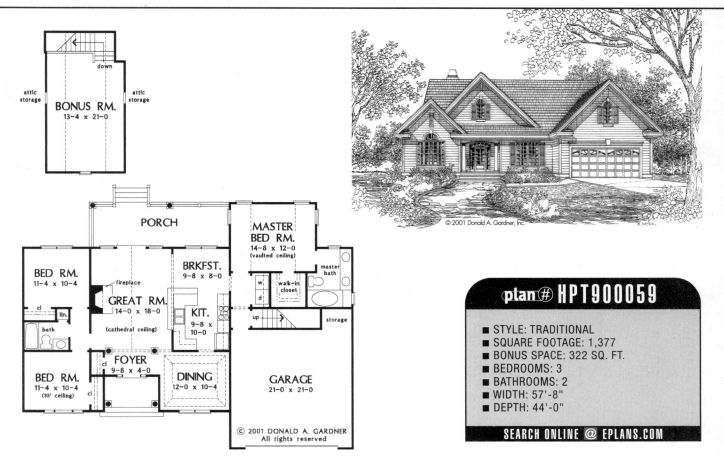

© 2001 Donald A. Gardner, Inc.

plan # HPT900059

- **STYLE:** TRADITIONAL
- **SQUARE FOOTAGE:** 1,377
- **BONUS SPACE:** 322 SQ. FT.
- **BEDROOMS:** 3
- **BATHROOMS:** 2
- **WIDTH:** 57'-8"
- **DEPTH:** 44'-0"

SEARCH ONLINE @ EPLANS.COM

plan # HPT900060

- STYLE: TRADITIONAL
- SQUARE FOOTAGE: 1,401
- BEDROOMS: 3
- BATHROOMS: 2
- WIDTH: 30'-0"
- DEPTH: 59'-10"
- FOUNDATION: SLAB

SEARCH ONLINE @ EPLANS.COM

A prominent front gable and country-style shutters lend rustic flair to this otherwise traditional home. A sensible floor plan separates living areas—located on the left side of the plan—from sleeping quarters, which sit to the right of the home. Special amenities in the living spaces include a fireplace and tray ceiling in the family room and a pantry in the kitchen; a rear covered porch offers space for outdoor activities. Each family bedroom includes a closet and access to a full bath; the master suite provides a walk-in closet and a lavish private bath.

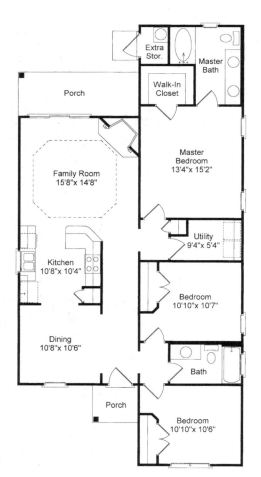

plan# HPT900061

- **STYLE: LAKEFRONT**
- **FIRST FLOOR: 1,212 SQ. FT.**
- **SECOND FLOOR: 620 SQ. FT.**
- **TOTAL: 1,832 SQ. FT.**
- **BEDROOMS: 3**
- **BATHROOMS: 2**
- **WIDTH: 38'-0"**
- **DEPTH: 40'-0"**
- **FOUNDATION: BASEMENT**

SEARCH ONLINE @ EPLANS.COM

This comfortable vacation design provides two levels of relaxing family space. The main level offers a wrapping front porch and an abundance of windows, filling interior spaces with the summer sunshine. A two-sided fireplace warms the living room/dining room combination and a master bedroom that features a roomy walk-in closet. Nearby, the hall bath offers a relaxing whirlpool tub. The kitchen is open and features an island snack bar and pantry storage. A cozy sun room accesses the wrapping deck. Upstairs, two additional bedrooms feature ample closet space and share a second-floor bath.

FIRST FLOOR

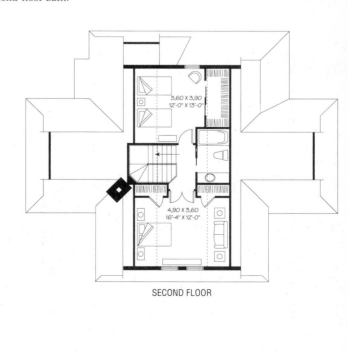

SECOND FLOOR

A flower box, covered front porch and horizontal siding combine to give this home plenty of appeal. Inside, the foyer is designed as an air lock, preventing cold air from disturbing the family. An open living area provides a spacious feeling, with the dining area defined by columns. The corner kitchen features an island snack bar, a window sink and tons of cabinet and counter space. Note the covered porch just off the dining area—perfect for dining alfresco. Upstairs, three bedrooms—each with a walk-in closet—share a lavish bath.

plan# HPT900062

- STYLE: COUNTRY
- FIRST FLOOR: 896 SQ. FT.
- SECOND FLOOR: 948 SQ. FT.
- TOTAL: 1,844 SQ. FT.
- BEDROOMS: 3
- BATHROOMS: 1½
- WIDTH: 35'-4"
- DEPTH: 39'-8"
- FOUNDATION: BASEMENT

SEARCH ONLINE @ EPLANS.COM

FIRST FLOOR

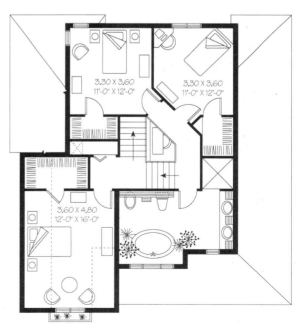

SECOND FLOOR

plan# HPT900063

- **STYLE:** TRADITIONAL
- **FIRST FLOOR:** 1,281 SQ. FT.
- **SECOND FLOOR:** 1,049 SQ. FT.
- **TOTAL:** 2,330 SQ. FT.
- **BEDROOMS:** 3
- **BATHROOMS:** 2½
- **WIDTH:** 68'-0"
- **DEPTH:** 34'-0"
- **FOUNDATION:** BASEMENT

SEARCH ONLINE @ EPLANS.COM

SECOND FLOOR

Multiple rooflines and attractive window treatments introduce this fine three-bedroom home to any neighborhood. Inside, a two-story foyer opens to a sunken living space to the left, which in turn presents a wonderful sun-room. A cozy office is to the right of the foyer—a perfect location for privacy. The spacious kitchen offers a window sink, built-in planning desk, a serving bar and easy access to the formal dining room. Note the porch access from both the living and the dining rooms. Upstairs, the lavish master suite shares a deck with one of the family bedrooms, while featuring a private bath, a fireplace and a huge walk-in closet. The two other family bedrooms share a hall bath.

FIRST FLOOR

plan# HPT900064

- **STYLE: PLANTATION**
- **FIRST FLOOR: 2,142 SQ. FT.**
- **SECOND FLOOR: 960 SQ. FT.**
- **TOTAL: 3,102 SQ. FT.**
- **BONUS SPACE: 327 SQ. FT.**
- **BEDROOMS: 4**
- **BATHROOMS: 3½**
- **WIDTH: 75'-8"**
- **DEPTH: 53'-0"**
- **FOUNDATION: CRAWLSPACE**

SEARCH ONLINE @ EPLANS.COM

Imagine driving up to this cottage beauty at the end of a long week. The long wraparound porch, hipped rooflines and shuttered windows will transport you. Inside, the foyer is flanked by a living room on the left and a formal dining room on the right. Across the gallery hall, the hearth-warmed family room will surely become the hub of the home. To the right, the spacious kitchen boasts a worktop island counter, ample pantry space and a breakfast area. A short hallway opens to the utility room and the two-car garage. The master suite takes up the entire left wing of the home, enjoying an elegant private bath and a walk-in closet that goes on and on. Upstairs, three more bedrooms reside, sharing two full baths. Expandable future space awaits on the right.

SECOND FLOOR

FIRST FLOOR

plan# HPT900065

- **STYLE:** COUNTRY COTTAGE
- **FIRST FLOOR:** 2,891 SQ. FT.
- **SECOND FLOOR:** 1,336 SQ. FT.
- **TOTAL:** 4,227 SQ. FT.
- **BONUS SPACE:** 380 SQ. FT.
- **BEDROOMS:** 4
- **BATHROOMS:** 3½ + ½
- **WIDTH:** 90'-8"
- **DEPTH:** 56'-4"
- **FOUNDATION:** BASEMENT, CRAWLSPACE

SEARCH ONLINE @ EPLANS.COM

This Southern coastal cottage radiates charm and elegance. Step inside from the covered porch and discover a floor plan with practicality and architectural interest. The foyer has a raised ceiling and is partially open to above. The library and great room offer fireplaces and built-in shelves; the great room also provides rear porch access. The kitchen, featuring an island with a separate sink, is adjacent to the breakfast room and a study with a built-in desk. On the far right, the master bedroom will amaze, with a sumptuous bath and enormous walk-in closet. Three upstairs bedrooms share a loft and recreation room. Note the convenient storage opportunities.

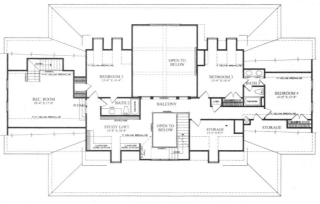

SECOND FLOOR

FIRST FLOOR

SECOND FLOOR

FIRST FLOOR

BASEMENT

plan# HPT900067

- **STYLE:** SOUTHERN COLONIAL
- **FIRST FLOOR:** 1,901 SQ. FT.
- **SECOND FLOOR:** 1,874 SQ. FT.
- **TOTAL:** 3,775 SQ. FT.
- **BEDROOMS:** 4
- **BATHROOMS:** 3½
- **WIDTH:** 50'-0"
- **DEPTH:** 70'-0"
- **FOUNDATION:** PIER

SEARCH ONLINE @ EPLANS.COM

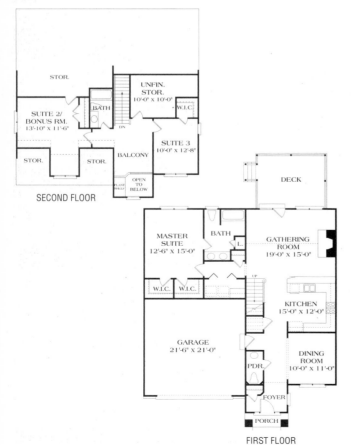

SECOND FLOOR

FIRST FLOOR

plan# HPT900066

- **STYLE:** CRAFTSMAN
- **FIRST FLOOR:** 1,258 SQ. FT.
- **SECOND FLOOR:** 662 SQ. FT.
- **TOTAL:** 1,920 SQ. FT.
- **BONUS SPACE:** 254 SQ. FT.
- **BEDROOMS:** 2
- **BATHROOMS:** 2½
- **WIDTH:** 41'-6"
- **DEPTH:** 48'-0"
- **FOUNDATION:** CRAWLSPACE

SEARCH ONLINE @ EPLANS.COM

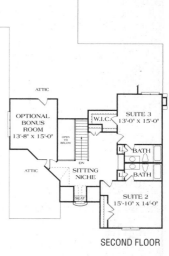

FIRST FLOOR

SECOND FLOOR

plan# HPT900069

- STYLE: EUROPEAN COTTAGE
- FIRST FLOOR: 2,326 SQ. FT.
- SECOND FLOOR: 955 SQ. FT.
- TOTAL: 3,281 SQ. FT.
- BONUS SPACE: 253 SQ. FT.
- BEDROOMS: 3
- BATHROOMS: 4
- WIDTH: 84'-2"
- DEPTH: 51'-4"
- FOUNDATION: CRAWLSPACE

SEARCH ONLINE @ EPLANS.COM

FIRST FLOOR

SECOND FLOOR

plan# HPT900068

- STYLE: FRENCH COUNTRY
- FIRST FLOOR: 2,000 SQ. FT.
- SECOND FLOOR: 934 SQ. FT.
- TOTAL: 2,934 SQ. FT.
- BONUS SPACE: 363 SQ. FT.
- BEDROOMS: 3
- BATHROOMS: 2½
- WIDTH: 42'-0"
- DEPTH: 94'-8"
- FOUNDATION: CRAWLSPACE

SEARCH ONLINE @ EPLANS.COM

PHOTO COURTESY OF: BOB GREENSPAN

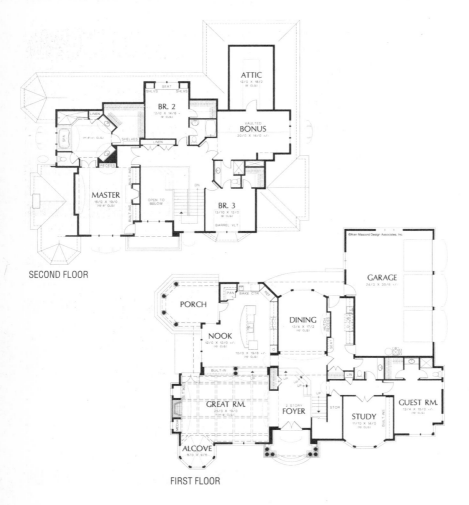

SECOND FLOOR

FIRST FLOOR

plan # HPT900070

- STYLE: CRAFTSMAN
- FIRST FLOOR: 2,572 SQ. FT.
- SECOND FLOOR: 1,578 SQ. FT.
- TOTAL: 4,150 SQ. FT.
- BONUS SPACE: 315 SQ. FT.
- BEDROOMS: 4
- BATHROOMS: 4½
- WIDTH: 78'-2"
- DEPTH: 68'-0"
- FOUNDATION: CRAWLSPACE

SEARCH ONLINE @ EPLANS.COM

Craftsman detailing and a hint of French flair make this home a standout in any neighborhood. An impressive foyer opens to the left to the great room, with a coffered ceiling, warming fireplace and a charming alcove, set in a turret. The kitchen is designed for entertaining, with an island that doubles as a snack bar and plenty of room to move. An adjacent porch invites dining alfresco. The bayed study is peaceful and quiet. A nearby guest room enjoys a private bath. Upstairs, the master suite is awe inspiring. A romantic fireplace sets the mood and natural light pours in. A sumptuous spa bath leaves homeowners pampered and relaxed. Two bedroom suites share a vaulted bonus room, perfect as a home gym.

© 2001 Donald A. Gardner, Inc.

Stone and horizontal siding give a definite country flavor to this two-story home. The front study makes an ideal guest room with the adjoining powder room. The formal dining room is accented with decorative columns that define its perimeter. The great room boasts a fireplace, built-ins and a magnificent view of the backyard beyond one of two rear porches. The master suite boasts two walk-in closets and a private bath. Two bedrooms share a full bath on the second floor.

plan# HPT900071

- **STYLE: CRAFTSMAN**
- **FIRST FLOOR: 1,707 SQ. FT.**
- **SECOND FLOOR: 514 SQ. FT.**
- **TOTAL: 2,221 SQ. FT.**
- **BONUS SPACE: 211 SQ. FT.**
- **BEDROOMS: 4**
- **BATHROOMS: 2½**
- **WIDTH: 50'-0"**
- **DEPTH: 71'-8"**

SEARCH ONLINE @ EPLANS.COM

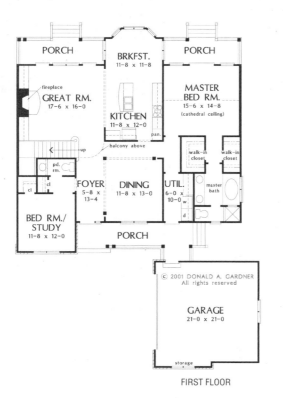

FIRST FLOOR

SECOND FLOOR

© 2002 Donald A. Gardner, Inc.

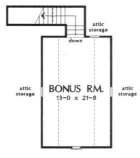

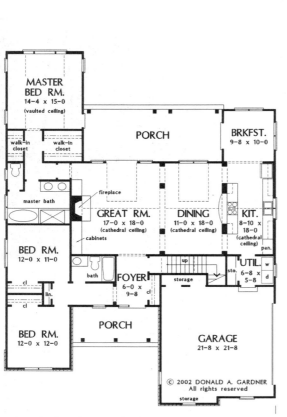

plan # HPT900072

- STYLE: CRAFTSMAN
- SQUARE FOOTAGE: 1,911
- BONUS SPACE: 366 SQ. FT.
- BEDROOMS: 3
- BATHROOMS: 2
- WIDTH: 52'-0"
- DEPTH: 69'-10"

SEARCH ONLINE @ EPLANS.COM

This Craftsman-inspired delight combines stone with delicately detailed windows for a rustic yet refined look. Enter from the columned porch to the foyer, which leads into the enormous great room. Here, a fireplace and open access to the dining room make entertaining a breeze. Both the great room and dining room feature soaring cathedral ceilings, as does the galley kitchen to the right. A petite breakfast nook off the kitchen opens to the rear porch. Sleeping quarters are sequestered to the left of the plan. Two bedrooms share a bath at the front, and the grand master suite is tucked in back. Two walk-in closets and a compartmented bath make the master suite a luxurious retreat. Upstairs, bonus space can be made into an extra guest room.

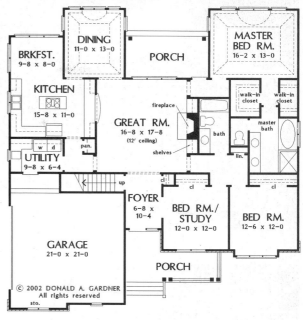

DINING
11-0 x 13-0

PORCH

MASTER
BED RM.
16-2 x 13-0

BRKFST.
9-8 x 8-0

KITCHEN
15-8 x 11-0

walk-in
closet

walk-in
closet

master
bath

fireplace

GREAT RM.
16-8 x 17-8
(12' ceiling)

bath

shelves

UTILITY
9-8 x 6-4

pan.

w d

lin.

up

cl

cl

cl

FOYER
6-8 x
10-4

BED RM./
STUDY
12-0 x 12-0

BED RM.
12-6 x 12-0

GARAGE
21-0 x 21-0

PORCH

sto.

plan# HPT900074

- STYLE: CRAFTSMAN
- SQUARE FOOTAGE: 1,904
- BONUS SPACE: 366 SQ. FT.
- BEDROOMS: 3
- BATHROOMS: 2
- WIDTH: 53'-10"
- DEPTH: 57'-8"

SEARCH ONLINE @ EPLANS.COM

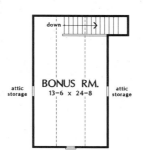

down

BONUS RM.
13-6 x 24-8

attic
storage

attic
storage

BED RM.
11-8 x 13-0

BED RM.
11-8 x 12-0

great room
below

cl

lin.

bath

railing

foyer
below

down

down

attic
storage

attic
storage

BONUS RM.
13-2 x 31-0

SECOND FLOOR

PORCH

MASTER
BED RM.
14-0 x 16-0

DINING
12-0 x 14-4

(vaulted ceiling)

GREAT RM.
23-0 x 15-10

SCREEN
PORCH
10-0 x 11-8

fireplace

balcony above

KITCHEN
12-0 x 14-2

walk-in
closet

master bath

lin.

BRKFST.
10-0 x 10-0

FOYER
6-8 x 7-7

pd. rm.

cl

down

up

UTILITY
8-4 x 5-8

d w

cl

PORCH

sto.

GARAGE
22-0 x 24-0

FIRST FLOOR

STORAGE
14-0 x 11-10

PATIO

STORAGE
13-4 x 15-6
(unfinished)

FAMILY RM.
17-10 x 15-4

fireplace

wet bar

cl

BED RM./
STUDY
12-0 x 10-0

bath

sto.

up

BASEMENT

plan# HPT900073

- STYLE: CRAFTSMAN
- MAIN LEVEL: 1682 SQ. FT.
- UPPER LEVEL: 577 SQ. FT.
- LOWER LEVEL: 690 SQ. FT.
- TOTAL: 2,949 SQ. FT.
- BONUS SPACE: 459 SQ. FT.
- BEDROOMS: 4
- BATHROOMS: 3½
- WIDTH: 79'-0"
- DEPTH: 68'-2"

SEARCH ONLINE @ EPLANS.COM

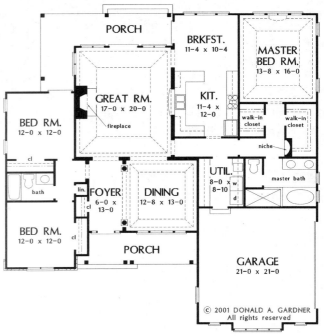

© 2001 Donald A. Gardner, Inc.

plan# HPT900076

- STYLE: CRAFTSMAN
- SQUARE FOOTAGE: 1,974
- BEDROOMS: 3
- BATHROOMS: 2
- WIDTH: 56'-0"
- DEPTH: 58'-4"

SEARCH ONLINE @ EPLANS.COM

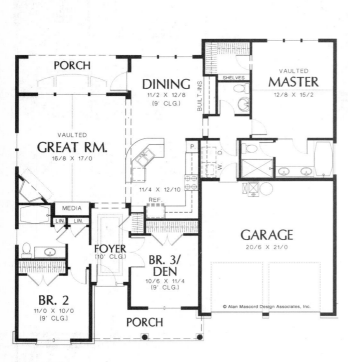

© Alan Mascord Design Associates, Inc.

plan# HPT900075

- STYLE: CRAFTSMAN
- SQUARE FOOTAGE: 1,580
- BEDROOMS: 3
- BATHROOMS: 2½
- WIDTH: 50'-0"
- DEPTH: 48'-0"
- FOUNDATION: CRAWLSPACE

SEARCH ONLINE @ EPLANS.COM

© 2002 Donald A. Gardner, Inc.

plan# HPT900077

- STYLE: CRAFTSMAN
- SQUARE FOOTAGE: 1,580
- BONUS SPACE: 367 SQ. FT.
- BEDROOMS: 3
- BATHROOMS: 2
- WIDTH: 55'-6"
- DEPTH: 46'-0"

SEARCH ONLINE @ EPLANS.COM

Stone accents and a copper bay bring a fresh look to this traditional facade. Sidelights around the door make the recessed entry a stunning centerpiece. Inside, the great room's fireplace brings warmth to the heart of the home, while the cathedral ceiling and deck access make it elegant. The kitchen enjoys views from the adjacent dining room's picture window. The comfy master suite in back enjoys a tray ceiling, walk-in closet and luxurious bath. The two bedrooms up front—or you can make one a study—share a full hall bath. Bonus space awaits expansion above the two-car garage.

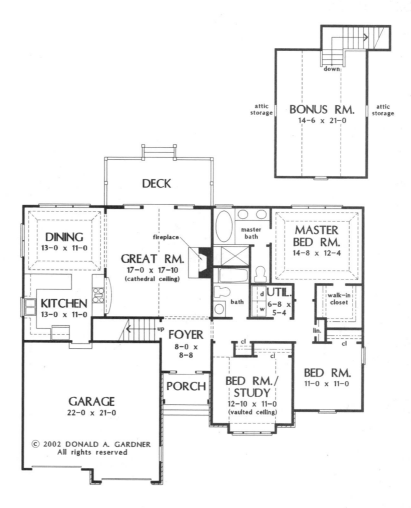

© 2001 Donald A. Gardner, Inc.

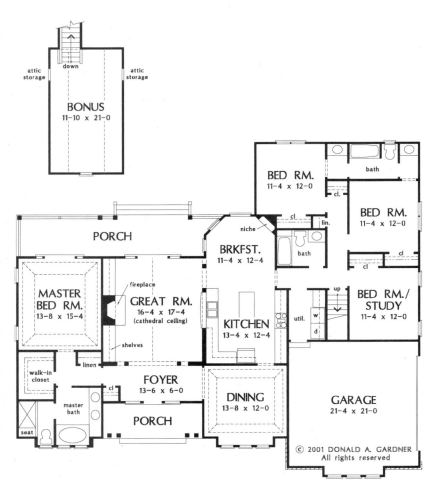

plan # HPT900078

- STYLE: CRAFTSMAN
- SQUARE FOOTAGE: 2,174
- BONUS SPACE: 299 SQ. FT.
- BEDROOMS: 4
- BATHROOMS: 3
- WIDTH: 66'-8"
- DEPTH: 56'-6"

SEARCH ONLINE @ EPLANS.COM

This striking house combines traditional design with Craftsman materials. Twin dormers and columns establish a symmetrical frame to the entryway, and stone accents the garage's box-bay window. Built-ins, a vaulted ceiling and a fireplace highlight the great room, which is connected to the kitchen by a handy pass-through. Tray ceilings crown both the dining room and master bedroom, while French doors in the master bedroom and great room lead to the rear porch. A study/bedroom and bonus room allow for versatility, and the master suite is located for optimum privacy.

plan# HPT900079

- STYLE: TRADITIONAL
- FIRST FLOOR: 1,925 SQ. FT.
- SECOND FLOOR: 1,173 SQ. FT.
- TOTAL: 3,098 SQ. FT.
- BEDROOMS: 4
- BATHROOMS: 3½
- WIDTH: 78'-0"
- DEPTH: 52'-0"
- FOUNDATION: CRAWLSPACE, SLAB

SEARCH ONLINE @ EPLANS.COM

This rustic countryside design offers a simple floor plan and charming exterior details. A covered front porch welcomes you inside to a foyer flanked on either side by formal living and dining rooms. The rear offers a family-size den warmed by a fireplace and a study to the left. The master suite enjoys porch access and a sumptuous private bath. The second floor is home to the three remaining bedrooms, each of which features a dormer window and a walk-in closet. Two full baths and a balcony overlook complete this floor.

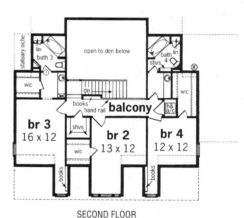

SECOND FLOOR

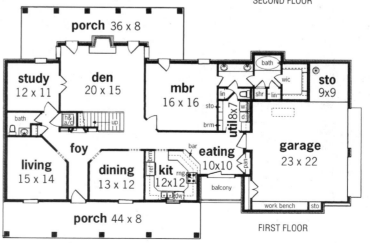

FIRST FLOOR

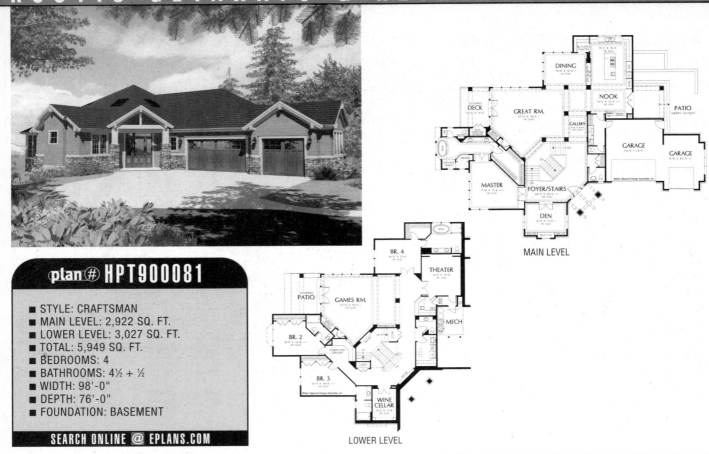

MAIN LEVEL

LOWER LEVEL

plan# HPT900081

- **STYLE:** CRAFTSMAN
- **MAIN LEVEL:** 2,922 SQ. FT.
- **LOWER LEVEL:** 3,027 SQ. FT.
- **TOTAL:** 5,949 SQ. FT.
- **BEDROOMS:** 4
- **BATHROOMS:** 4½ + ½
- **WIDTH:** 98'-0"
- **DEPTH:** 76'-0"
- **FOUNDATION:** BASEMENT

SEARCH ONLINE @ EPLANS.COM

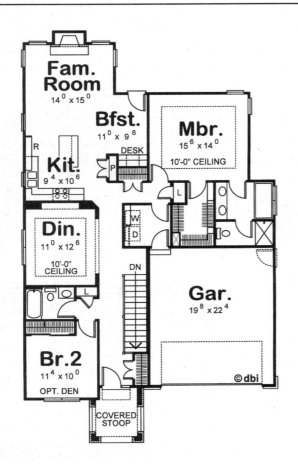

plan# HPT900080

- **STYLE:** FRENCH COUNTRY
- **SQUARE FOOTAGE:** 1,556
- **BEDROOMS:** 2
- **BATHROOMS:** 2
- **WIDTH:** 40'-0"
- **DEPTH:** 58'-4"

SEARCH ONLINE @ EPLANS.COM

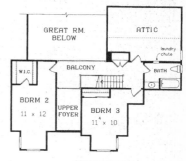

SECOND FLOOR

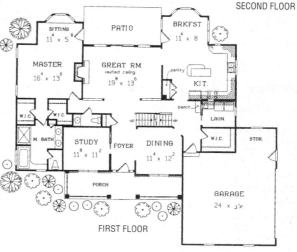

FIRST FLOOR

plan # HPT900082

- STYLE: COUNTRY COTTAGE
- FIRST FLOOR: 1,966 SQ. FT.
- SECOND FLOOR: 726 SQ. FT.
- TOTAL: 2,692 SQ. FT.
- BEDROOMS: 3
- BATHROOMS: 2½
- WIDTH: 66'-0"
- DEPTH: 59'-8"
- FOUNDATION: BASEMENT

SEARCH ONLINE @ EPLANS.COM

SECOND FLOOR

FIRST FLOOR

plan # HPT900083

- STYLE: TRADITIONAL
- FIRST FLOOR: 1,461 SQ. FT.
- SECOND FLOOR: 628 SQ. FT.
- TOTAL: 2,089 SQ. FT.
- BEDROOMS: 3
- BATHROOMS: 2½
- WIDTH: 48'-0"
- DEPTH: 59'-0"

SEARCH ONLINE @ EPLANS.COM

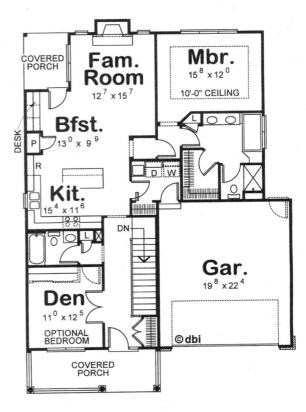

plan# HPT900085

- STYLE: CRAFTSMAN
- SQUARE FOOTAGE: 1,344
- BEDROOMS: 1
- BATHROOMS: 2
- WIDTH: 40'-0"
- DEPTH: 55'-8"

SEARCH ONLINE @ EPLANS.COM

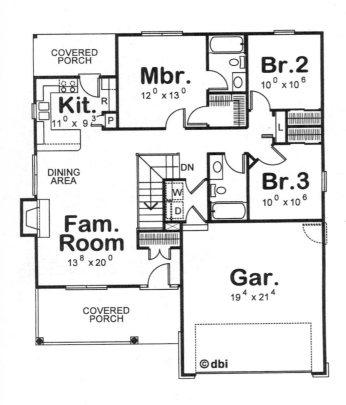

plan# HPT900084

- STYLE: CRAFTSMAN
- SQUARE FOOTAGE: 1,195
- BEDROOMS: 3
- BATHROOMS: 2
- WIDTH: 40'-0"
- DEPTH: 48'-8"

SEARCH ONLINE @ EPLANS.COM

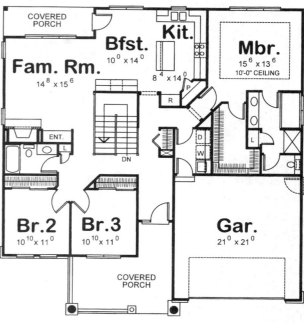

plan# HPT900086

- STYLE: CRAFTSMAN
- SQUARE FOOTAGE: 1,724
- BEDROOMS: 3
- BATHROOMS: 2
- WIDTH: 50'-0"
- DEPTH: 50'-0"

SEARCH ONLINE @ EPLANS.COM

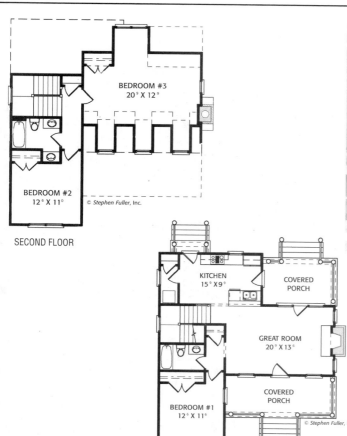

plan# HPT900087

- STYLE: FARMHOUSE
- FIRST FLOOR: 862 SQ. FT.
- SECOND FLOOR: 654 SQ. FT.
- TOTAL: 1,516 SQ. FT.
- BEDROOMS: 3
- BATHROOMS: 2
- WIDTH: 34'-0"
- DEPTH: 39'-6"
- FOUNDATION: CRAWLSPACE

SEARCH ONLINE @ EPLANS.COM

SECOND FLOOR

FIRST FLOOR

plan# HPT900088

- STYLE: NW CONTEMPORARY
- FIRST FLOOR: 852 SQ. FT.
- SECOND FLOOR: 374 SQ. FT.
- TOTAL: 1,226 SQ. FT.
- BEDROOMS: 2
- BATHROOMS: 2
- WIDTH: 37'-10"
- DEPTH: 33'-4"
- FOUNDATION: CRAWLSPACE

SEARCH ONLINE @ EPLANS.COM

SECOND FLOOR

FIRST FLOOR

plan# HPT900089

- STYLE: MEDITERRANEAN
- FIRST FLOOR: 617 SQ. FT.
- SECOND FLOOR: 474 SQ. FT.
- TOTAL: 1,091 SQ. FT.
- BEDROOMS: 2
- BATHROOMS: 2½
- WIDTH: 32'-0"
- DEPTH: 31'-0"
- FOUNDATION: CRAWLSPACE

SEARCH ONLINE @ EPLANS.COM

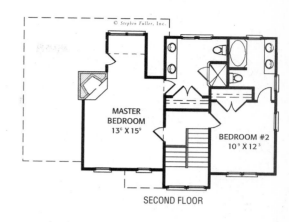

SECOND FLOOR

plan# HPT900091

- STYLE: EUROPEAN COTTAGE
- FIRST FLOOR: 648 SQ. FT.
- SECOND FLOOR: 683 SQ. FT.
- TOTAL: 1,331 SQ. FT.
- BEDROOMS: 2
- BATHROOMS: 2½
- WIDTH: 42'-0"
- DEPTH: 29'-6"
- FOUNDATION: CRAWLSPACE

SEARCH ONLINE @ EPLANS.COM

FIRST FLOOR

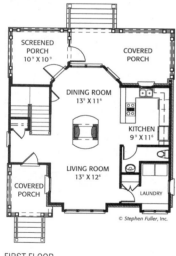

FIRST FLOOR

SECOND FLOOR

plan# HPT900090

- STYLE: TUDOR
- FIRST FLOOR: 756 SQ. FT.
- SECOND FLOOR: 580 SQ. FT.
- TOTAL: 1,336 SQ. FT.
- BEDROOMS: 2
- BATHROOMS: 2½
- WIDTH: 32'-0"
- DEPTH: 36'-9"
- FOUNDATION: CRAWLSPACE

SEARCH ONLINE @ EPLANS.COM

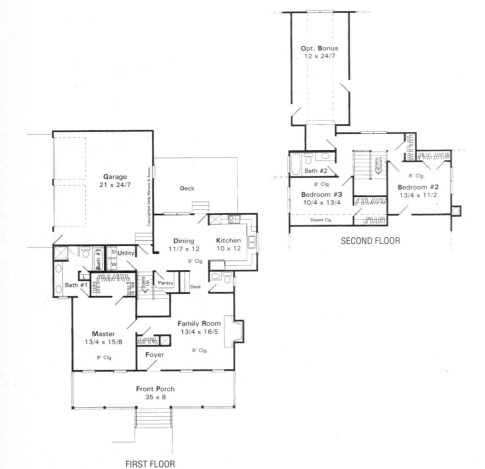

FIRST FLOOR

SECOND FLOOR

plan# HPT900092

- **STYLE:** COUNTRY COTTAGE
- **FIRST FLOOR:** 1,189 SQ. FT.
- **SECOND FLOOR:** 546 SQ. FT.
- **TOTAL:** 1,735 SQ. FT.
- **BONUS SPACE:** 355 SQ. FT.
- **BEDROOMS:** 3
- **BATHROOMS:** 2½
- **WIDTH:** 44'-0"
- **DEPTH:** 60'-5"
- **FOUNDATION:** CRAWLSPACE

SEARCH ONLINE @ EPLANS.COM

This rustic country cottage works great as a primary home or as a vacation getaway. Past the covered front porch, the foyer opens into the family room, warmed by an extended-hearth fireplace. A built-in planning desk and walk-in pantry are wonderful amenities for the U-shaped kitchen. Bright windows over the sink and in the dining area bring in lots of natural light. The first-floor master suite enjoys a pampering bath and walk-in closet. Upstairs, two bedrooms share a full bath and optional bonus space, perfect as a home office, gym or playroom.

TO ORDER BLUEPRINTS CALL TOLL FREE 1-800-521-6797

plan # HPT900093

- STYLE: LAKEFRONT
- SQUARE FOOTAGE: 840
- BEDROOMS: 1
- BATHROOMS: 1
- WIDTH: 33'-0"
- DEPTH: 31'-0"
- FOUNDATION: BASEMENT

SEARCH ONLINE @ EPLANS.COM

This charming home is ideal for waterfront property with a generous wraparound porch. The porch features a corner gazebo that's perfect for outdoor living. The vestibule offers an energy- and space-efficient pocket door that opens to the island kitchen and dining room where sliding glass doors open to the gazebo. The living room views in three directions, bringing the outside in. A bedroom and lavish bath complete the floor plan.

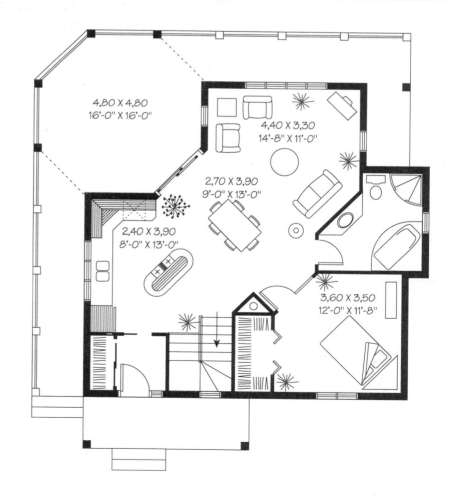

4,80 X 4,80
16'-0" X 16'-0"

4,40 X 3,30
14'-8" X 11'-0"

2,70 X 3,90
9'-0" X 13'-0"

2,40 X 3,90
8'-0" X 13'-0"

3,60 X 3,50
12'-0" X 11'-8"

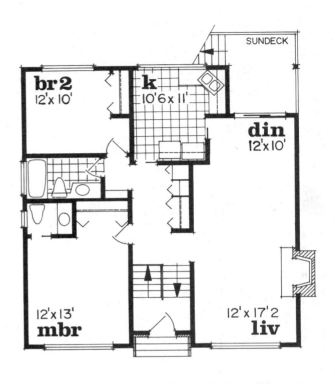

plan# **HPT900094**

- **STYLE:** BUNGALOW
- **SQUARE FOOTAGE:** 1,031
- **BEDROOMS:** 2
- **BATHROOMS:** 1½
- **WIDTH:** 32'-0"
- **DEPTH:** 34'-0"
- **FOUNDATION:** BASEMENT

SEARCH ONLINE @ EPLANS.COM

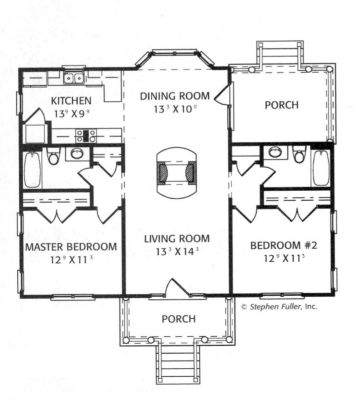

plan# **HPT900095**

- **STYLE:** MOUNTAIN
- **SQUARE FOOTAGE:** 1,070
- **BEDROOMS:** 2
- **BATHROOMS:** 2
- **WIDTH:** 40'-0"
- **DEPTH:** 36'-6"
- **FOUNDATION:** CRAWLSPACE

SEARCH ONLINE @ EPLANS.COM

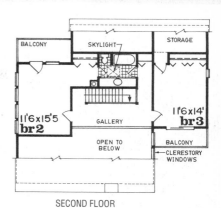

SECOND FLOOR

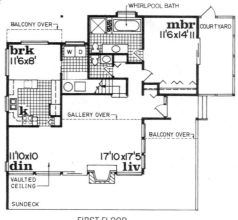

FIRST FLOOR

plan# HPT900097

- STYLE: COUNTRY COTTAGE
- FIRST FLOOR: 1,242 SQ. FT.
- SECOND FLOOR: 704 SQ. FT.
- TOTAL: 1,946 SQ. FT.
- BEDROOMS: 2
- BATHROOMS: 2½
- WIDTH: 42'-6"
- DEPTH: 36'-0"
- FOUNDATION: CRAWLSPACE

SEARCH ONLINE @ EPLANS.COM

plan# HPT900096

- STYLE: RANCH
- SQUARE FOOTAGE: 1,196
- BEDROOMS: 3
- BATHROOMS: 1½
- WIDTH: 46'-0"
- DEPTH: 26'-0"
- FOUNDATION: BASEMENT

SEARCH ONLINE @ EPLANS.COM

© 1985 Donald A. Gardner Architects, Inc.

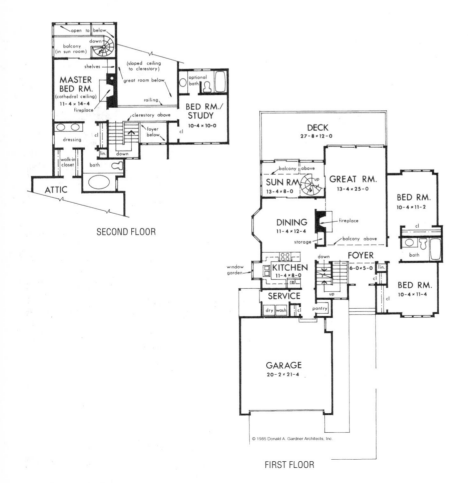

SECOND FLOOR

FIRST FLOOR

© 1985 Donald A. Gardner Architects, Inc.

plan # HPT900098

- STYLE: CONTEMPORARY
- FIRST FLOOR: 1,340 SQ. FT.
- SECOND FLOOR: 651 SQ. FT.
- TOTAL: 1,991 SQ. FT.
- BEDROOMS: 4
- BATHROOMS: 3
- WIDTH: 45'-4"
- DEPTH: 60'-0"

SEARCH ONLINE @ EPLANS.COM

This contemporary design will make a wonderful visual impact on any neighborhood. Inside, the foyer opens to an impressive two-story great room with a large view of the rear yard and a warming fireplace. A sun room and a dining room sit to the left of the great room. Note the window garden over the kitchen sink—perfect for an herb garden. Two family bedrooms share a full bath on the right of the foyer, while the master suite and a third family bedroom (or a study) reside on the second level. This amazing master suite features a balcony with spiral stairs down to the sun room, a fireplace with built-in shelves and a roomy bath.

© 1986 Donald A. Gardner Architects, Inc.

plan# HPT900099

- STYLE: CONTEMPORARY
- FIRST FLOOR: 1,434 SQ. FT.
- SECOND FLOOR: 604 SQ. FT.
- TOTAL: 2,038 SQ. FT.
- BEDROOMS: 3
- BATHROOMS: 2
- WIDTH: 47'-4"
- DEPTH: 69'-0"

SEARCH ONLINE @ EPLANS.COM

This home is a stunner in any setting—build it in the woods or in the most urban neighborhood. Wood and stone blend with contemporary lines for a fresh yet natural look. The interior was designed for optimum leisure with its enormous hearth-warmed great room at the center and a spectacular sun room that leads out to a phenomenal rear deck. The kitchen—which boasts a window garden—is bookended by a casual breakfast nook and a formal dining room for special occasions. Two bedrooms share a bath on the right and a utility room off the breakfast nook opens to the two-car garage. Upstairs, the deluxe master suite awaits. Among its many amenities are a cathedral ceiling, fireplace, spacious skylit bath with corner tub, a huge walk-in closet and an adjacent study. And as an extra touch of custom luxury, a petite balcony off the bedroom looks down into the sun room.

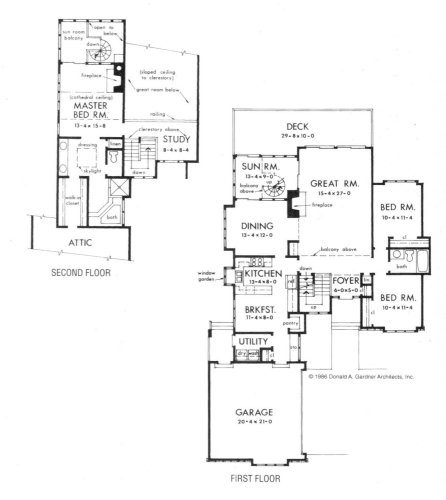

© 1986 Donald A. Gardner Architects, Inc.

© 2001 Donald A. Gardner, Inc.

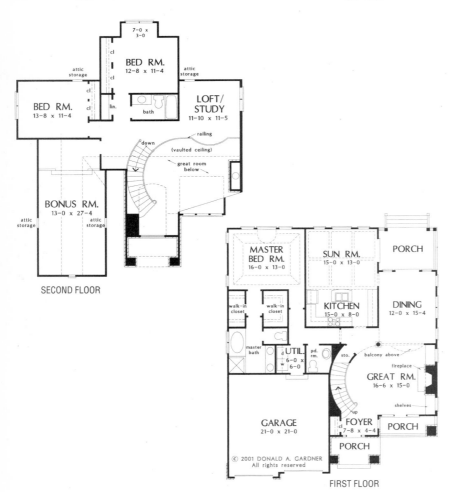

SECOND FLOOR

FIRST FLOOR

© 2001 DONALD A. GARDNER
All rights reserved

plan# HPT900100

- STYLE: CRAFTSMAN
- FIRST FLOOR: 1,542 SQ. FT.
- SECOND FLOOR: 752 SQ. FT.
- TOTAL: 2,294 SQ. FT.
- BONUS SPACE: 370 SQ. FT.
- BEDROOMS: 3
- BATHROOMS: 2½
- WIDTH: 44'-4"
- DEPTH: 54'-0"

SEARCH ONLINE @ EPLANS.COM

A unique mixture of stone, siding, and windows create character in this Arts and Crafts design. Columns, decorative railing and a metal roof add architectural interest to an intimate front porch, while a rock entryway frames a French door flanked by side-lights and crowned with a transom. An elegant, curved staircase highlights the grand two-story foyer and great room. A clerestory floods both the great room and second-floor loft with light. A delightful sunroom can be accessed from the dining room and is open to the kitchen. Upstairs, closets act as noise barriers between two bedrooms, and the bonus room can be used as a home theatre or recreation room.

plan# HPT900101

- **STYLE:** COUNTRY COTTAGE
- **FIRST FLOOR:** 1,904 SQ. FT.
- **SECOND FLOOR:** 1,098 SQ. FT.
- **TOTAL:** 3,002 SQ. FT.
- **BONUS SPACE:** 522 SQ. FT.
- **BEDROOMS:** 4
- **BATHROOMS:** 4½
- **WIDTH:** 88'-2"
- **DEPTH:** 54'-0"
- **FOUNDATION:** BASEMENT, CRAWLSPACE

SEARCH ONLINE @ EPLANS.COM

This unique exterior design presents an open, yet cozy floor plan. A built-in entertainment center and a cathedral ceiling create a spacious great room that leads to the breakfast area and island kitchen. The terrace is accessible from the breakfast area. Privacy is afforded to the master bedroom, placed to the far right of the design; it's complemented by a master bath built for two and a walk-in closet with a window seat. At the top of the stairs, a balcony and a hall lead to a future recreation room. Three bedrooms, each with full baths, are also available on the second floor.

SECOND FLOOR

FIRST FLOOR

© 2002 Donald A. Gardner, Inc.

BED RM.
12-0 x 12-0

great room below

attic storage

railing down

bath lin. cl

BONUS RM.
21-0 x 14-4

down

bath

BED RM.
12-0 x 11-0

lin. cl

foyer below

BED RM.
12-0 x 11-0

attic storage

SECOND FLOOR

plan # HPT900102

- STYLE: FARMHOUSE
- FIRST FLOOR: 1,798 SQ. FT.
- SECOND FLOOR: 723 SQ. FT.
- TOTAL: 2,521 SQ. FT.
- BONUS SPACE: 349 SQ. FT.
- BEDROOMS: 4
- BATHROOMS: 3½
- WIDTH: 66'-8"
- DEPTH: 49'-8"

SEARCH ONLINE @ EPLANS.COM

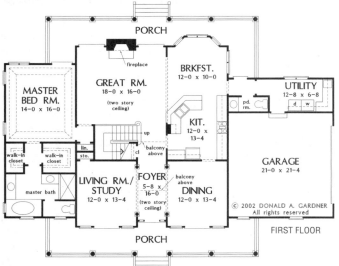

PORCH

fireplace

MASTER BED RM.
14-0 x 16-0

GREAT RM.
18-0 x 16-0
(two story ceiling)

BRKFST.
12-0 x 10-0

UTILITY
12-8 x 6-8

pd. rm. d | w

up

balcony above

KIT.
12-0 x 13-4

lin. sto.

walk-in closet

walk-in closet

master bath

LIVING RM./
STUDY
12-0 x 13-4

FOYER
5-8 x 16-0
(two story ceiling)

balcony above

DINING
12-0 x 13-4

GARAGE
21-0 x 21-4

© 2002 DONALD A. GARDNER
All rights reserved

PORCH

FIRST FLOOR

With spacious front and rear porches, twin gables and an arched entrance, this home has overwhelming charm and curb appeal. Columns make a grand impression both inside and outside, and transoms above French doors brighten both the front and rear of the floor plan. An angled counter separates the kitchen from the great room and breakfast area, while the mudroom/utility area is complete with a sink. A tray ceiling tops the master bedroom, and the formal living room/study and bonus room are flexible spaces, tailoring to family needs. A balcony overlooks the foyer and great room, while an additional upstairs bedroom has its own bath and can be used as a guest suite.

© 2001 Donald A. Gardner, Inc.

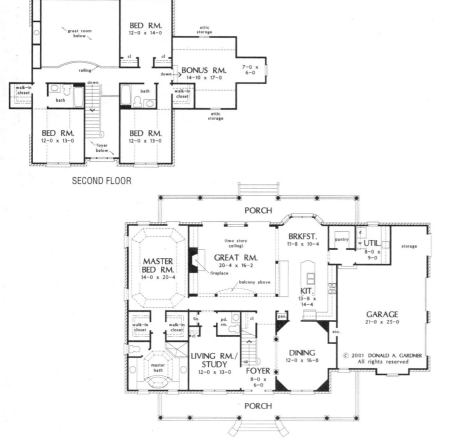

SECOND FLOOR

FIRST FLOOR

plan# HPT900103

- STYLE: TRADITIONAL
- FIRST FLOOR: 2,194 SQ. FT.
- SECOND FLOOR: 973 SQ. FT.
- TOTAL: 3,167 SQ. FT.
- BONUS SPACE: 281 SQ. FT.
- BEDROOMS: 4
- BATHROOMS: 3½
- WIDTH: 71'-11"
- DEPTH: 54'-4"

SEARCH ONLINE @ EPLANS.COM

This updated farmhouse has been given additional custom-styled features. Twin gables, sidelights, and an arched entryway accent the facade, while decorative ceiling treatments, bay windows, and French doors adorn the interior. From an abundance of counter space and large walk-in pantry to the built-ins and storage areas, this design makes the most of space. Supported by columns, a curved balcony overlooks the stunning two-story great room. The powder room is easily accessible from the common rooms, and angled corners soften the dining room.

plan # HPT900104

- **STYLE: COUNTRY COTTAGE**
- **FIRST FLOOR: 1,900 SQ. FT.**
- **SECOND FLOOR: 827 SQ. FT.**
- **TOTAL: 2,727 SQ. FT.**
- **BONUS SPACE: 165 SQ. FT.**
- **BEDROOMS: 4**
- **BATHROOMS: 3½**
- **WIDTH: 56'-0"**
- **DEPTH: 51'-4"**
- **FOUNDATION: BASEMENT, CRAWLSPACE**

SEARCH ONLINE @ EPLANS.COM

Traditional Craftsman flavor makes this beautiful brick and siding home a treasure in any neighborhood. From the covered front porch, the two-story foyer gives way to a soaring vaulted family room, made cozy by a fireplace framed by radius windows. An intriguing kitchen spreads out to accommodate multiple chefs, making meal preparation a fun family event (while offering a convenient layout that adapts to quick meals). The keeping room, with a warming fireplace, is surrounded by windows topped with transoms, bringing in floods of natural light. The first-floor master suite is indulgent, providing a beautiful vaulted bath and an immense walk-in closet. Upstairs, three bedrooms share access to bonus space.

FIRST FLOOR

SECOND FLOOR

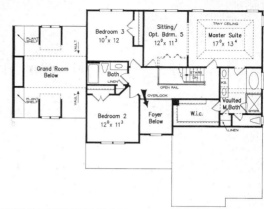

SECOND FLOOR

FIRST FLOOR

plan# HPT900105

- **STYLE:** COUNTRY
- **FIRST FLOOR:** 1,447 SQ. FT.
- **SECOND FLOOR:** 1,109 SQ. FT.
- **TOTAL:** 2,556 SQ. FT.
- **BEDROOMS:** 5
- **BATHROOMS:** 3
- **WIDTH:** 58'-0"
- **DEPTH:** 47'-0"
- **FOUNDATION:** BASEMENT, CRAWLSPACE

SEARCH ONLINE @ EPLANS.COM

SECOND FLOOR

© 2001 Donald A. Gardner, Inc.

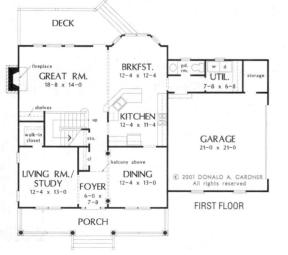

FIRST FLOOR

plan# HPT900106

- **STYLE:** COUNTRY
- **FIRST FLOOR:** 1,282 SQ. FT.
- **SECOND FLOOR:** 985 SQ. FT.
- **TOTAL:** 2,267 SQ. FT.
- **BONUS SPACE:** 395 SQ. FT.
- **BEDROOMS:** 3
- **BATHROOMS:** 2½
- **WIDTH:** 55'-10"
- **DEPTH:** 43'-8"

SEARCH ONLINE @ EPLANS.COM

SECOND FLOOR

FIRST FLOOR

plan# HPT900108

- STYLE: FARMHOUSE
- FIRST FLOOR: 1,127 SQ. FT.
- SECOND FLOOR: 485 SQ. FT.
- TOTAL: 1,612 SQ. FT.
- BEDROOMS: 3
- BATHROOMS: 2½
- WIDTH: 58'-8"
- DEPTH: 42'-0"
- FOUNDATION: BASEMENT

SEARCH ONLINE @ EPLANS.COM

SECOND FLOOR

© 2002 Donald A. Gardner, Inc.

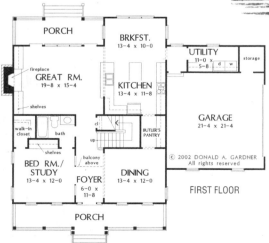

FIRST FLOOR

© 2002 DONALD A. GARDNER
All rights reserved

plan# HPT900107

- STYLE: COUNTRY
- FIRST FLOOR: 1,420 SQ. FT.
- SECOND FLOOR: 1,065 SQ. FT.
- TOTAL: 2,485 SQ. FT.
- BONUS SPACE: 411 SQ. FT.
- BEDROOMS: 4
- BATHROOMS: 3
- WIDTH: 57'-8"
- DEPTH: 49'-0"

SEARCH ONLINE @ EPLANS.COM

TO ORDER BLUEPRINTS CALL TOLL FREE 1-800-521-6797

plan# HPT900109

- STYLE: TRADITIONAL
- FIRST FLOOR: 1,378 SQ. FT.
- SECOND FLOOR: 669 SQ. FT.
- TOTAL: 2,047 SQ. FT.
- BEDROOMS: 4
- BATHROOMS: 2½
- WIDTH: 48'-4"
- DEPTH: 53'-6"
- FOUNDATION: BASEMENT, CRAWLSPACE

SEARCH ONLINE @ EPLANS.COM

The traditional farmhouse gets a fresh outlook with this updated plan. The covered porch opens to an elegant two-story foyer, which opens to the formal dining room on the left. Straight ahead lies the vaulted great room, featuring a fireplace and a ribbon of windows to view the rear property. To the right, the bayed breakfast nook accesses the outside through a French door. The kitchen enjoys pantry space and an ample serving bar. Both a powder room and laundry area are convenient to the kitchen. The deluxe master suite takes up the entire right wing of the first floor, boasting a tray ceiling and an enormous private bath with a walk-in closet. Upstairs, three bedrooms share a full bath and an overlook to the family room below.

© 2001 Donald A. Gardner Architects, Inc.

Country accents and farmhouse style enhance the facade of this lovely two-story home. The first floor provides a formal dining room and great room warmed by a fireplace. The kitchen connects to a breakfast bay—perfect for casual morning meals. The first-floor master suite includes two walk-in closets and a private bath. Upstairs, a loft overlooks the two-story great room. Three second-floor bedrooms share a hall bath. The bonus room above the garage is great for a home office or guest suite.

plan# HPT900110

- **STYLE: COUNTRY**
- **FIRST FLOOR: 1,667 SQ. FT.**
- **SECOND FLOOR: 803 SQ. FT.**
- **TOTAL: 2,470 SQ. FT.**
- **BONUS SPACE: 318 SQ. FT.**
- **BEDROOMS: 4**
- **BATHROOMS: 2½**
- **WIDTH: 52'-4"**
- **DEPTH: 57'-0"**

SEARCH ONLINE @ EPLANS.COM

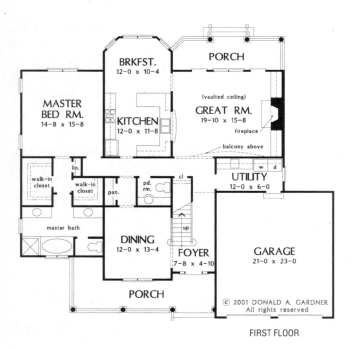

FIRST FLOOR

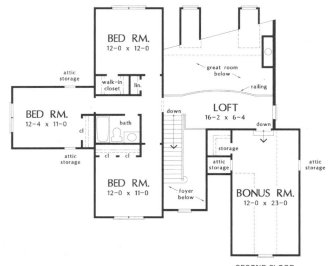

SECOND FLOOR

TO ORDER BLUEPRINTS CALL TOLL FREE 1-800-521-6797

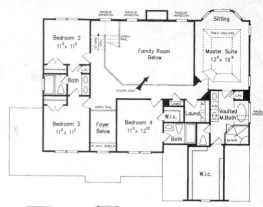

SECOND FLOOR

FIRST FLOOR

plan# HPT900112

- **STYLE: TRADITIONAL**
- **FIRST FLOOR: 1,393 SQ. FT.**
- **SECOND FLOOR: 1,330 SQ. FT.**
- **TOTAL: 2,723 SQ. FT.**
- **BEDROOMS: 5**
- **BATHROOMS: 4**
- **WIDTH: 58'-0"**
- **DEPTH: 47'-6"**
- **FOUNDATION: BASEMENT, CRAWLSPACE**

SEARCH ONLINE @ EPLANS.COM

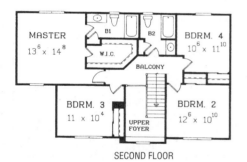

SECOND FLOOR

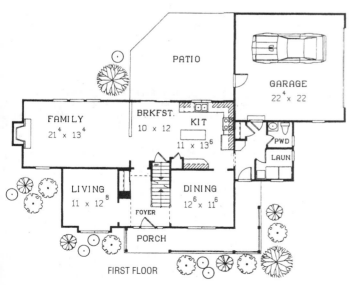

FIRST FLOOR

plan# HPT900111

- **STYLE: TRADITIONAL**
- **FIRST FLOOR: 1,165 SQ. FT.**
- **SECOND FLOOR: 974 SQ. FT.**
- **TOTAL: 2,139 SQ. FT.**
- **BEDROOMS: 4**
- **BATHROOMS: 2½**
- **WIDTH: 65'-0"**
- **DEPTH: 48'-8"**
- **FOUNDATION: BASEMENT**

SEARCH ONLINE @ EPLANS.COM

SECOND FLOOR

plan# HPT900114

- **STYLE:** CAPE COD
- **FIRST FLOOR:** 1,974 SQ. FT.
- **SECOND FLOOR:** 1,038 SQ. FT.
- **TOTAL:** 3,012 SQ. FT.
- **BEDROOMS:** 4
- **BATHROOMS:** 3½
- **WIDTH:** 72'-0"
- **DEPTH:** 57'-0"
- **FOUNDATION:** BASEMENT, CRAWLSPACE

SEARCH ONLINE @ EPLANS.COM

FIRST FLOOR

SECOND FLOOR

FIRST FLOOR

plan# HPT900113

- **STYLE:** FARMHOUSE
- **FIRST FLOOR:** 1,745 SQ. FT.
- **SECOND FLOOR:** 887 SQ. FT.
- **TOTAL:** 2,632 SQ. FT.
- **BONUS SPACE:** 297 SQ. FT.
- **BEDROOMS:** 4
- **BATHROOMS:** 3½
- **WIDTH:** 60'-8"
- **DEPTH:** 50'-10"

SEARCH ONLINE @ EPLANS.COM

TO ORDER BLUEPRINTS CALL TOLL FREE 1-800-521-6797

plan# HPT900115

- **STYLE:** VICTORIAN
- **FIRST FLOOR:** 1,146 SQ. FT.
- **SECOND FLOOR:** 943 SQ. FT.
- **TOTAL:** 2,089 SQ. FT.
- **BONUS SPACE:** 324 SQ. FT.
- **BEDROOMS:** 3
- **BATHROOMS:** 2½
- **WIDTH:** 56'-0"
- **DEPTH:** 38'-0"
- **FOUNDATION:** BASEMENT

SEARCH ONLINE @ EPLANS.COM

This beautiful three-bedroom home boasts many attractive features. Two covered porches will entice you outside, while inside, a special sun room on the first floor brings the outdoors in. The foyer opens on the right to a comfortable family room that may be used as a home office. On the left, the living area is warmed by the sun room and a cozy corner fireplace. A formal dining area lies adjacent to an efficient kitchen with a central island and breakfast nook overlooking the back porch. The second level offers two family bedrooms served by a full bath. A spacious master suite with a walk-in closet and luxurious bath completes the second floor.

FIRST FLOOR

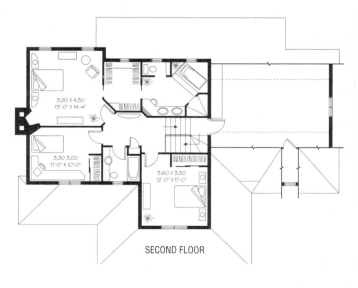

SECOND FLOOR

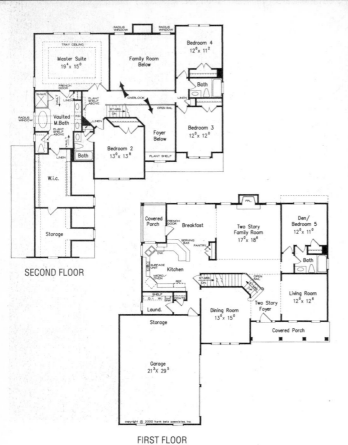

SECOND FLOOR

FIRST FLOOR

plan # HPT900117

- STYLE: COUNTRY COTTAGE
- FIRST FLOOR: 1,570 SQ. FT.
- SECOND FLOOR: 1,650 SQ. FT.
- TOTAL: 3,220 SQ. FT.
- BEDROOMS: 5
- BATHROOMS: 4
- WIDTH: 55'-6"
- DEPTH: 60'-0"
- FOUNDATION: BASEMENT, CRAWLSPACE

SEARCH ONLINE @ EPLANS.COM

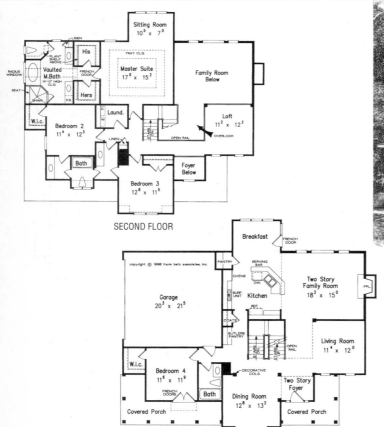

SECOND FLOOR

FIRST FLOOR

plan # HPT900116

- STYLE: COUNTRY COTTAGE
- FIRST FLOOR: 1,435 SQ. FT.
- SECOND FLOOR: 1,452 SQ. FT.
- TOTAL: 2,887 SQ. FT.
- BONUS SPACE: 82 SQ. FT.
- BEDROOMS: 4
- BATHROOMS: 3
- WIDTH: 56'-4"
- DEPTH: 48'-6"
- FOUNDATION: BASEMENT, CRAWLSPACE

SEARCH ONLINE @ EPLANS.COM

plan# HPT900118

- **STYLE: CAPE COD**
- **FIRST FLOOR: 846 SQ. FT.**
- **SECOND FLOOR: 998 SQ. FT.**
- **TOTAL: 1,844 SQ. FT.**
- **BEDROOMS: 3**
- **BATHROOMS: 2½**
- **WIDTH: 49'-4"**
- **DEPTH: 38'-0"**
- **FOUNDATION: BASEMENT, CRAWLSPACE**

SEARCH ONLINE @ EPLANS.COM

New England's seaside is dotted with cottages like this one. Its classic good looks—showcased by dormers and window detailing—will adapt beautifully to any region. The covered porch opens to a two-story foyer, flanked by a dining room and a convenient half-bath. Straight ahead—past the handy coat closet—is the grand hearth-warmed family room, enjoying views of the outdoors through a ribbon of windows. The kitchen features a serving-bar counter to the breakfast area, which has access to the outdoors. Sleeping quarters are secluded upstairs. Two family or guest bedrooms share a full bath. The elegant tray-ceilinged master suite enjoys a private vaulted bath with a windowed tub and walk-in closet. The second floor also features a loft area that cleverly conceals the laundry room.

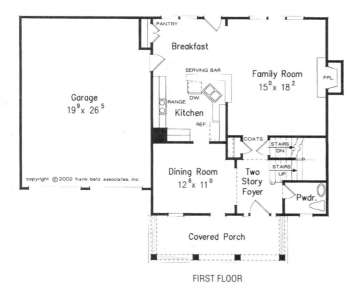

FIRST FLOOR

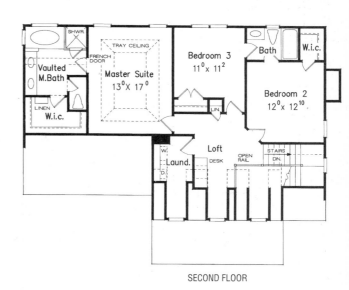

SECOND FLOOR

plan# HPT900119

- **STYLE:** VICTORIAN
- **FIRST FLOOR:** 1,464 SQ. FT.
- **SECOND FLOOR:** 1,054 SQ. FT.
- **TOTAL:** 2,518 SQ. FT.
- **BONUS SPACE:** 332 SQ. FT.
- **BEDROOMS:** 4
- **BATHROOMS:** 3
- **WIDTH:** 59'-0"
- **DEPTH:** 51'-6"
- **FOUNDATION:** CRAWLSPACE

SEARCH ONLINE @ EPLANS.COM

Country Victoriana embellishes this beautiful home. Perfect for a corner lot, this home begs for porch swings and lemonade. Inside, extra-high ceilings expand the space, as a thoughtful floor plan invites family and friends. The two-story great room enjoys a warming fireplace and wonderful rear views. The country kitchen has a preparation island and easily serves the sunny bayed nook and the formal dining room. To the far left, a bedroom serves as a perfect guest room; to the far right, a turret houses a private den. Upstairs, two bedrooms (one in a turret) share a full bath and ample bonus space. The master suite opens through French doors to reveal a grand bedroom and a sumptuous bath with a bumped-out spa tub.

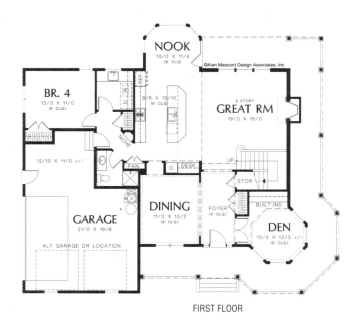

FIRST FLOOR

SECOND FLOOR

plan# HPT900120

- **STYLE:** VICTORIAN FARMHOUSE
- **FIRST FLOOR:** 960 SQ. FT.
- **SECOND FLOOR:** 841 SQ. FT.
- **TOTAL:** 1,801 SQ. FT.
- **BEDROOMS:** 3
- **BATHROOMS:** 1½
- **WIDTH:** 36'-0"
- **DEPTH:** 30'-0"
- **FOUNDATION:** BASEMENT

SEARCH ONLINE @ EPLANS.COM

This romantic cottage design is ideal for any countryside setting. Lively Victorian details enhance the exterior. A wrapping porch with a gazebo-style sitting area encourages refreshing outdoor relaxation, while interior spaces are open to each other. The kitchen with a snack bar is open to both the dining area and the living room area. A powder bath with laundry facilities completes the first floor. The second floor offers space for three family bedrooms with walk-in closets and a pampering whirlpool bath.

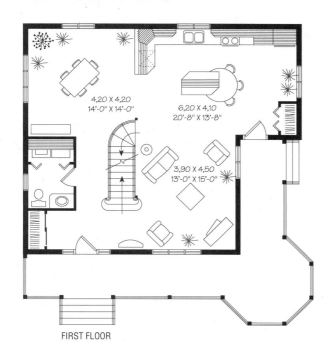

FIRST FLOOR

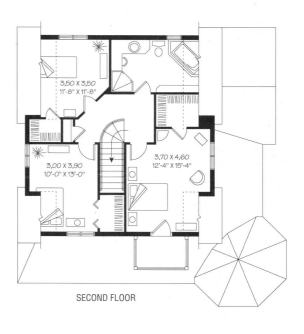

SECOND FLOOR

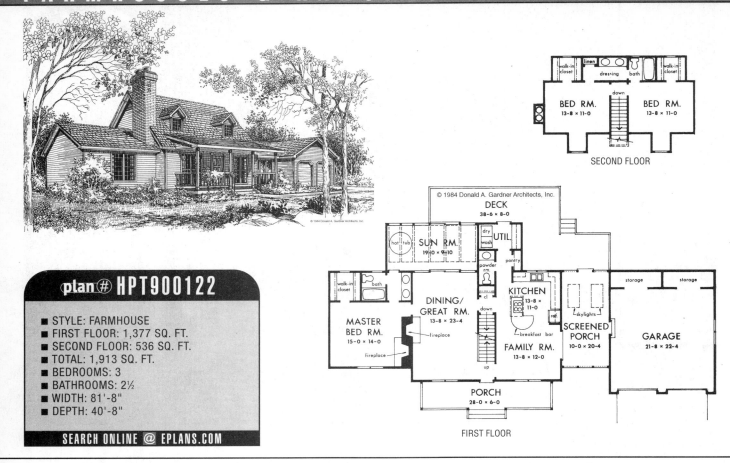

SECOND FLOOR

© 1984 Donald A. Gardner Architects, Inc.

DECK
38-6 × 8-0

SUN RM.
19-0 × 9-10

UTIL.

MASTER BED RM.
15-0 × 14-0

DINING/GREAT RM.
13-8 × 23-4

KITCHEN
13-8 × 11-0

FAMILY RM.
13-8 × 12-0

SCREENED PORCH
10-0 × 20-4

GARAGE
21-8 × 22-4

PORCH
28-0 × 6-0

FIRST FLOOR

BED RM.
13-8 × 11-0

BED RM.
13-8 × 11-0

plan# HPT900122

- STYLE: FARMHOUSE
- FIRST FLOOR: 1,377 SQ. FT.
- SECOND FLOOR: 536 SQ. FT.
- TOTAL: 1,913 SQ. FT.
- BEDROOMS: 3
- BATHROOMS: 2½
- WIDTH: 81'-8"
- DEPTH: 40'-8"

SEARCH ONLINE @ EPLANS.COM

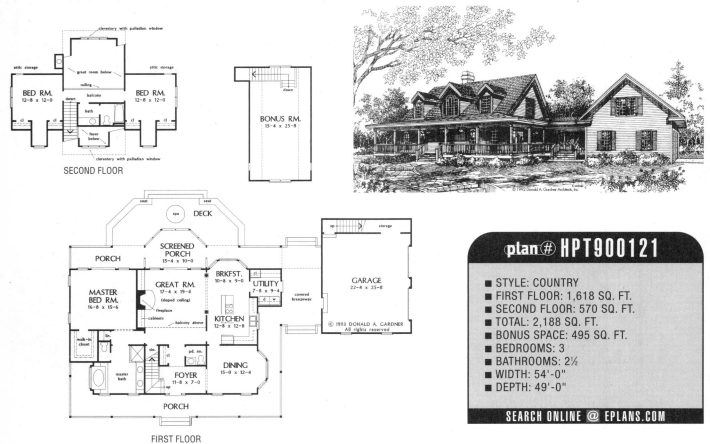

SECOND FLOOR

BED RM.
12-8 × 12-0

BED RM.
12-8 × 12-0

BONUS RM.
15-4 × 25-8

© 1992 Donald A. Gardner Architects, Inc.

DECK

SCREENED PORCH
15-4 × 10-0

GREAT RM.
17-4 × 19-4
(sloped ceiling)

MASTER BED RM.
16-8 × 15-6

BRKFST.
10-8 × 9-0

UTILITY
7-8 × 9-4

GARAGE
22-4 × 25-8

KITCHEN
12-8 × 12-8

DINING
15-0 × 12-4

FOYER
11-8 × 7-0

© 1993 DONALD A. GARDNER
All rights reserved

PORCH

FIRST FLOOR

plan# HPT900121

- STYLE: COUNTRY
- FIRST FLOOR: 1,618 SQ. FT.
- SECOND FLOOR: 570 SQ. FT.
- TOTAL: 2,188 SQ. FT.
- BONUS SPACE: 495 SQ. FT.
- BEDROOMS: 3
- BATHROOMS: 2½
- WIDTH: 54'-0"
- DEPTH: 49'-0"

SEARCH ONLINE @ EPLANS.COM

plan# HPT900123

- STYLE: TRADITIONAL
- SQUARE FOOTAGE: 2,225
- BONUS SPACE: 1,253 SQ. FT.
- BEDROOMS: 3
- BATHROOMS: 2½
- WIDTH: 71'-5"
- DEPTH: 62'-5"
- FOUNDATION: BASEMENT, CRAWLSPACE, SLAB

SEARCH ONLINE @ EPLANS.COM

An inviting porch is only a prelude to the entertaining possibilities inside. Enter to find a dining room, set off by columns, to the immediate right. Ahead, the great room—with a vaulted ceiling, a fireplace and patio access—will host many an event. The kitchen allows for guests to gather and socialize, while the breakfast nook provides a wonderful space for informal meals. The master bedroom will delight with a large walk-in closet and a bath with dual sinks and a separate tub and shower. Two more bedrooms on the first floor share a hall bath. Upstairs, future space leaves it all up to your imagination.

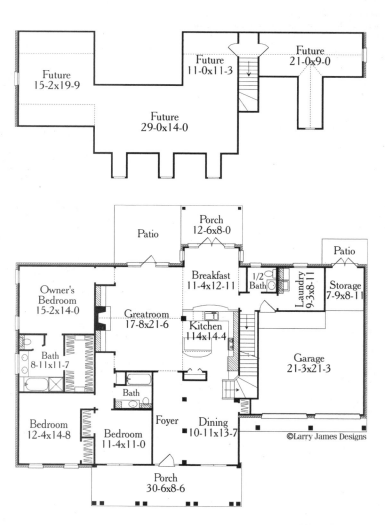

©Larry James Designs

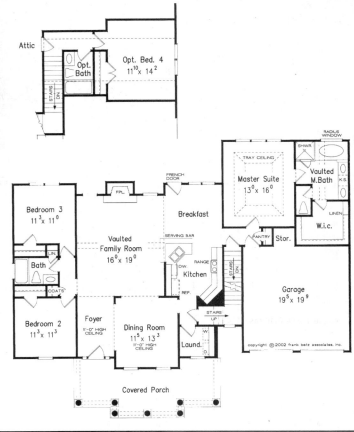

plan# HPT900124

- STYLE: WILLIAMSBURG
- SQUARE FOOTAGE: 1,769
- BONUS SPACE: 160 SQ. FT.
- BEDROOMS: 3
- BATHROOMS: 2
- WIDTH: 62'-0"
- DEPTH: 51'-8"
- FOUNDATION: BASEMENT, CRAWLSPACE

SEARCH ONLINE @ EPLANS.COM

plan# HPT900125

- STYLE: COUNTRY
- SQUARE FOOTAGE: 2,178
- BONUS SPACE: 287 SQ. FT.
- BEDROOMS: 3
- BATHROOMS: 2
- WIDTH: 65'-4"
- DEPTH: 61'-6"
- FOUNDATION: BASEMENT, CRAWLSPACE

SEARCH ONLINE @ EPLANS.COM

TO ORDER BLUEPRINTS CALL TOLL FREE 1-800-521-6797

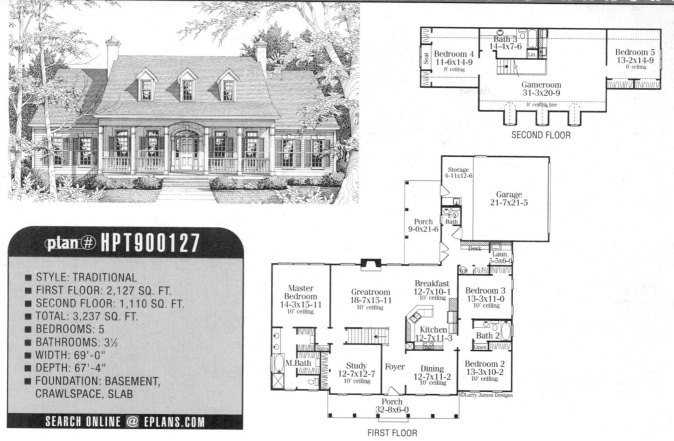

plan# HPT900127

- STYLE: TRADITIONAL
- FIRST FLOOR: 2,127 SQ. FT.
- SECOND FLOOR: 1,110 SQ. FT.
- TOTAL: 3,237 SQ. FT.
- BEDROOMS: 5
- BATHROOMS: 3½
- WIDTH: 69'-0"
- DEPTH: 67'-4"
- FOUNDATION: BASEMENT, CRAWLSPACE, SLAB

SEARCH ONLINE @ EPLANS.COM

SECOND FLOOR

Bedroom 4 11-6x14-9 8' ceiling
Bath 3 14-4x7-6
Bedroom 5 13-2x14-9 8' ceiling
Gameroom 31-3x20-9 8' ceiling line

Storage 4-11x12-6
Garage 21-7x21-5
Porch 9-0x21-6
Laun. 5-5x6-0

Master Bedroom 14-3x15-11 10' ceiling
Greatroom 18-7x15-11 10' ceiling
Breakfast 12-7x10-1 10' ceiling
Bedroom 3 13-3x11-0 10' ceiling
Kitchen 12-7x11-3
Bath 2
M.Bath
Study 12-7x12-7 10' ceiling
Foyer
Dining 12-7x11-2 10' ceiling
Bedroom 2 13-3x10-2 10' ceiling
Porch 32-8x6-0

©Larry James Designs

FIRST FLOOR

Storage 21-4x7-4
Greatroom 16-8x17-6 9' ceiling
Basement Stair Location
Carport 22-0x22-0
Patio 18-0x12-0
Bedroom 11-6x11-6 9' ceiling
Shelves Pantry
Dining 11-0x11-6 9' ceiling
Kitchen 10-10x11-6
M.Bath 9' ceiling
Bedroom 11-6x13-6 9' ceiling
Bath
Greatroom 21-10x17-6 9' ceiling
Owner's Bedroom 15-6x17-6 9' ceiling
Porch 39-4x8-6

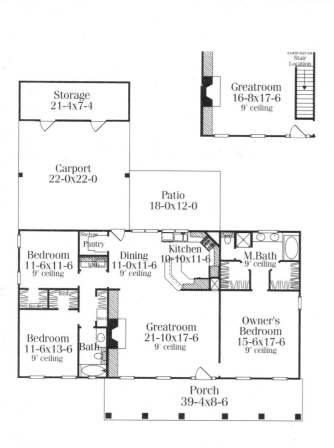

plan# HPT900126

- STYLE: TRADITIONAL
- SQUARE FOOTAGE: 1,680
- BEDROOMS: 3
- BATHROOMS: 2
- WIDTH: 56'-6"
- DEPTH: 68'-6"
- FOUNDATION: BASEMENT, CRAWLSPACE, SLAB

SEARCH ONLINE @ EPLANS.COM

© 2001 Donald A. Gardner, Inc.

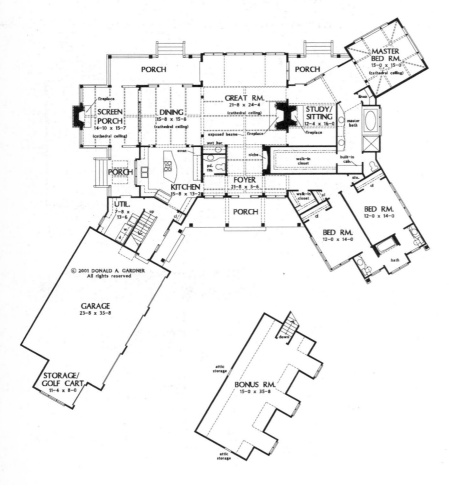

© 2001 DONALD A. GARDNER
All rights reserved

plan# HPT900128

- STYLE: CRAFTSMAN
- SQUARE FOOTAGE: 3,188
- BONUS SPACE: 615 SQ. FT.
- BEDROOMS: 3
- BATHROOMS: 2½
- WIDTH: 106'-4"
- DEPTH: 104'-1"

SEARCH ONLINE @ EPLANS.COM

This incredible home evokes images of stately Southwestern ranches with classic wood detailing and deep eaves. An arched entryway mimics the large clerestory above it, while a trio of dormers and multiple gables add architectural interest. Equally impressive, the interior boasts three fireplaces—one within a scenic screened porch—while a long cathedral ceiling extends from the great room to the screened porch and is highlighted by exposed beams. An art niche complements the foyer, and a wet bar enhances the great room. Columns help distinguish rooms without enclosing space. The extraordinary master suite features a large study/sitting area, bedroom with exposed beams in a hipped cathedral ceiling, huge walk-in closet and spacious master bath.

plan# HPT900129

- STYLE: COUNTRY
- SQUARE FOOTAGE: 1,674
- BONUS SPACE: 336 SQ. FT.
- BEDROOMS: 3
- BATHROOMS: 2
- WIDTH: 56'-4"
- DEPTH: 50'-0"

SEARCH ONLINE @ EPLANS.COM

A trio of dormers, metal porch covering and a mixture of stone and siding create a modern version of the traditional American home. The front porch is bordered by columns and features a trio of arches. A fireplace and built-ins, along with a cathedral ceiling that flows to the kitchen, highlight the great room. Tray ceilings crown the dining room and master bedroom, while visually expanding space. The bonus room makes a perfect playroom for kids, separating the noise from the common living areas and master bedroom. The master bath is complete with a sizable shower, double vanity, garden tub and a private privy.

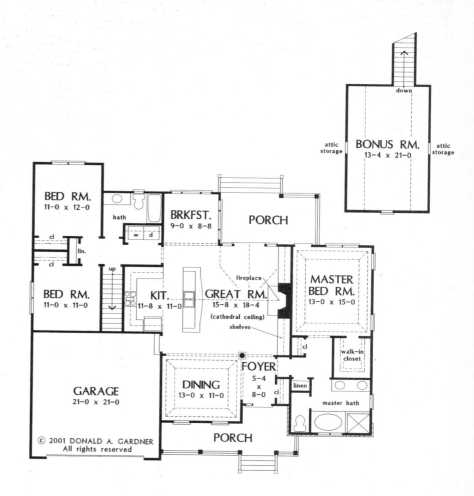

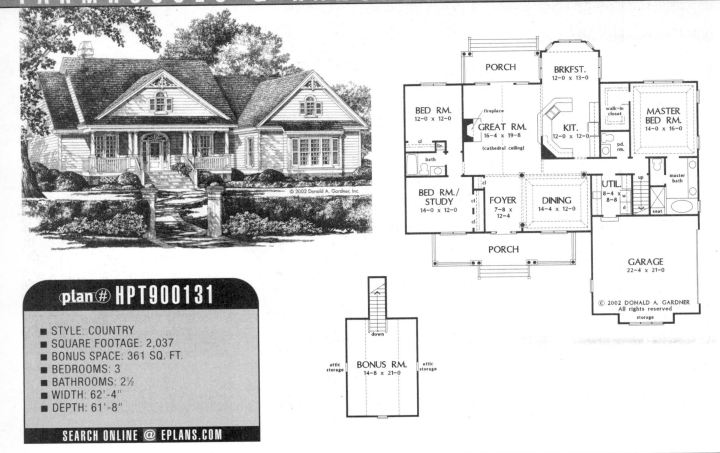

PORCH

BRKFST.
12-0 x 13-0

BED RM.
12-0 x 12-0

fireplace

GREAT RM.
16-4 x 19-8
(cathedral ceiling)

KIT.
12-0 x 12-0

walk-in closet

MASTER BED RM.
14-0 x 16-0

cl

lin.

bath

pd. rm.

BED RM./STUDY
14-0 x 12-0

cl

FOYER
7-8 x 12-4

cl

DINING
14-4 x 12-0

UTIL.
8-4 x 8-8

up

master bath

w
d

seat

PORCH

GARAGE
22-4 x 21-0

storage

down

attic storage

BONUS RM.
14-8 x 21-0

attic storage

plan # HPT900131

- STYLE: COUNTRY
- SQUARE FOOTAGE: 2,037
- BONUS SPACE: 361 SQ. FT.
- BEDROOMS: 3
- BATHROOMS: 2½
- WIDTH: 62'-4"
- DEPTH: 61'-8"

SEARCH ONLINE @ EPLANS.COM

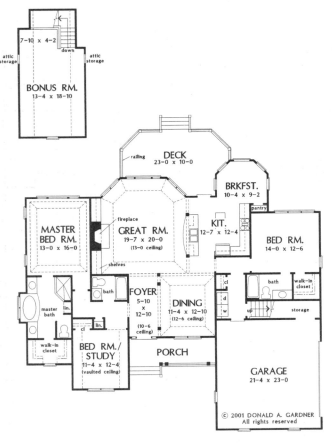

7-10 x 4-2

down

attic storage

attic storage

BONUS RM.
13-4 x 18-10

railing

DECK
23-0 x 10-0

BRKFST.
10-4 x 9-2

pantry

MASTER BED RM.
13-0 x 16-0

fireplace

GREAT RM.
19-7 x 20-0
(13-0 ceiling)

shelves

KIT.
12-7 x 12-4

BED RM.
14-0 x 12-6

cl

bath

walk-in closet

master bath

lin.

bath

FOYER
5-10 x 12-10
(10-6 ceiling)

DINING
11-4 x 12-10
(12-6 ceiling)

d

w

up

storage

walk-in closet

cl

lin.

BED RM./STUDY
11-4 x 12-4
(vaulted ceiling)

PORCH

GARAGE
21-4 x 23-0

plan # HPT900130

- STYLE: COUNTRY
- SQUARE FOOTAGE: 1,971
- BONUS SPACE: 358 SQ. FT.
- BEDROOMS: 3
- BATHROOMS: 3
- WIDTH: 62'-6"
- DEPTH: 57'-2"

SEARCH ONLINE @ EPLANS.COM

TO ORDER BLUEPRINTS CALL TOLL FREE 1-800-521-6797

plan# HPT900132

- **STYLE:** COUNTRY
- **SQUARE FOOTAGE:** 1,827
- **BONUS SPACE:** 384 SQ. FT.
- **BEDROOMS:** 3
- **BATHROOMS:** 2
- **WIDTH:** 61'-8"
- **DEPTH:** 62'-8"

SEARCH ONLINE @ EPLANS.COM

With its welcoming front porch, Palladian windows and siding, this home adds curb appeal to any streetscape. Columns and a tray ceiling define the dining room, while columns make a grand entrance to the great room, which features built-ins, a fireplace, a kitchen pass-through, and French doors leading outside. A breakfast room off the kitchen makes the perfect place to enjoy early morning coffee. Located for privacy, the master suite has a tray ceiling in the bedroom, a spacious walk-in closet, and a master bath equipped with a double vanity, private toilet, large shower and garden tub. The utility/mud room is complete with a sink.

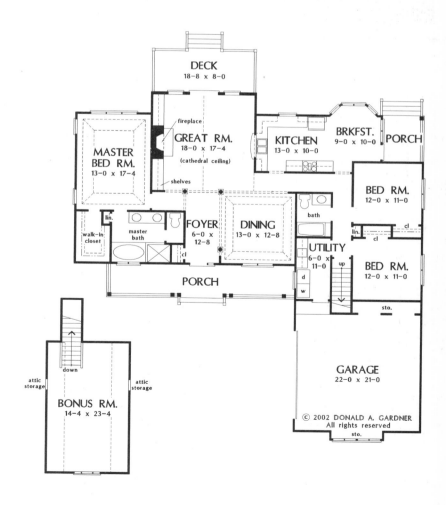

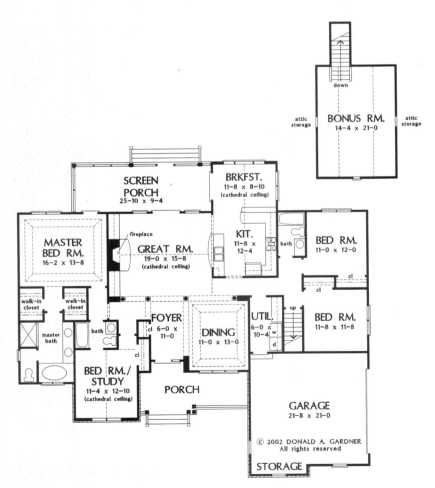

BONUS RM.
14-4 x 21-0

attic storage

attic storage

down

SCREEN PORCH
25-10 x 9-4

BRKFST.
11-8 x 8-10
(cathedral ceiling)

MASTER BED RM.
16-2 x 13-8

fireplace

GREAT RM.
19-0 x 15-8
(cathedral ceiling)

KIT.
11-8 x 12-4

bath

BED RM.
11-0 x 12-0

walk-in closet

walk-in closet

cl

cl

master bath

bath

FOYER
cl 6-0 x 11-0

DINING
11-0 x 13-0

UTIL.
6-0 x 10-4

up

BED RM.
11-8 x 11-8

cl

BED RM./ STUDY
11-4 x 12-10
(cathedral ceiling)

PORCH

GARAGE
21-8 x 21-0

STORAGE

plan # HPT900133

- **STYLE:** COUNTRY
- **SQUARE FOOTAGE:** 2,097
- **BONUS SPACE:** 352 SQ. FT.
- **BEDROOMS:** 4
- **BATHROOMS:** 3
- **WIDTH:** 64'-10"
- **DEPTH:** 59'-6"

SEARCH ONLINE @ EPLANS.COM

Graceful arches contrast with high gables for a stunning exterior on this Craftsman home. Windows with decorative transoms and several French doors flood the open floor plan with natural light. Tray ceilings in the dining room and master bedroom as well as cathedral ceilings in the bedroom/study, great room, kitchen and breakfast area create architectural interest and visual space. Built-ins in the great room and additional space in the garage offer convenient storage. A screened porch allows for comfortable outdoor entertaining; a bonus room, near two additional bedrooms, offers flexibility. Positioned for privacy, the master suite features access to the screened porch, dual walk-in closets and a well-appointed bath, including a private toilet, garden tub, double vanity and spacious shower.

TO ORDER BLUEPRINTS CALL TOLL FREE 1-800-521-6797

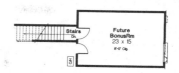

plan# HPT900135

- **STYLE:** FARMHOUSE
- **SQUARE FOOTAGE:** 2,102
- **BONUS SPACE:** 351 SQ. FT.
- **BEDROOMS:** 3
- **BATHROOMS:** 2
- **WIDTH:** 75'-0"
- **DEPTH:** 44'-8"
- **FOUNDATION:** CRAWLSPACE, SLAB

SEARCH ONLINE @ EPLANS.COM

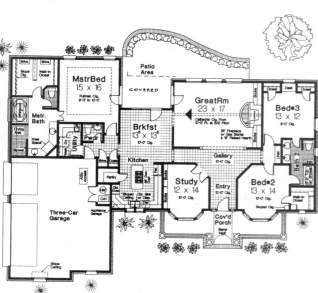

plan# HPT900134

- **STYLE:** FARMHOUSE
- **SQUARE FOOTAGE:** 2,501
- **BEDROOMS:** 3
- **BATHROOMS:** 2½
- **WIDTH:** 78'-10"
- **DEPTH:** 57'-7"
- **FOUNDATION:** SLAB

SEARCH ONLINE @ EPLANS.COM

A stone and brick facade complements European country-cottage style with a decorative cupola, French doors, and a bay window. Inside, you are greeted by a vaulted great room with a stone-hearth fireplace. The gourmet kitchen and breakfast nook have tile flooring for simple maintenance. The master suite is separated for privacy; it features a luxurious bath and grand walk-in closet. Two additional bedrooms and a bayed study share a full bath and convenient powder room.

plan# HPT900136

- **STYLE:** FARMHOUSE
- **SQUARE FOOTAGE:** 2,299
- **BEDROOMS:** 3
- **BATHROOMS:** 2½
- **WIDTH:** 88'-11"
- **DEPTH:** 47'-3"
- **FOUNDATION:** CRAWLSPACE, SLAB

SEARCH ONLINE @ EPLANS.COM

plan # HPT900137

- **STYLE:** FRENCH COUNTRY
- **SQUARE FOOTAGE:** 2,620
- **BEDROOMS:** 4
- **BATHROOMS:** 3
- **WIDTH:** 65'-0"
- **DEPTH:** 70'-0"
- **FOUNDATION:** SLAB

SEARCH ONLINE @ EPLANS.COM

Peaks and pinnacles add storybook charm to this European country cottage. Stonework and multipane windows accent the exterior, while inside, thoughtful details make this a home you'll want to call your own. At the rear of the plan, the family room is enchanting, with a raised ceiling, a stone fireplace that echoes the facade, and access to the covered patio. The semi-bayed breakfast nook flows into the kitchen for easy serving and clean-up. The vaulted master suite is a romantic hideaway with a spa-tub and a shower built for two. Two family bedrooms are separated for privacy, while a third is situated for use as a study, nursery or guest room.

MAIN LEVEL

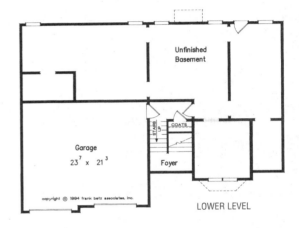

LOWER LEVEL

plan# HPT900139

- STYLE: NEOCLASSIC
- MAIN LEVEL: 1,677 SQ. FT.
- LOWER LEVEL ENTRY: 40 SQ. FT.
- TOTAL: 1,717 SQ. FT.
- BEDROOMS: 3
- BATHROOMS: 2
- WIDTH: 50'-0"
- DEPTH: 39'-4"
- FOUNDATION: BASEMENT

SEARCH ONLINE @ EPLANS.COM

SECOND FLOOR

FIRST FLOOR

plan# HPT900138

- STYLE: TRADITIONAL
- FIRST FLOOR: 2,130 SQ. FT.
- SECOND FLOOR: 897 SQ. FT.
- TOTAL: 3,027 SQ. FT.
- BEDROOMS: 4
- BATHROOMS: 3½
- WIDTH: 62'-4"
- DEPTH: 54'-6"
- FOUNDATION: BASEMENT, CRAWLSPACE, SLAB

SEARCH ONLINE @ EPLANS.COM

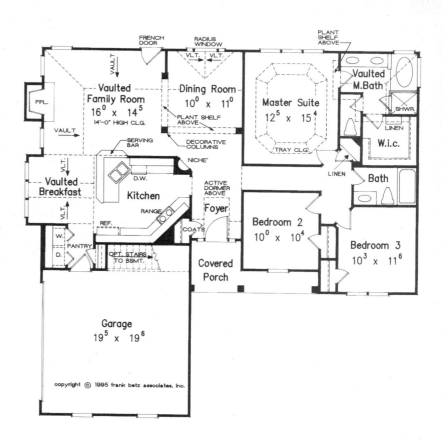

plan # HPT900140

- STYLE: COUNTRY
- SQUARE FOOTAGE: 1,497
- BEDROOMS: 3
- BATHROOMS: 2
- WIDTH: 52'-4"
- DEPTH: 50'-0"
- FOUNDATION: CRAWLSPACE

SEARCH ONLINE @ EPLANS.COM

This charming home presents a quaint exterior, yet a spacious, modern plan awaits inside. With decorative pillars around the dining room and a vaulted breakfast area, the family chef will enjoy entertaining and serving up gourmet meals. Vaulted ceilings throughout add ambiance and grandeur. The master suite will please, with a wonderful private bath and a tray ceiling. Two additional family bedrooms share a hall bath.

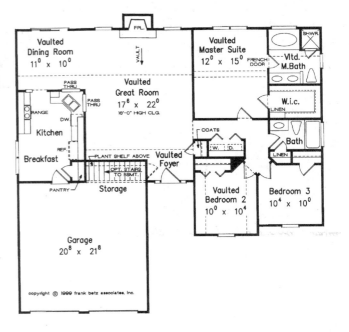

copyright © 1999 frank betz associates, inc.

plan# HPT900141

- STYLE: TRADITIONAL
- SQUARE FOOTAGE: 2,882
- BEDROOMS: 3
- BATHROOMS: 2
- WIDTH: 50'-0"
- DEPTH: 50'-4"
- FOUNDATION: BASEMENT, CRAWLSPACE

SEARCH ONLINE @ EPLANS.COM

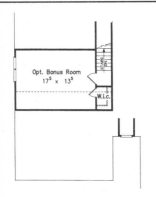

copyright © 2000 frank betz associates, inc.

plan# HPT900142

- STYLE: TRADITIONAL
- SQUARE FOOTAGE: 1,633
- BONUS SPACE: 285 SQ. FT.
- BEDROOMS: 3
- BATHROOMS: 2
- WIDTH: 47'-6"
- DEPTH: 54'-4"
- FOUNDATION: BASEMENT, CRAWLSPACE

SEARCH ONLINE @ EPLANS.COM

© 2001 Donald A. Gardner, Inc.

B. NATHAN

plan# HPT900143

- **STYLE:** COUNTRY
- **SQUARE FOOTAGE:** 2,080
- **BONUS SPACE:** 348 SQ. FT.
- **BEDROOMS:** 4
- **BATHROOMS:** 2
- **WIDTH:** 63'-8"
- **DEPTH:** 54'-4"

SEARCH ONLINE @ EPLANS.COM

Architectural detail and traffic flow are the two most important elements in this design. A stone wall is enhanced by a box-bay window that is capped with a metal roof. Stone visually anchors an additional box-bay window. A prominent dormer features a Palladian-style window, which mimics the arches found on the front porch. Family efficiency is created by an open, yet defined floorplan. Decorative tray ceilings add custom appeal, while the flexibility of a study/bedroom provides options. Ample counter space is found in the utility/mud room and kitchen. Elegant doors lead into the master suite where dual walk-ins and vanities add to the suite experience.

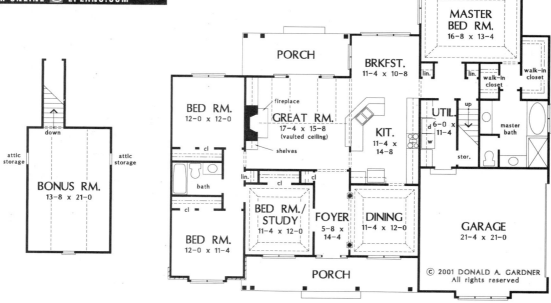

© 2001 Donald A. Gardner, Inc.

B. NATHAN

Dormers set above a charming porch and beautiful entry door with arched transoms lend eye appeal to this wonderful four-bedroom design. The foyer leads to the dining room to the right and a bedroom or study to the left—both featuring exciting ceiling treatments. The hearth-warmed great room shares an open area with the island kitchen and bayed breakfast nook. The master suite enjoys plenty of privacy, tucked to the rear of the garage. The master bath includes a tub set in a corner window and a walk-in closet. Two family bedrooms sharing a full bath reside to the left of the plan.

plan# HPT900144

- STYLE: TRADITIONAL
- SQUARE FOOTAGE: 2,413
- BONUS SPACE: 417 SQ. FT.
- BEDROOMS: 4
- BATHROOMS: 2½
- WIDTH: 78'-8"
- DEPTH: 57'-8"

SEARCH ONLINE @ EPLANS.COM

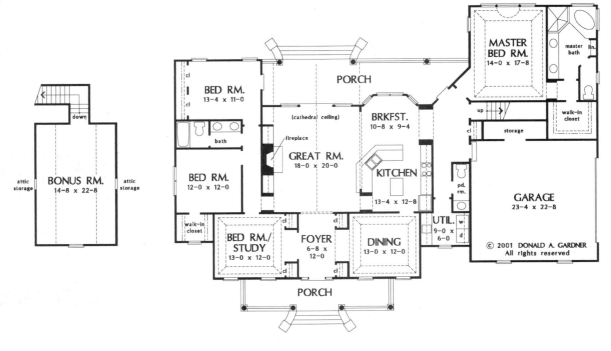

TO ORDER BLUEPRINTS CALL TOLL FREE 1-800-521-6797

plan # HPT900145

- **STYLE:** COUNTRY
- **SQUARE FOOTAGE:** 1,643
- **BONUS SPACE:** 338 SQ. FT.
- **BEDROOMS:** 3
- **BATHROOMS:** 2
- **WIDTH:** 50'-4"
- **DEPTH:** 58'-6"

SEARCH ONLINE @ EPLANS.COM

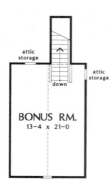

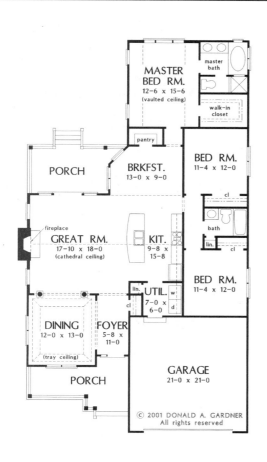

plan # HPT900146

- **STYLE:** TRADITIONAL
- **SQUARE FOOTAGE:** 1,726
- **BEDROOMS:** 3
- **BATHROOMS:** 2
- **WIDTH:** 41'-8"
- **DEPTH:** 72'-4"

SEARCH ONLINE @ EPLANS.COM

With all the charm of country living, this siding bungalow makes a great first home, retirement home, or vacation retreat. From the covered front porch, the living room soars with a cathedral ceiling. Straight ahead, a U-shaped kitchen and sunny dining room are perfect for casual meals or elegant dining. Two bedrooms—or make one a study—share a full bath. The master bedroom enjoys a private bath and a walk-in closet. Storage space behind the carport has room for gardening and recreation equipment, or use it as a workshed.

plan# HPT900147

- **STYLE:** TRANSITIONAL
- **SQUARE FOOTAGE:** 1,375
- **BEDROOMS:** 3
- **BATHROOMS:** 2
- **WIDTH:** 61'-0"
- **DEPTH:** 35'-0"
- **FOUNDATION:** CRAWLSPACE, SLAB

SEARCH ONLINE @ EPLANS.COM

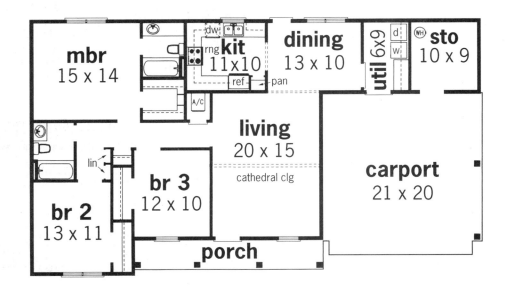

© 1995 Donald A. Gardner Architects, Inc.

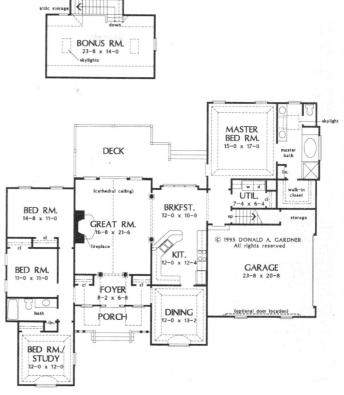

BONUS RM.
23-8 x 14-0
skylights

attic storage
down

MASTER BED RM.
15-0 x 17-0

master bath

skylight

DECK

(cathedral ceiling)

BED RM.
14-8 x 11-0

cl

GREAT RM.
16-8 x 21-6
fireplace

BED RM.
11-0 x 11-0

cl

FOYER
8-2 x 6-8

PORCH

bath

BED RM./STUDY
12-0 x 12-0

BRKFST.
12-0 x 10-0

KIT.
12-0 x 12-4

DINING
12-0 x 13-2

UTIL.
7-4 x 6-4

walk-in closet

storage

up

© 1995 DONALD A. GARDNER
All rights reserved

GARAGE
23-8 x 20-8

(optional door location)

plan # HPT900148

- STYLE: COUNTRY
- SQUARE FOOTAGE: 2,225
- BONUS SPACE: 401 SQ. FT.
- BEDROOMS: 4
- BATHROOMS: 2
- WIDTH: 69'-4"
- DEPTH: 65'-0"

SEARCH ONLINE @ EPLANS.COM

Rear Porch
14/2 x 8

8' Clg.

Bedroom #3
11/4 x 10
8' Clg.

Family Room
18 x 15
Vaulted Clg. 11'-9"

Breakfast
13/7 x 10/8
Snack Bar

Master
13/6 x 15/6
10' Reccessed Clg.

Bath #2

Kitchen
13/7 x 9/2

Dining
10 x 12
8' Clg

Foyer
5/4 x 12

Stairs Down

P

D   W

Bath #1

L

Bedroom #2
11/4 x 11
8' Clg

Front Porch
19/8 x 4

Copyright Greg Marloss & Assoc.

Garage
21/4 x 21/8

plan # HPT900149

- STYLE: FARMHOUSE
- SQUARE FOOTAGE: 1,681
- BEDROOMS: 3
- BATHROOMS: 2
- WIDTH: 58'-0"
- DEPTH: 58'-0"
- FOUNDATION: BASEMENT

SEARCH ONLINE @ EPLANS.COM

plan # HPT900150

- STYLE: RANCH
- SQUARE FOOTAGE: 1,484
- BEDROOMS: 3
- BATHROOMS: 2
- WIDTH: 53'-6"
- DEPTH: 28'-0"
- FOUNDATION: BASEMENT, CRAWLSPACE

SEARCH ONLINE @ EPLANS.COM

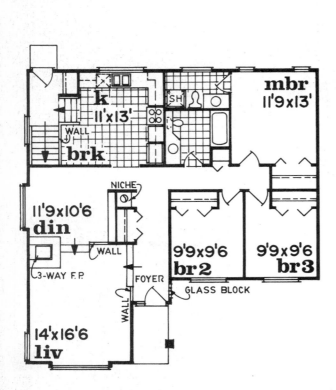

plan # HPT900151

- STYLE: RANCH
- SQUARE FOOTAGE: 1,434
- BEDROOMS: 3
- BATHROOMS: 2
- WIDTH: 41'-4"
- DEPTH: 42'-4"
- FOUNDATION: BASEMENT, CRAWLSPACE

SEARCH ONLINE @ EPLANS.COM

Bedroom
10-11x13-6

Basement Stair
Location

plan # HPT900153

- STYLE: VICTORIAN
- SQUARE FOOTAGE: 1,966
- BEDROOMS: 3
- BATHROOMS: 2½
- WIDTH: 72'-0"
- DEPTH: 55'-8"
- FOUNDATION: BASEMENT, CRAWLSPACE, SLAB

SEARCH ONLINE @ EPLANS.COM

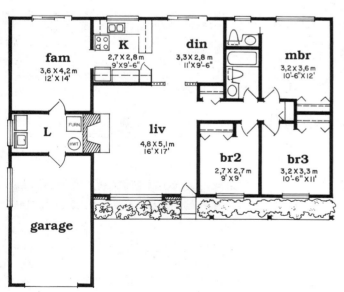

plan # HPT900152

- STYLE: RANCH
- SQUARE FOOTAGE: 1,319
- BEDROOMS: 3
- BATHROOMS: 1½
- WIDTH: 50'-0"
- DEPTH: 42'-0"
- FOUNDATION: BASEMENT

SEARCH ONLINE @ EPLANS.COM

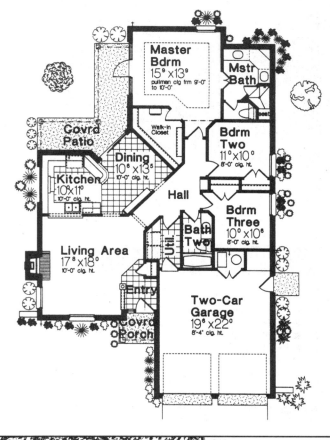

plan# HPT900154

- STYLE: EUROPEAN COTTAGE
- SQUARE FOOTAGE: 1,495
- BEDROOMS: 3
- BATHROOMS: 2
- WIDTH: 40'-0"
- DEPTH: 65'-0"
- FOUNDATION: SLAB

SEARCH ONLINE @ EPLANS.COM

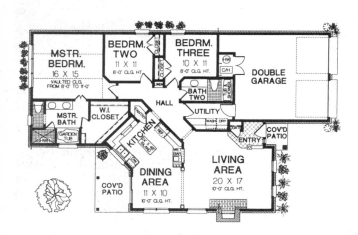

plan# HPT900155

- STYLE: EUROPEAN COTTAGE
- SQUARE FOOTAGE: 1,648
- BEDROOMS: 3
- BATHROOMS: 2
- WIDTH: 40'-0"
- DEPTH: 66'-8"
- FOUNDATION: SLAB

SEARCH ONLINE @ EPLANS.COM

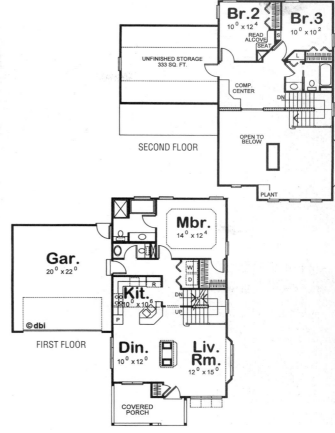

SECOND FLOOR

FIRST FLOOR

plan# HPT900156

- **STYLE:** TRADITIONAL
- **FIRST FLOOR:** 979 SQ. FT.
- **SECOND FLOOR:** 511 SQ. FT.
- **TOTAL:** 1,490 SQ. FT.
- **BEDROOMS:** 3
- **BATHROOMS:** 2½
- **WIDTH:** 45'-0"
- **DEPTH:** 48'-0"

SEARCH ONLINE @ EPLANS.COM

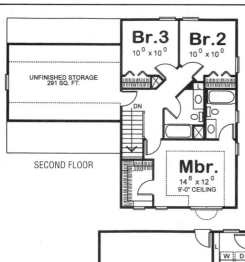

SECOND FLOOR

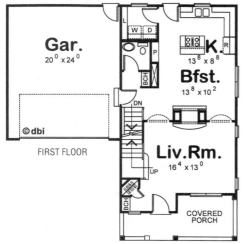

FIRST FLOOR

plan# HPT900157

- **STYLE:** FARMHOUSE
- **FIRST FLOOR:** 762 SQ. FT.
- **SECOND FLOOR:** 691 SQ. FT.
- **TOTAL:** 1,453 SQ. FT.
- **BEDROOMS:** 3
- **BATHROOMS:** 2½
- **WIDTH:** 41'-4"
- **DEPTH:** 43'-0"

SEARCH ONLINE @ EPLANS.COM

This updated farmhouse features the best of country and modern looks. The bayed dining room is showcased on the front covered porch. Just beyond is the hearth-warmed great room, which opens to the galley kitchen. A powder room and washer-and-dryer area are both convenient to the kitchen. Tucked privately in back is the master suite, which enjoys a spacious private bath and access to its own covered porch. A second suite resides upstairs, boasting a tray ceiling, huge walk-in closet and another private porch.

plan# HPT900158

- STYLE: FARMHOUSE
- FIRST FLOOR: 451 SQ. FT.
- SECOND FLOOR: 949 SQ. FT.
- TOTAL: 1,400 SQ. FT.
- BONUS SPACE: 113 SQ. FT.
- BEDROOMS: 2
- BATHROOMS: 2
- WIDTH: 45'-4"
- DEPTH: 49'-4"

SEARCH ONLINE @ EPLANS.COM

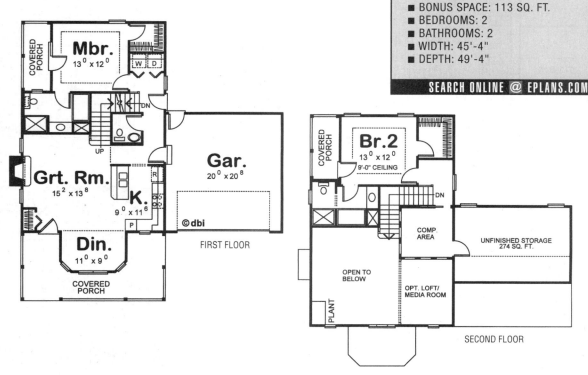

plan# HPT900159

- **STYLE: TRADITIONAL**
- **FIRST FLOOR: 1,448 SQ. FT.**
- **SECOND FLOOR: 1,714 SQ. FT.**
- **TOTAL: 3,162 SQ. FT.**
- **BEDROOMS: 5**
- **BATHROOMS: 4**
- **WIDTH: 60'-0"**
- **DEPTH: 43'-10"**
- **FOUNDATION: BASEMENT, CRAWLSPACE**

SEARCH ONLINE @ EPLANS.COM

Stones and clapboard siding adorn this roomy home. Inside, the two-story foyer introduces a private study with double-door entry and a large formal dining room. Straight ahead decorative columns welcome visitors to the family room, which features a coffered ceiling, fireplace and open planning. The breakfast room and kitchen work well together. A first-floor bedroom is perfect as a guest suite. Upstairs, three family bedrooms—one with a private bath—enjoy a children's retreat that functions as a bonus space. The master suite is the picture of luxury with a sumptuous bath and oversized walk-in closet.

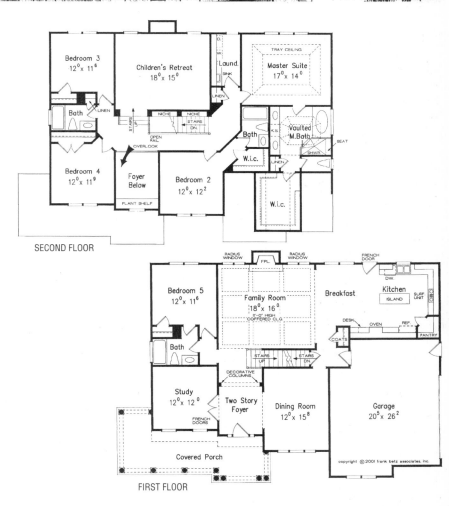

SECOND FLOOR

FIRST FLOOR

Space efficiency is the strong suit of this European cottage. The main level contains the everyday living space, while the upstairs level presents four bedrooms—including the master bedroom, which enjoys its own sitting area and vaulted bath. Ample window area allows every corner to bask in natural light. The whole family can enjoy meals in the formal dining room, the breakfast area or at the serving bar. The fifth bedroom can double as an office, and is tucked away from common areas to afford privacy.

plan # HPT900160

- STYLE: TRADITIONAL
- FIRST FLOOR: 1,240 SQ. FT.
- SECOND FLOOR: 1,273 SQ. FT.
- TOTAL: 2,513 SQ. FT.
- BEDROOMS: 5
- BATHROOMS: 3
- WIDTH: 46'-0"
- DEPTH: 45'-6"
- FOUNDATION: BASEMENT, CRAWLSPACE

SEARCH ONLINE @ EPLANS.COM

FIRST FLOOR

SECOND FLOOR

SECOND FLOOR

plan# HPT900161

- **STYLE:** TRADITIONAL
- **FIRST FLOOR:** 1,803 SQ. FT.
- **SECOND FLOOR:** 548 SQ. FT.
- **TOTAL:** 2,351 SQ. FT.
- **BONUS SPACE:** 277 SQ. FT.
- **BEDROOMS:** 4
- **BATHROOMS:** 3
- **WIDTH:** 55'-0"
- **DEPTH:** 48'-0"
- **FOUNDATION:** BASEMENT, CRAWLSPACE, SLAB

SEARCH ONLINE @ EPLANS.COM

FIRST FLOOR

copyright © 2002 frank betz associates, inc

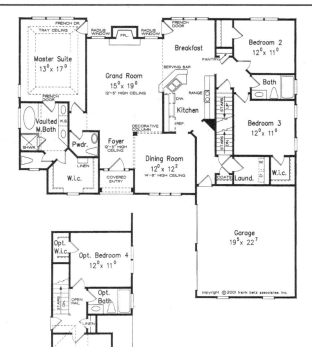

copyright © 2001 frank betz associates, inc.

plan# HPT900162

- **STYLE:** TRADITIONAL
- **SQUARE FOOTAGE:** 1,823
- **BONUS SPACE:** 579 SQ. FT.
- **BEDROOMS:** 3
- **BATHROOMS:** 2½
- **WIDTH:** 55'-0"
- **DEPTH:** 57'-0"
- **FOUNDATION:** BASEMENT, CRAWLSPACE

SEARCH ONLINE @ EPLANS.COM

Brick and shake blend for a beautiful Cape Cod-style home that will be a joy and a comfort for generations to come. Inside, the floor plan is warm and inviting, bathed in natural light. The two-story foyer opens on the right to a formal dining room and ahead to reveal a soaring vaulted family room with an extended-hearth fireplace framed by radius windows. A vaulted ceiling in the bayed breakfast nook adds an elegant touch to casual meals. In the kitchen, an island and plenty of counter space makes food preparation easier than ever. The first-floor master suite enjoys a bayed sitting area, vaulted bath and a walk-in closet with space designated for a mirror and linen closet. Upstairs, two bedrooms share a full bath, bonus room, and a loft/desk area.

plan# HPT900163

- **STYLE: TRADITIONAL**
- **FIRST FLOOR: 2,060 SQ. FT.**
- **SECOND FLOOR: 688 SQ. FT.**
- **TOTAL: 2,748 SQ. FT.**
- **BONUS SPACE: 258 SQ. FT.**
- **BEDROOMS: 4**
- **BATHROOMS: 3**
- **WIDTH: 57'-0"**
- **DEPTH: 56'-6"**
- **FOUNDATION: BASEMENT, CRAWLSPACE**

SEARCH ONLINE @ EPLANS.COM

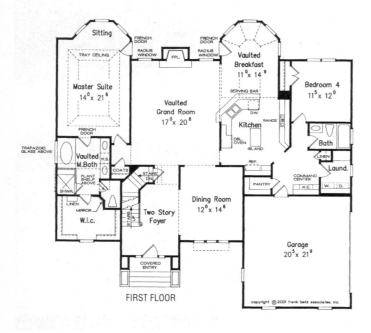

FIRST FLOOR

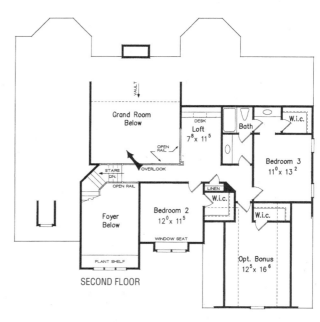

SECOND FLOOR

SECOND FLOOR

FIRST FLOOR

plan# HPT900013

- STYLE: TRADITIONAL
- FIRST FLOOR: 2,285 SQ. FT.
- SECOND FLOOR: 956 SQ. FT.
- TOTAL: 3,241 SQ. FT.
- BONUS SPACE: 555 SQ. FT.
- BEDROOMS: 5
- BATHROOMS: 4
- WIDTH: 57'-3"
- DEPTH: 65'-5"

SEARCH ONLINE @ EPLANS.COM

SECOND FLOOR

FIRST FLOOR

plan# HPT900164

- STYLE: TRADITIONAL
- FIRST FLOOR: 1,736 SQ. FT.
- SECOND FLOOR: 1,650 SQ. FT.
- TOTAL: 3,386 SQ. FT.
- BEDROOMS: 5
- BATHROOMS: 4½
- WIDTH: 62'-0"
- DEPTH: 56'-0"
- FOUNDATION: BASEMENT, CRAWLSPACE

SEARCH ONLINE @ EPLANS.COM

Bedroom 3
10^0 x 11^5

Bedroom 2
10^7 x 11^2

Family Room
Below

OVERLOOK

Bath

PLANT
SHELF

Foyer
Below

LINEN

Opt. Bonus
11^5 x 20^6

SECOND FLOOR

Breakfast

SERVING BAR

Vaulted
Family Room
14^0 x 16^6

TRAY CEILING

Master Suite
16^0 x 13^0

RANGE
Kitchen
DW.

REF.

PANT.

Pwdr.

Vaulted
M.Bath

W.i.c.

LINEN SHWR

Dining Room
10^0 x 11^6

OPEN
RAIL

COATS

Laund.

STORAGE

Two Story
Foyer

COVERED
ENTRY

Garage
19^5 x 21^9

copyright © 2002 frank betz associates, inc.

FIRST FLOOR

plan # HPT900165

- STYLE: TRADITIONAL
- FIRST FLOOR: 1,177 SQ. FT.
- SECOND FLOOR: 457 SQ. FT.
- TOTAL: 2,811 SQ. FT.
- BONUS SPACE: 249 SQ. FT.
- BEDROOMS: 3
- BATHROOMS: 2½
- WIDTH: 41'-0"
- DEPTH: 48'-4"
- FOUNDATION: BASEMENT, CRAWLSPACE

SEARCH ONLINE @ EPLANS.COM

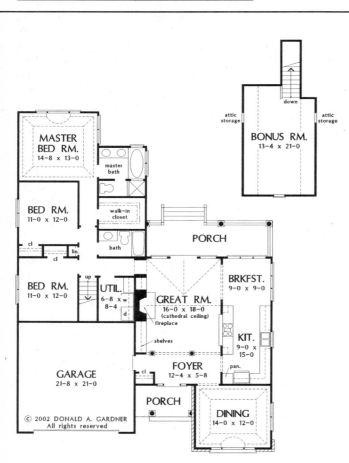

MASTER
BED RM.
14-8 x 13-0

master
bath

walk-in
closet

bath

BED RM.
11-0 x 12-0

cl

lin.

cl

PORCH

BED RM.
11-0 x 12-0

up

UTIL.
6-8 x
8-4

w

d

GREAT RM.
16-0 x 18-0
(cathedral ceiling)
fireplace

shelves

BRKFST.
9-0 x 9-0

KIT.
9-0 x
15-0

GARAGE
21-8 x 21-0

cl

FOYER
12-4 x 5-8

pan.

PORCH

DINING
14-0 x 12-0

attic
storage

down

attic
storage

BONUS RM.
13-4 x 21-0

© 2002 DONALD A. GARDNER
All rights reserved

© 2002 Donald A. Gardner, Inc.

plan # HPT900166

- STYLE: TRADITIONAL
- SQUARE FOOTAGE: 1,707
- BONUS SPACE: 323 SQ. FT.
- BEDROOMS: 3
- BATHROOMS: 2
- WIDTH: 48'-6"
- DEPTH: 65'-6"

SEARCH ONLINE @ EPLANS.COM

TO ORDER BLUEPRINTS CALL TOLL FREE 1-800-521-6797

plan # HPT900167

- **STYLE:** COUNTRY COTTAGE
- **FIRST FLOOR:** 1,056 SQ. FT.
- **SECOND FLOOR:** 929 SQ. FT.
- **TOTAL:** 1,985 SQ. FT.
- **BONUS SPACE:** 246 SQ. FT.
- **BEDROOMS:** 4
- **BATHROOMS:** 3
- **WIDTH:** 52'-4"
- **DEPTH:** 38'-6"
- **FOUNDATION:** BASEMENT, CRAWLSPACE

SEARCH ONLINE @ EPLANS.COM

Stone and shingles lend rustic drama to this cottage-style traditional that lives large in under 2,000 square feet. A vaulted, hearth-warmed family room opens from the two-story foyer and features a wall of windows to the rear property. To the left is an open-flow area—the bay-windowed breakfast nook, vaulted keeping room complete with fireplace, and of course the kitchen itself. This kitchen is a cook's dream, spacious with abundant work and storage space. An adjacent laundry room accesses both segments of the triple garage. Secluded to the right of the first floor is the ultimate in master-suite luxury, featuring a tray ceiling, bayed sitting area and deluxe private bath. Upstairs, three additional bedrooms enjoy ample closet space and share two baths.

FIRST FLOOR

SECOND FLOOR

SECOND FLOOR

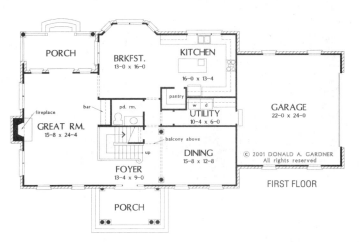

FIRST FLOOR

plan# HPT900169

- **STYLE:** TRADITIONAL
- **FIRST FLOOR:** 1,486 SQ. FT.
- **SECOND FLOOR:** 1,248 SQ. FT.
- **TOTAL:** 2,734 SQ. FT.
- **BONUS SPACE:** 455 SQ. FT.
- **BEDROOMS:** 3
- **BATHROOMS:** 2½
- **WIDTH:** 70'-11"
- **DEPTH:** 44'-7"

SEARCH ONLINE @ EPLANS.COM

SECOND FLOOR

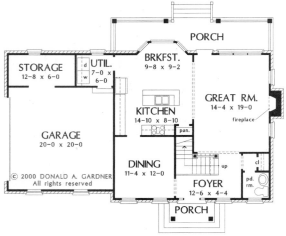

FIRST FLOOR

plan# HPT900168

- **STYLE:** TRADITIONAL
- **FIRST FLOOR:** 985 SQ. FT.
- **SECOND FLOOR:** 870 SQ. FT.
- **TOTAL:** 1,855 SQ. FT.
- **BONUS SPACE:** 331 SQ. FT.
- **BEDROOMS:** 3
- **BATHROOMS:** 2½
- **WIDTH:** 53'-5"
- **DEPTH:** 36'-2"

SEARCH ONLINE @ EPLANS.COM

B. NATHAN
© 2001 Donald A. Gardner, Inc.

This updated classic features a beautiful facade with gables, Palladian-style windows and stately columns. On the interior, the open floorplan creates an easy traffic-flow pattern, making it a family-efficient layout. Tray ceilings cap the master bedroom and master bath, while columns and countertops distinguish areas without enclosing space. The second-floor balcony overlooks both the great room and foyer, and the utility/mudroom includes a sink and closet storage. The master suite incorporates a sitting bay, two walk-in closets and a luxurious bath with a spacious shower, double vanity, garden tub and private privy. The screen porch and bonus room add flexibility and extra living areas.

plan# HPT900170

- STYLE: TRADITIONAL
- FIRST FLOOR: 1,684 SQ. FT.
- SECOND FLOOR: 538 SQ. FT.
- TOTAL: 2,222 SQ. FT.
- BONUS SPACE: 415 SQ. FT.
- BEDROOMS: 3
- BATHROOMS: 2½
- WIDTH: 46'-3"
- DEPTH: 64'-7"

SEARCH ONLINE @ EPLANS.COM

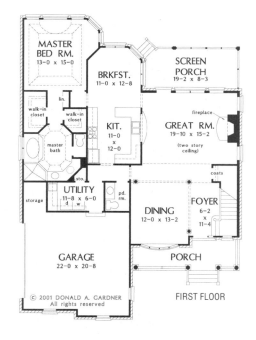

FIRST FLOOR

SECOND FLOOR

plan# HPT900171

- **STYLE:** TRADITIONAL
- **FIRST FLOOR:** 1,231 SQ. FT.
- **SECOND FLOOR:** 1,225 SQ. FT.
- **TOTAL:** 2,456 SQ. FT.
- **BONUS SPACE:** 296 SQ. FT.
- **BEDROOMS:** 4
- **BATHROOMS:** 2½
- **WIDTH:** 52'-8"
- **DEPTH:** 38'-4"
- **FOUNDATION:** BASEMENT, CRAWLSPACE, SLAB

SEARCH ONLINE @ EPLANS.COM

A stately brick facade and lateral siding bring Southern elegance to this traditional neighborhood home. From the two-story foyer, this plan unfolds as family oriented and ready for your busy lifestyle. To the right, a library with an arched opening enjoys a multi-pane window. On the left, the living room flows into the dining room, through an arched entry. The gourmet kitchen has an island for easy preparation and a desk area for organization. The family room, with a fireplace and lots of natural light, accesses the deck/patio. Upstairs, the master suite is resplendent with a spa bath. Three additional bedrooms share a full bath; an upstairs laundry is an added luxury.

FIRST FLOOR

SECOND FLOOR

SECOND FLOOR

FIRST FLOOR

© 2001 DONALD A. GARDNER
All rights reserved

plan# HPT900172

- STYLE: TRADITIONAL
- FIRST FLOOR: 1,536 SQ. FT.
- SECOND FLOOR: 613 SQ. FT.
- TOTAL: 2,149 SQ. FT.
- BONUS SPACE: 262 SQ. FT.
- BEDROOMS: 3
- BATHROOMS: 2½
- WIDTH: 48'-0"
- DEPTH: 51'-6"

SEARCH ONLINE @ EPLANS.COM

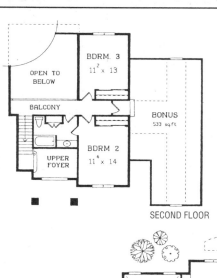

SECOND FLOOR

FIRST FLOOR

plan# HPT900173

- STYLE: TRADITIONAL
- FIRST FLOOR: 1,574 SQ. FT.
- SECOND FLOOR: 639 SQ. FT.
- TOTAL: 2,213 SQ. FT.
- BONUS SPACE: 533 SQ. FT.
- BEDROOMS: 3
- BATHROOMS: 2½
- WIDTH: 65'-0"
- DEPTH: 43'-0"
- FOUNDATION: BASEMENT

SEARCH ONLINE @ EPLANS.COM

plan# HPT900174

- **STYLE: TRADITIONAL**
- **FIRST FLOOR: 1,680 SQ. FT.**
- **SECOND FLOOR: 513 SQ. FT.**
- **TOTAL: 2,193 SQ. FT.**
- **BONUS SPACE: 300 SQ. FT.**
- **BEDROOMS: 4**
- **BATHROOMS: 3**
- **WIDTH: 57'-0"**
- **DEPTH: 47'-10"**
- **FOUNDATION: BASEMENT, CRAWLSPACE**

SEARCH ONLINE @ EPLANS.COM

Brick, shutters and keystone lintels bring out the best in this elegant traditional. A petite covered entry leads to the vaulted foyer, opening to the vaulted great room featuring a fireplace. The roomy kitchen is flanked by a formal dining room at the front and a breakfast area to the back, which enjoys French-door access to the outdoors. A bedroom and full bath are tucked away behind the kitchen, convenient to the laundry area. To the left of the plan, a swanky master suite boasts a tray ceiling and vaulted private bath with an enormous walk-in closet—it's practically a room of its own! Upstairs, two bedrooms share a full bath, optional bonus space and a balcony overlook to the great room.

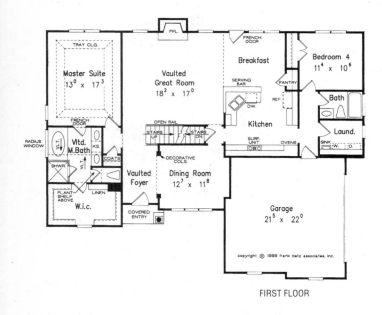

FIRST FLOOR

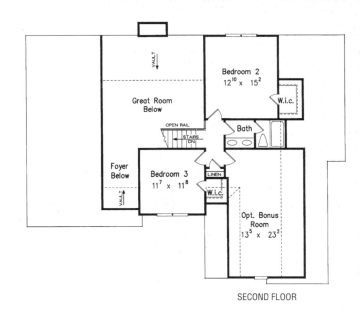

SECOND FLOOR

plan# HPT900175

- **STYLE: TRADITIONAL**
- **SQUARE FOOTAGE: 2,111**
- **BEDROOMS: 2**
- **BATHROOMS: 2**
- **WIDTH: 75'-0"**
- **DEPTH: 64'-8"**
- **FOUNDATION: BASEMENT**

SEARCH ONLINE @ EPLANS.COM

This ranch-style home is designed with today's most up-to-date trends. The open floor plan allows for a casual and comfortable lifestyle. The enormous great room, featuring a fourteen-foot vaulted ceiling, is open to the kitchen and adjoining breakfast area. Split bedrooms include a master suite that features His and Hers walk-in closets, a private bath with a whirlpool tub, and convenient access to the laundry room. Bedroom 2 has a walk-in closet and full bath nearby—the third bedroom can be converted to a den and boasts a cathedral ceiling. Don't overlook the formal dining room, which provides ample space for special dinners.

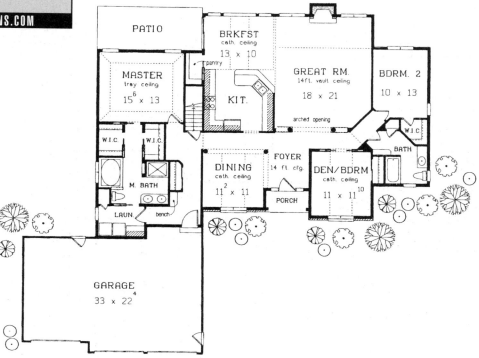

© 2001 Donald A. Gardner, Inc.

With an elegant brick facade and a standing-seam roof that shelters the front porch, this traditional design brings back the stately homes of the past. Inside, the floor plan gives a nod to history in the parlor with a cathedral ceiling just to the left of the foyer; refined columns separate this room from the dining room. Less formal rooms—the kitchen, great room and breakfast area—all open to each other. The first-floor master suite includes a tray ceiling, walk-in closet and private bath. Upstairs, three bedrooms—one with a private bath—share a balcony that overlooks the great room.

plan# HPT900176

- **STYLE:** TRADITIONAL
- **FIRST FLOOR:** 1,809 SQ. FT.
- **SECOND FLOOR:** 869 SQ. FT.
- **TOTAL:** 2,678 SQ. FT.
- **BONUS SPACE:** 320 SQ. FT.
- **BEDROOMS:** 4
- **BATHROOMS:** 3½
- **WIDTH:** 50'-7"
- **DEPTH:** 52'-7"

SEARCH ONLINE @ EPLANS.COM

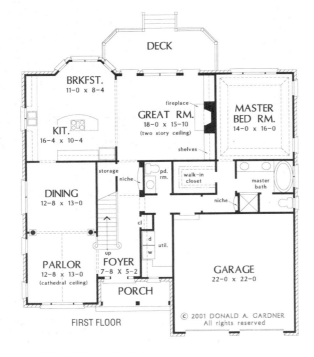

FIRST FLOOR

© 2001 DONALD A. GARDNER
All rights reserved

SECOND FLOOR

TO ORDER BLUEPRINTS CALL TOLL FREE 1-800-521-6797

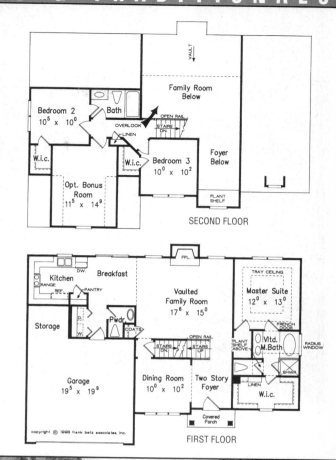

SECOND FLOOR

FIRST FLOOR

copyright © 1998 frank betz associates, inc.

plan# HPT900177

- **STYLE:** TRADITIONAL
- **FIRST FLOOR:** 1,134 SQ. FT.
- **SECOND FLOOR:** 375 SQ. FT.
- **TOTAL:** 2,643 SQ. FT.
- **BONUS SPACE:** 181 SQ. FT.
- **BEDROOMS:** 3
- **BATHROOMS:** 2½
- **WIDTH:** 50'-0"
- **DEPTH:** 37'-10"
- **FOUNDATION:** BASEMENT, CRAWLSPACE

SEARCH ONLINE @ EPLANS.COM

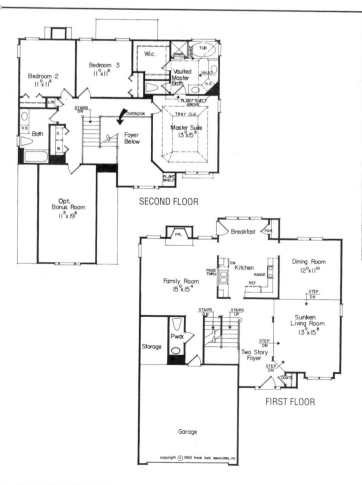

SECOND FLOOR

FIRST FLOOR

copyright © 1992 frank betz associates, inc.

plan# HPT900178

- **STYLE:** TRADITIONAL
- **FIRST FLOOR:** 1,078 SQ. FT.
- **SECOND FLOOR:** 908 SQ. FT.
- **TOTAL:** 1,986 SQ. FT.
- **BONUS SPACE:** 240 SQ. FT.
- **BEDROOMS:** 3
- **BATHROOMS:** 2½
- **WIDTH:** 40'-0"
- **DEPTH:** 49'-6"
- **FOUNDATION:** BASEMENT, CRAWLSPACE, SLAB

SEARCH ONLINE @ EPLANS.COM

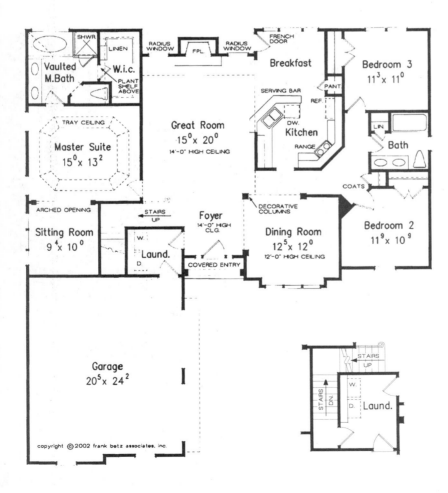

plan # HPT900179

- **STYLE: TRADITIONAL**
- **SQUARE FOOTAGE: 1,768**
- **BONUS SPACE: 347 SQ. FT.**
- **BEDROOMS: 3**
- **BATHROOMS: 2**
- **WIDTH: 54'-0"**
- **DEPTH: 59'-6"**
- **FOUNDATION: CRAWLSPACE, SLAB**

SEARCH ONLINE @ EPLANS.COM

This cozy traditional features amenities galore. The hearth-warmed great room will be the center of family life, opening to the kitchen and breakfast nook as well as the formal dining room. The breakfast nook enjoys French-door access to the rear property. Two bedrooms sharing a full bath are tucked to the right of the plan. On the opposite side sits the luxurious master suite, boasting a tray ceiling, vaulted bath with windowed tub and walk-in closet, and a private sitting room. A convenient laundry room accesses the two-car garage.

© 2001 Donald A. Gardner, Inc.

plan# HPT900180

- **STYLE:** TRADITIONAL
- **SQUARE FOOTAGE:** 1,929
- **BEDROOMS:** 3
- **BATHROOMS:** 2
- **WIDTH:** 46'-11"
- **DEPTH:** 71'-11"

SEARCH ONLINE @ EPLANS.COM

This traditional design features a hipped roof, multiple gables and brick accents. Sidelights expand the front entrance and allow an abundance of natural light. The top of the front Palladian-style window visually reinforces the window above the door. Topped with a vaulted ceiling, the dining room displays a Palladian-style window that leads eyes up to the ceiling. The kitchen includes a counter that acts as a partition, separating the kitchen from the great room. The great room displays a striking fireplace, built-in shelves and French doors that access the porch. The master suite exhibits a vaulted ceiling in the bedroom and an exquisitely designed bath with dual lavatories, a large shower and garden tub.

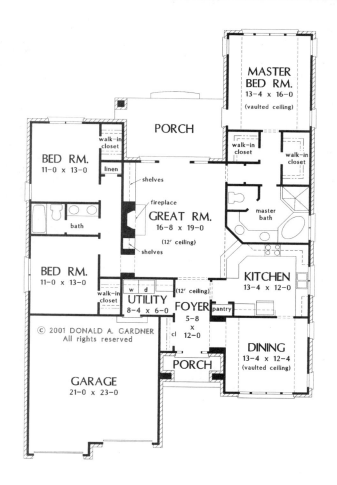

plan# HPT900181

- STYLE: TRADITIONAL
- SQUARE FOOTAGE: 1,506
- BEDROOMS: 3
- BATHROOMS: 2
- WIDTH: 40'-0"
- DEPTH: 52'-4"
- FOUNDATION: CRAWLSPACE

SEARCH ONLINE @ EPLANS.COM

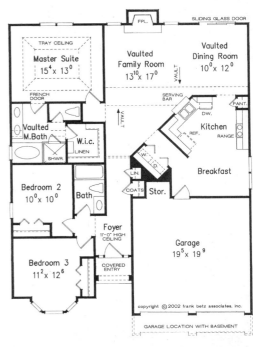

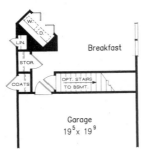

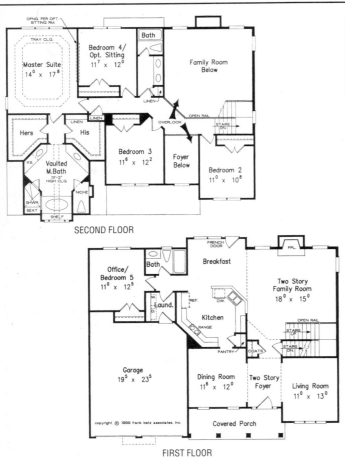

SECOND FLOOR

FIRST FLOOR

plan# HPT900182

- STYLE: TRADITIONAL
- FIRST FLOOR: 1,351 SQ. FT.
- SECOND FLOOR: 1,312 SQ. FT.
- TOTAL: 2,663 SQ. FT.
- BEDROOMS: 4
- BATHROOMS: 3
- WIDTH: 50'-0"
- DEPTH: 41'-4"
- FOUNDATION: BASEMENT, CRAWLSPACE

SEARCH ONLINE @ EPLANS.COM

TO ORDER BLUEPRINTS CALL TOLL FREE 1-800-521-6797

© 2001 Donald A. Gardner, Inc.

plan# HPT900183

- STYLE: TRADITIONAL
- SQUARE FOOTAGE: 2,358
- BONUS SPACE: 373 SQ. FT.
- BEDROOMS: 4
- BATHROOMS: 3
- WIDTH: 58'-11"
- DEPTH: 66'-3"

SEARCH ONLINE @ EPLANS.COM

A hipped roof and the varying gable heights give this traditional home a much larger feel, while a box-bay window is crowned with a metal roof. Inside, twelve-foot ceilings abound. A single column defines the tray-ceilinged dining room. The great room presents a fireplace and built-ins and is connected to the kitchen via a pass-through. Bonus-room access is near the gathering areas, and the study/bedroom features a vaulted ceiling. The master suite is set apart by a private foyer it shares with the rear porch. A bay window creates a sitting area, and an octagonal tray ceiling adds visual appeal. Note the large shower and garden tub in the master bath.

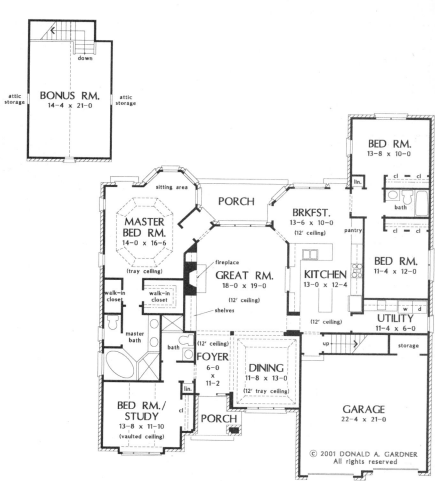

plan# HPT900185

- **STYLE:** TRADITIONAL
- **SQUARE FOOTAGE:** 2,992
- **BEDROOMS:** 4
- **BATHROOMS:** 2½
- **WIDTH:** 79'-4"
- **DEPTH:** 83'-4"
- **FOUNDATION:** BASEMENT

SEARCH ONLINE @ EPLANS.COM

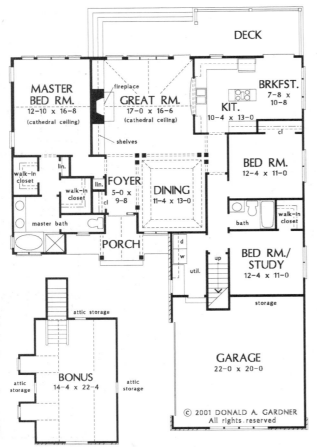

plan# HPT900184

- **STYLE:** CRAFTSMAN
- **SQUARE FOOTAGE:** 1,753
- **BONUS SPACE:** 389 SQ. FT.
- **BEDROOMS:** 3
- **BATHROOMS:** 2
- **WIDTH:** 49'-4"
- **DEPTH:** 64'-4"

SEARCH ONLINE @ EPLANS.COM

TO ORDER BLUEPRINTS CALL TOLL FREE 1-800-521-6797

© 2001 Donald A. Gardner, Inc.

plan# HPT900186

- STYLE: TRADITIONAL
- SQUARE FOOTAGE: 2,330
- BONUS SPACE: 364 SQ. FT.
- BEDROOMS: 3
- BATHROOMS: 2½
- WIDTH: 62'-3"
- DEPTH: 60'-6"

SEARCH ONLINE @ EPLANS.COM

Quaint and simple, this country home with front dormers will charm the whole neighborhood. Inside, the foyer is flanked on either side by a formal dining room and a study. A cathedral ceiling enlarges the great room, which is warmed by a fireplace flanked by built-ins. The master suite is located to the right and includes two walk-in closets and a private bath.

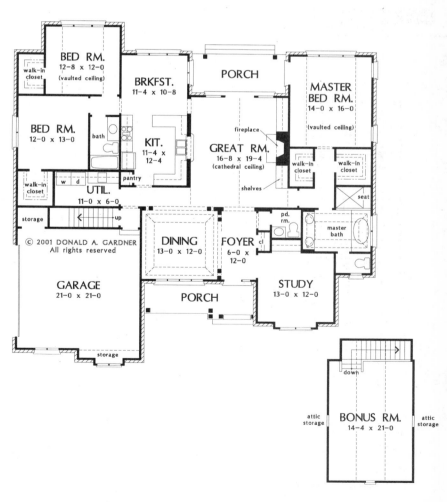

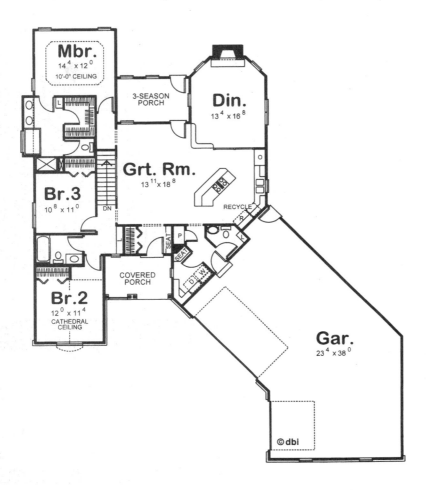

plan# HPT900187

- STYLE: TRADITIONAL
- SQUARE FOOTAGE: 1,709
- BEDROOMS: 3
- BATHROOMS: 2½
- WIDTH: 63'-3"
- DEPTH: 79'-9"

SEARCH ONLINE @ EPLANS.COM

Stucco and keystones blend well with the neighborhood facades, while tradition gets a new twist in this novel rearrangement of space. Saunter past the three-car garage to the covered front porch, which leads through a petite foyer to the open great room/kitchen combination. The kitchen's cooktop island divides the space, while both areas access the bayed, hearth-warmed dining room. The great room also opens to the three-season porch. The left wing of the plan holds the sleeping quarters, including two family bedrooms sharing a full bath and an elegant master suite, which enjoys a spacious private bath with a walk-in closet and a windowed tub.

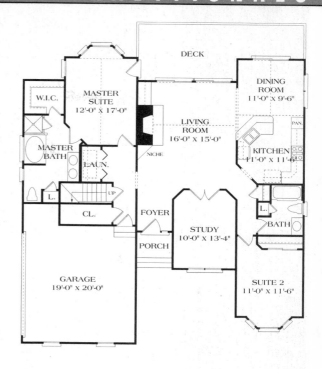

plan# HPT900188

- STYLE: CRAFTSMAN
- SQUARE FOOTAGE: 1,570
- BONUS SPACE: 326 SQ. FT.
- BEDROOMS: 2
- BATHROOMS: 2
- WIDTH: 47'-6"
- DEPTH: 52'-0"
- FOUNDATION: CRAWLSPACE

SEARCH ONLINE @ EPLANS.COM

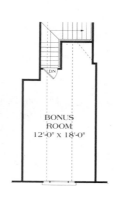

BONUS ROOM
12'-0" X 18'-0"

plan# HPT900189

- STYLE: TRADITIONAL
- SQUARE FOOTAGE: 1,504
- BEDROOMS: 3
- BATHROOMS: 2
- WIDTH: 55'-2"
- DEPTH: 46'-10"
- FOUNDATION: CRAWLSPACE, SLAB

SEARCH ONLINE @ EPLANS.COM

© 2002 Donald A. Gardner, Inc

Incorporating Old World style and elements, this house combines stone and stucco with gable peaks and arched windows for a stunning European facade. The grand portico leads to an open floor plan, which is equally impressive. Built-in cabinetry, French doors and a fireplace enhance the great room; an angled counter separates the kitchen from the breakfast nook. The first-floor master suite is located in the quiet zone with no rooms above it. Upstairs, a balcony overlooks the great room. The bonus room features convenient second-floor access, and shares a full bath with two upstairs bathrooms.

plan# HPT900190

- **STYLE: TRADITIONAL**
- **FIRST FLOOR: 1,345 SQ. FT.**
- **SECOND FLOOR: 452 SQ. FT.**
- **TOTAL: 1,797 SQ. FT.**
- **BONUS SPACE: 349 SQ. FT.**
- **BEDROOMS: 3**
- **BATHROOMS: 2½**
- **WIDTH: 63'-0"**
- **DEPTH: 40'-0"**

SEARCH ONLINE @ EPLANS.COM

FIRST FLOOR

SECOND FLOOR

plan# HPT900191

- STYLE: TRADITIONAL
- SQUARE FOOTAGE: 1,606
- BONUS SPACE: 338 SQ. FT.
- BEDROOMS: 3
- BATHROOMS: 2
- WIDTH: 50'-0"
- DEPTH: 54'-0"

SEARCH ONLINE @ EPLANS.COM

This smart, traditional plan packs a lot of living space into its modest square footage. A stately columned porch leads to the foyer, which boasts a convenient coat closet to its left. Just ahead, the great room's cathedral ceiling amplifies elegance while its cozy hearth offers the warmth of home. The kitchen features ample counter space and is bookended by a formal dining room and a sunny breakfast nook. The rear deck will provide many seasons of fun and relaxation. Two bedrooms—one that could be converted to a study—share a full bath on the left of the plan. A divine master suite is secluded behind the garage, with a vaulted ceiling, stunning master bath and walk-in closet. The utility room is convenient to both the kitchen and the garage. Bonus space awaits expansion upstairs.

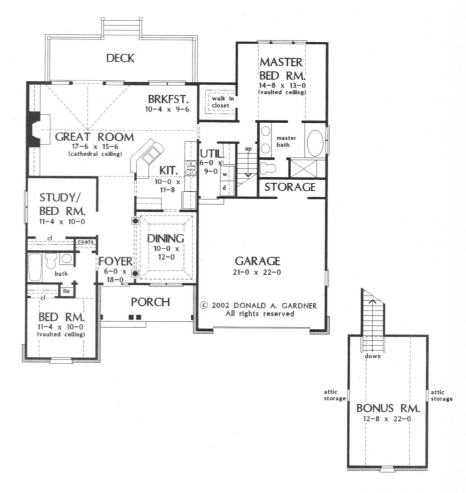

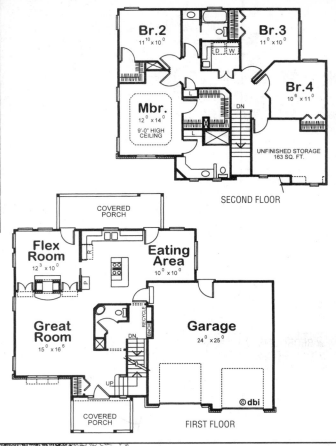

SECOND FLOOR

PHOTOGRAPHY BY DESIGN BASICS, INC.

COVERED PORCH

Flex Room 12³ x 10⁰

Eating Area 10⁰ x 10⁰

Great Room 15⁰ x 16⁵

Garage 24⁰ x 25⁰

COVERED PORCH

©dbi

FIRST FLOOR

plan# HPT900192

- ■ STYLE: TRADITIONAL
- ■ FIRST FLOOR: 929 SQ. FT.
- ■ SECOND FLOOR: 1,058 SQ. FT.
- ■ TOTAL: 1,987 SQ. FT.
- ■ BEDROOMS: 4
- ■ BATHROOMS: 2½
- ■ WIDTH: 50'-4"
- ■ DEPTH: 47'-4"

SEARCH ONLINE @ EPLANS.COM

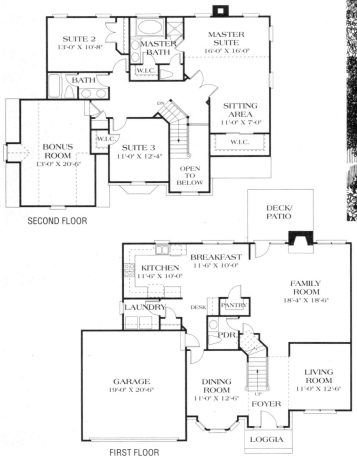

SECOND FLOOR

FIRST FLOOR

plan# HPT900193

- ■ STYLE: TRANSITIONAL
- ■ FIRST FLOOR: 1,200 SQ. FT.
- ■ SECOND FLOOR: 1,039 SQ. FT.
- ■ TOTAL: 2,239 SQ. FT.
- ■ BONUS SPACE: 309 SQ. FT.
- ■ BEDROOMS: 3
- ■ BATHROOMS: 2½
- ■ WIDTH: 50'-0"
- ■ DEPTH: 39'-6"
- ■ FOUNDATION: CRAWLSPACE, SLAB

SEARCH ONLINE @ EPLANS.COM

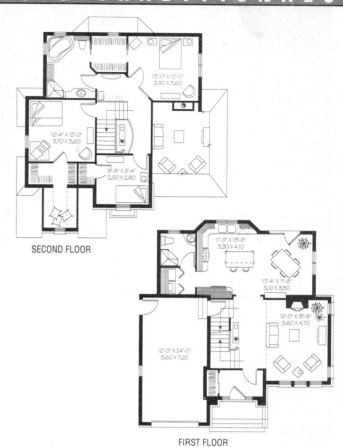

SECOND FLOOR

FIRST FLOOR

plan# HPT900194

- ■ STYLE: TRADITIONAL
- ■ FIRST FLOOR: 838 SQ. FT.
- ■ SECOND FLOOR: 879 SQ. FT.
- ■ TOTAL: 1,717 SQ. FT.
- ■ BEDROOMS: 3
- ■ BATHROOMS: 2
- ■ WIDTH: 36'-0"
- ■ DEPTH: 39'-8"
- ■ FOUNDATION: BASEMENT

SEARCH ONLINE @ EPLANS.COM

SECOND FLOOR

FIRST FLOOR

plan# HPT900195

- ■ STYLE: TRADITIONAL
- ■ FIRST FLOOR: 1,112 SQ. FT.
- ■ SECOND FLOOR: 882 SQ. FT.
- ■ TOTAL: 1,994 SQ. FT.
- ■ BEDROOMS: 3
- ■ BATHROOMS: 2½
- ■ WIDTH: 40'-0"
- ■ DEPTH: 43'-0"
- ■ FOUNDATION: CRAWLSPACE

SEARCH ONLINE @ EPLANS.COM

© 2001 Donald A. Gardner, Inc.

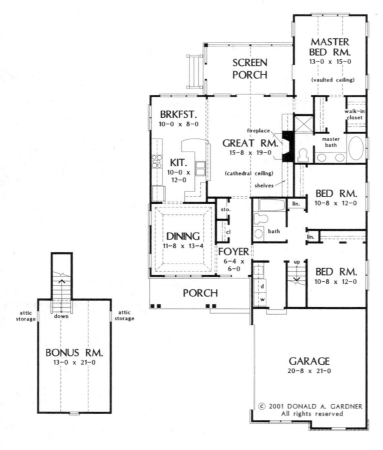

SCREEN PORCH

MASTER BED RM.
13-0 x 15-0
(vaulted ceiling)

walk-in closet

BRKFST.
10-0 x 8-0

fireplace

master bath

GREAT RM.
15-8 x 19-0

KIT.
10-0 x 12-0

(cathedral ceiling)

shelves

sto.

cl

lin.

BED RM.
10-8 x 12-0

bath

lin.

DINING
11-8 x 13-4

FOYER
6-4 x 6-0

up

BED RM.
10-8 x 12-0

PORCH

d
w

attic storage

down

attic storage

BONUS RM.
13-0 x 21-0

GARAGE
20-8 x 21-0

plan# HPT900196

- STYLE: CRAFTSMAN
- SQUARE FOOTAGE: 1,682
- BONUS SPACE: 320 SQ. FT.
- BEDROOMS: 3
- BATHROOMS: 2
- WIDTH: 40'-0"
- DEPTH: 78'-4"

SEARCH ONLINE @ EPLANS.COM

This Arts and Crafts cottage combines stone and stucco to create an Old World feel. From decorative wood brackets and columns to arched windows and shutters, the details produce architectural interest and absolute charm. This design features plenty of windows and French doors to invite nature inside. Built-in cabinetry enhances the interior and provides convenience. Topping the great room is a cathedral ceiling, and a tray ceiling completes the dining room. The master suite, which features a vaulted ceiling in the bedroom and an ample master bath, lies next to the screened porch, while a bonus room, accessible from two additional bedrooms, would make a perfect game room for the family.

© 2001 Donald A. Gardner, Inc.

plan # HPT900197

- **STYLE:** TRADITIONAL
- **SQUARE FOOTAGE:** 1,610
- **BONUS SPACE:** 353 SQ. FT.
- **BEDROOMS:** 3
- **BATHROOMS:** 2
- **WIDTH:** 49'-11"
- **DEPTH:** 55'-1"

SEARCH ONLINE @ EPLANS.COM

Flower boxes, shuttered windows and a cozy front porch lend a country feel to this brick traditional home. Inside, a bedroom/study sits to the left of the foyer; directly ahead, the great room opens to a small side porch and features a fireplace flanked by built-in bookshelves. An efficient kitchen easily serves the dining room, which boasts a tray ceiling. Sleeping quarters to the left of the plan include a master suite, with a large walk-in closet and private bath, and one family bedroom with access to a nearby full bath. Upstairs, a bonus room can serve as a third bedroom, recreation room or game room.

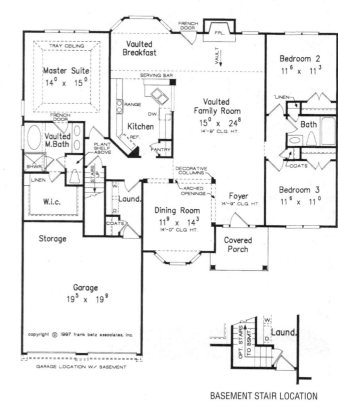

plan# HPT900198

- **STYLE: NEOCLASSIC**
- **SQUARE FOOTAGE: 1,780**
- **BEDROOMS: 3**
- **BATHROOMS: 2**
- **WIDTH: 52'-0"**
- **DEPTH: 57'-6"**
- **FOUNDATION: BASEMENT, CRAWLSPACE**

SEARCH ONLINE @ EPLANS.COM

GARAGE LOCATION W/ BASEMENT

BASEMENT STAIR LOCATION

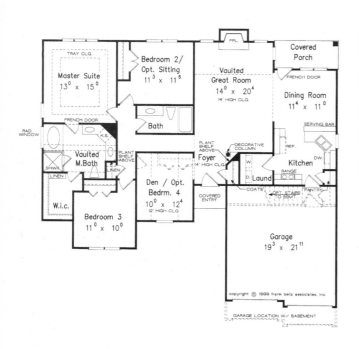

plan# HPT900199

- **STYLE: TRADITIONAL**
- **SQUARE FOOTAGE: 1,606**
- **BEDROOMS: 3**
- **BATHROOMS: 2**
- **WIDTH: 53'-0"**
- **DEPTH: 51'-4"**
- **FOUNDATION: BASEMENT, CRAWLSPACE**

SEARCH ONLINE @ EPLANS.COM

TO ORDER BLUEPRINTS CALL TOLL FREE 1-800-521-6797

plan# HPT900200

- **STYLE:** TRADITIONAL
- **FIRST FLOOR:** 2,497 SQ. FT.
- **SECOND FLOOR:** 1,028 SQ. FT.
- **TOTAL:** 3,525 SQ. FT.
- **BEDROOMS:** 5
- **BATHROOMS:** 4½
- **WIDTH:** 87'-0"
- **DEPTH:** 57'-5"
- **FOUNDATION:** BASEMENT, CRAWLSPACE, SLAB

SEARCH ONLINE @ EPLANS.COM

Perfect symmetry is pleasing in this Southern country cottage. Accent arches and two false chimneys add architectural interest outside; inside, a curving staircase and delicate touches lend charm and sophistication. The central great room will surely be a gathering place, with a fireplace framed by windows and easy access to the rest of the living areas. Two generous bedrooms, each with a private bath, precede the master suite. The vaulted master bedroom has a bayed window, enormous walk-in closet and pampering bath. Upstairs, two bedrooms and a playroom are flexible to meet your family's needs.

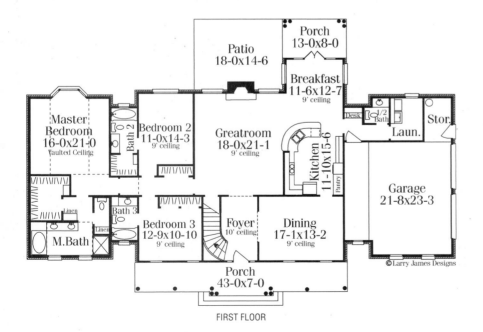

FIRST FLOOR

SECOND FLOOR

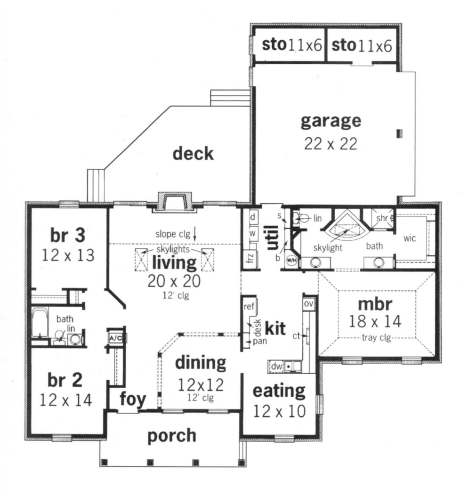

plan# HPT900201

- **STYLE:** TRADITIONAL
- **SQUARE FOOTAGE:** 1,936
- **BEDROOMS:** 3
- **BATHROOMS:** 2
- **WIDTH:** 62'-0"
- **DEPTH:** 68'-0"
- **FOUNDATION:** CRAWLSPACE, SLAB

SEARCH ONLINE @ EPLANS.COM

This traditional ranch-style home is enhanced by graceful southern accents. A front covered porch welcomes you inside to a foyer that introduces a formal dining room and living room brightened by skylights. The master suite provides a skylit bath and a roomy walk-in closet. Two additional family bedrooms are located on the opposite side of the home and share a hall bath. The rear deck provides plenty of outdoor entertainment options. A two-car garage with storage and a useful utility room complete this lovely one-story home.

plan# HPT900202

- **STYLE:** TRADITIONAL
- **SQUARE FOOTAGE:** 2,122
- **BONUS SPACE:** 965 SQ. FT.
- **BEDROOMS:** 3
- **BATHROOMS:** 2½
- **WIDTH:** 69'-0"
- **DEPTH:** 67'-10"
- **FOUNDATION:** BASEMENT, CRAWLSPACE, SLAB

SEARCH ONLINE @ EPLANS.COM

Symmetry and Southern charm combine to make this home a family favorite. Inside, natural light is a cheerful addition. Nine-foot ceilings bring height and grandeur to every room—the living room ceiling tops off at a soaring eleven feet! The U-shaped kitchen features a bonus side counter for extra workspace, and easily serves the breakfast and dining rooms. Separated for privacy, the master suite is a joy, with a spa-style bath and His and Hers walk-in closets. Two more bedrooms are located to the far right. A bonus room would be a perfect home office, guest room or nursery. Future space upstairs awaits your imagination.

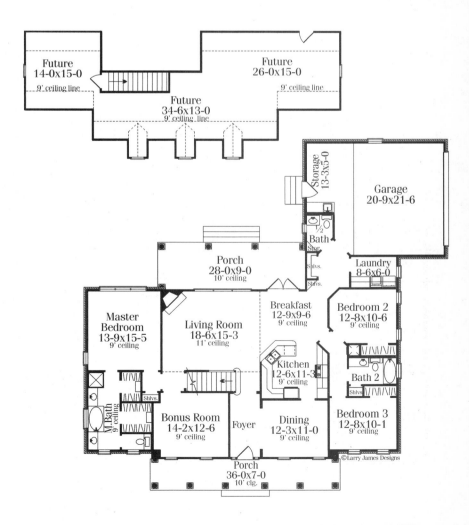

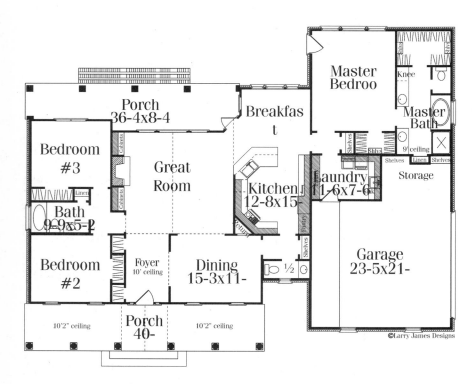

©Larry James Designs

plan# HPT900203

- **STYLE: TRADITIONAL**
- **SQUARE FOOTAGE: 2,197**
- **BEDROOMS: 3**
- **BATHROOMS: 2½**
- **WIDTH: 72'-10"**
- **DEPTH: 56'-6"**
- **FOUNDATION: BASEMENT, CRAWLSPACE, SLAB**

SEARCH ONLINE @ EPLANS.COM

Palladian-style windows and a barrel-vaulted portico are just the beginning of this lovely brick-and-stucco family home. Enter from the columned porch to find a dining room to the right and the vaulted great room straight ahead. Here, a lateral fireplace with surrounding built-in shelving won't block the fantastic views of the rear property. Two bedrooms, or make one a study, share a full bath on the left; on the far right, the master suite revels in a bright, sunny bedroom with backyard access and a wonderfully soothing bath. Don't miss the laundry room and storage space off the side-entry garage.

plan # HPT900204

- STYLE: GEORGIAN
- SQUARE FOOTAGE: 3,136
- BEDROOMS: 4
- BATHROOMS: 3½
- WIDTH: 80'-6"
- DEPTH: 72'-4"
- FOUNDATION: CRAWLSPACE

SEARCH ONLINE @ EPLANS.COM

Formal elegance may be the motif on the facade, but inside this home, family livability takes center stage. The foyer leads to a convenient coat closet and powder room before presenting the hearth-warmed family room. This room accesses a small side porch that leads out to the rear terrace. At the front left of the plan, a living room with a fireplace is adjacent to the formal dining room, which in turn opens to the spacious island kitchen. Ample counter space and a worktop island counter make this kitchen a cook's delight. Tucked behind the kitchen is a bedroom and full bath, and a laundry room that accesses the two-car garage. Three more bedrooms take up the right wing of the home, including a large master suite with an elegant private bath. Two bedrooms at the front share a spacious bath.

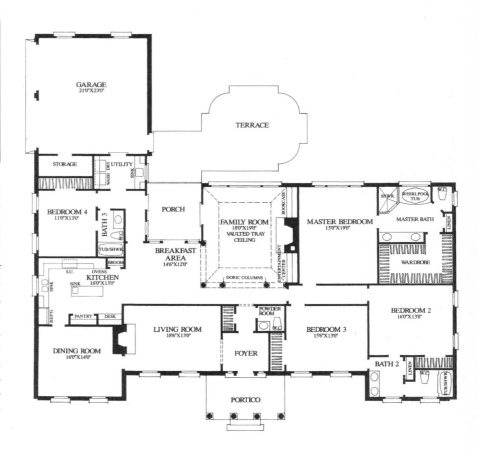

This home is sure to become the centerpiece of the neighborhood. Classic Early American features such as pedimented gables and shutters bring stately charm to the facade. Inside, formal space is designated at the front, where the foyer is flanked by a living room on the left and dining room on the right. Straight ahead is the hearth-warmed two-story family room, which flows into the breakfast room and island kitchen. A roomy laundry area and pantry space are convenient to the kitchen. On the opposite side of the plan is a guest bedroom that could be converted into a den. Upstairs, four bedrooms reside, including a spectacular master suite with its own sitting area and positively luxurious private bath.

plan# HPT900205

- STYLE: SOUTHERN COLONIAL
- FIRST FLOOR: 1,377 SQ. FT.
- SECOND FLOOR: 1,341 SQ. FT.
- TOTAL: 2,718 SQ. FT.
- BEDROOMS: 5
- BATHROOMS: 4
- WIDTH: 50'-0"
- DEPTH: 47'-4"
- FOUNDATION: BASEMENT, CRAWLSPACE

SEARCH ONLINE @ EPLANS.COM

FIRST FLOOR

SECOND FLOOR

© 2001 Donald A. Gardner, Inc.

plan# HPT900206

- STYLE: TRADITIONAL
- FIRST FLOOR: 1,500 SQ. FT.
- SECOND FLOOR: 1,106 SQ. FT.
- TOTAL: 2,606 SQ. FT.
- BONUS SPACE: 366 SQ. FT.
- BEDROOMS: 4
- BATHROOMS: 2½
- WIDTH: 63'-3"
- DEPTH: 48'-1"

SEARCH ONLINE @ EPLANS.COM

Elegant and stately, the exterior features a Palladian-style window, which accents the front facade and floods the two-story foyer with light. The floorplan features open spaces with more room definition for those seeking a truly Traditional design. Columns separate the formal living and dining rooms, while a bay window extends the breakfast area. French doors access the rear porch as well as connect the family room to the outdoors. Built-ins embrace the fireplace, and an angled counter allows the kitchen to take part in casual entertaining. The master bedroom features a tray ceiling, and additional bedrooms share a full bath with the bonus room. Note the second-floor balcony.

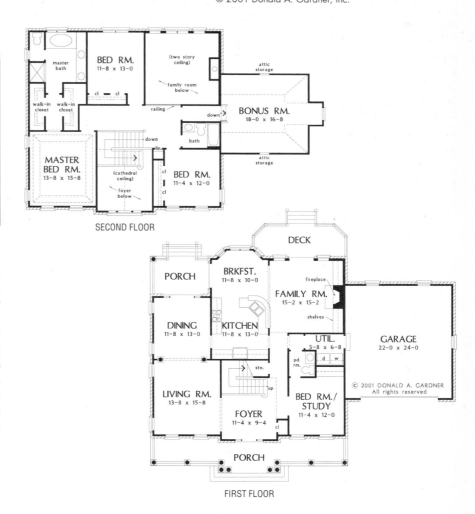

SECOND FLOOR

FIRST FLOOR

SECOND FLOOR

plan# HPT900207

- STYLE: SOUTHERN COLONIAL
- FIRST FLOOR: 1,217 SQ. FT.
- SECOND FLOOR: 1,390 SQ. FT.
- TOTAL: 2,607 SQ. FT.
- BEDROOMS: 5
- BATHROOMS: 3
- WIDTH: 50'-0"
- DEPTH: 40'-4"
- FOUNDATION: BASEMENT, CRAWLSPACE

SEARCH ONLINE @ EPLANS.COM

FIRST FLOOR

copyright © 2002 frank betz associates, inc.

SECOND FLOOR

FIRST FLOOR

plan# HPT900208

- STYLE: COLONIAL
- FIRST FLOOR: 680 SQ. FT.
- SECOND FLOOR: 674 SQ. FT.
- TOTAL: 1,354 SQ. FT.
- BEDROOMS: 3
- BATHROOMS: 2½
- WIDTH: 34'-5"
- DEPTH: 31'-3"
- FOUNDATION: SLAB

SEARCH ONLINE @ EPLANS.COM

plan# HPT900209

- STYLE: GEORGIAN
- FIRST FLOOR: 755 SQ. FT.
- SECOND FLOOR: 736 SQ. FT.
- TOTAL: 1,491 SQ. FT.
- BONUS SPACE: 293 SQ. FT.
- BEDROOMS: 3
- BATHROOMS: 2½
- WIDTH: 45'-10"
- DEPTH: 37'-5"
- FOUNDATION: BASEMENT, CRAWLSPACE

SEARCH ONLINE @ EPLANS.COM

Economical to build and a joy to live in, this Georgian-style home is sure to please. A portico entry leads to the family room, rich in natural light and warmed by an extended-hearth fireplace. The dining room is bright and open, flowing into the kitchen area. On the second floor, the master suite charms with a tray ceiling, oversize walk-in closet and a vaulted bath with a spa tub. Twin bedrooms share a full bath. An optional bonus room makes a great playroom, guest suite or home office.

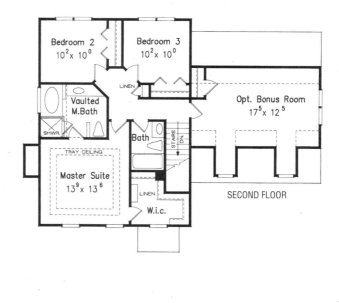

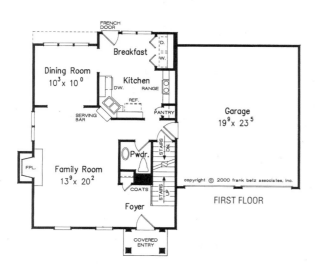

Cape Cod style and Georgian sensibilities set this stunning home apart from the rest. Upon entry, a lovely bayed dining room is to the right. The two-story great room includes a fireplace framed by windows. In the kitchen, a step-saving shape allows easy meal preparation. A bedroom/home office would also make a great guest room. Upstairs, the master suite is rich with natural light. The master bath has a vaulted ceiling and pampering spa tub. Two more bedrooms share a full bath. Located for ultimate convenience, a laundry room near the bedrooms encourages organization.

plan # HPT900210

- STYLE: GEORGIAN
- FIRST FLOOR: 1,233 SQ. FT.
- SECOND FLOOR: 1,045 SQ. FT.
- TOTAL: 2,278 SQ. FT.
- BEDROOMS: 4
- BATHROOMS: 3
- WIDTH: 49'-0"
- DEPTH: 42'-0"
- FOUNDATION: BASEMENT, CRAWLSPACE

SEARCH ONLINE @ EPLANS.COM

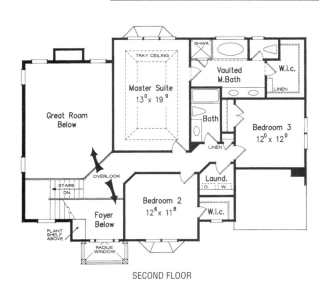

FIRST FLOOR

SECOND FLOOR

SECOND FLOOR

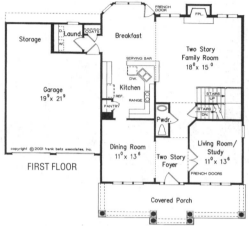

FIRST FLOOR

plan # HPT900211

- **STYLE:** SOUTHERN COLONIAL
- **FIRST FLOOR:** 1,186 SQ. FT.
- **SECOND FLOOR:** 1,210 SQ. FT.
- **TOTAL:** 2,396 SQ. FT.
- **BEDROOMS:** 4
- **BATHROOMS:** 2½
- **WIDTH:** 50'-0"
- **DEPTH:** 47'-6"
- **FOUNDATION:** BASEMENT, CRAWLSPACE

SEARCH ONLINE @ EPLANS.COM

SECOND FLOOR

FIRST FLOOR

plan # HPT900212

- **STYLE:** GEORGIAN
- **FIRST FLOOR:** 1,816 SQ. FT.
- **SECOND FLOOR:** 662 SQ. FT.
- **TOTAL:** 2,478 SQ. FT.
- **BONUS SPACE:** 342 SQ. FT.
- **BEDROOMS:** 3
- **BATHROOMS:** 2½
- **WIDTH:** 54'-0"
- **DEPTH:** 54'-0"
- **FOUNDATION:** BASEMENT, CRAWLSPACE

SEARCH ONLINE @ EPLANS.COM

This stately two-story beauty offers the utmost in style and livability. The grand columned entryway is topped by a railed roof, making it the centerpiece of the facade. Formal space resides at the front of the plan, with a living room and dining room flanking the foyer. Secluded behind the staircase is the elegant master suite, with a huge walk-in closet and swanky private bath. The hearth-warmed family room flows into the island kitchen and breakfast nook, making this space the comfortable hub of home life. A laundry room and half-bath are convenient to this area. Upstairs, three bedrooms all have access to separate baths and share space with a future recreation room.

plan# HPT900213

- STYLE: SOUTHERN COLONIAL
- FIRST FLOOR: 2,168 SQ. FT.
- SECOND FLOOR: 1,203 SQ. FT.
- TOTAL: 3,371 SQ. FT.
- BONUS SPACE: 452 SQ. FT.
- BEDROOMS: 4
- BATHROOMS: 4½
- WIDTH: 71'-2"
- DEPTH: 63'-4"
- FOUNDATION: BASEMENT, CRAWLSPACE

SEARCH ONLINE @ EPLANS.COM

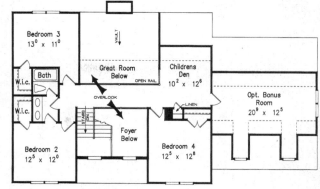

SECOND FLOOR

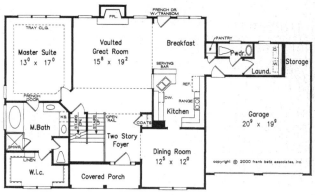

FIRST FLOOR

plan # HPT900215

- **STYLE:** SOUTHERN COLONIAL
- **FIRST FLOOR:** 1,440 SQ. FT.
- **SECOND FLOOR:** 886 SQ. FT.
- **TOTAL:** 2,326 SQ. FT.
- **BONUS SPACE:** 309 SQ. FT.
- **BEDROOMS:** 4
- **BATHROOMS:** 2½
- **WIDTH:** 61'-0"
- **DEPTH:** 37'-4"
- **FOUNDATION:** BASEMENT, CRAWLSPACE

SEARCH ONLINE @ EPLANS.COM

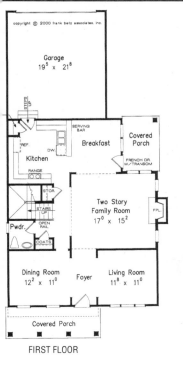

FIRST FLOOR

SECOND FLOOR

plan # HPT900214

- **STYLE:** SOUTHERN COLONIAL
- **FIRST FLOOR:** 1,064 SQ. FT.
- **SECOND FLOOR:** 1,216 SQ. FT.
- **TOTAL:** 2,280 SQ. FT.
- **BEDROOMS:** 3
- **BATHROOMS:** 2½
- **WIDTH:** 32'-0"
- **DEPTH:** 66'-0"
- **FOUNDATION:** BASEMENT, CRAWLSPACE

SEARCH ONLINE @ EPLANS.COM

SECOND FLOOR

FIRST FLOOR

plan# HPT900216

- STYLE: GEORGIAN
- FIRST FLOOR: 2,093 SQ. FT.
- SECOND FLOOR: 641 SQ. FT.
- TOTAL: 2,734 SQ. FT.
- BONUS SPACE: 258 SQ. FT.
- BEDROOMS: 3
- BATHROOMS: 2½
- WIDTH: 58'-4"
- DEPTH: 55'-8"
- FOUNDATION: BASEMENT, CRAWLSPACE

SEARCH ONLINE @ EPLANS.COM

SECOND FLOOR

FIRST FLOOR

plan# HPT900217

- STYLE: GEORGIAN
- FIRST FLOOR: 2,719 SQ. FT.
- SECOND FLOOR: 929 SQ. FT.
- TOTAL: 3,648 SQ. FT.
- BONUS SPACE: 530 SQ. FT.
- BEDROOMS: 3
- BATHROOMS: 4
- WIDTH: 62'-8"
- DEPTH: 83'-0"
- FOUNDATION: WALKOUT BASEMENT

SEARCH ONLINE @ EPLANS.COM

TO ORDER BLUEPRINTS CALL TOLL FREE 1-800-521-6797

© Stephen Fuller, Inc.

plan# HPT900218

- **STYLE:** GEORGIAN
- **FIRST FLOOR:** 1,981 SQ. FT.
- **SECOND FLOOR:** 1,935 SQ. FT.
- **TOTAL:** 3,916 SQ. FT.
- **BEDROOMS:** 5
- **BATHROOMS:** 4
- **WIDTH:** 65'-0"
- **DEPTH:** 64'-10"
- **FOUNDATION:** WALKOUT BASEMENT

SEARCH ONLINE @ EPLANS.COM

Take one look at this Early American Colonial home and you'll fall in love with it's beauty, functionality and luxuries. From the covered front porch, continue to the great room, where a fireplace and a bay window with wonderful rear-property views await. The kitchen will delight, with a wraparound counter that provides plenty of workspace for easy meal preparation. Up the grand staircase, the master suite revels in a private deck and pampering spa bath. Three additional bedrooms complete this level. Don't miss the first-floor guest room with an adjacent full bath.

SECOND FLOOR

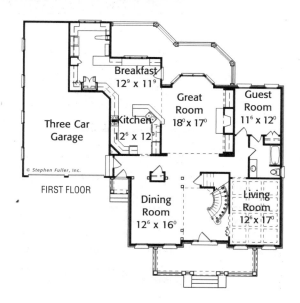

FIRST FLOOR

© Stephen Fuller, Inc.

Colonial details and a covered porch combine to give this home plenty of curb appeal. Inside, a formal dining room presides at the front of the plan, while more casual rooms wait in the back. Here, a family room with a fireplace works well with the C-shaped kitchen and adjacent breakfast area. The first-floor master suite ensures privacy and offers two walk-in closets and a lavish bath, as well a private access to the rear porch. Upstairs, three spacious bedrooms provide plenty of storage—Bedrooms 2 and 4 share a large bath, while Bedroom 3 is all about privacy. The two-car garage is wonderfully convenient to the kitchen, making the unloading of groceries a breeze.

plan# HPT900219

- STYLE: NORTHEAST COLONIAL
- FIRST FLOOR: 1,832 SQ. FT.
- SECOND FLOOR: 973 SQ. FT.
- TOTAL: 2,805 SQ. FT.
- BEDROOMS: 4
- BATHROOMS: 3½
- WIDTH: 49'-0"
- DEPTH: 66'-0"
- FOUNDATION: WALKOUT BASEMENT

SEARCH ONLINE @ EPLANS.COM

Master Bedroom 18³ x 14⁰

Breakfast 9³ x 10⁰

Family Room 16⁶ x 18⁰

Kitchen 11⁶ x 12³

Two Car Garage

Dining Room 13⁹ x 15⁶

© Stephen Fuller, Inc.

FIRST FLOOR

© Stephen Fuller, Inc.

Bedroom #4 21⁶ x 11⁹

Bedroom #3 13⁰ x 11⁹

Bedroom #2 13⁶ x 13⁰

SECOND FLOOR

SECOND FLOOR

plan# HPT900220

- **STYLE:** GEORGIAN
- **FIRST FLOOR:** 1,373 SQ. FT.
- **SECOND FLOOR:** 1,512 SQ. FT.
- **TOTAL:** 2,885 SQ. FT.
- **BEDROOMS:** 4
- **BATHROOMS:** 3½
- **WIDTH:** 56'-4"
- **DEPTH:** 44'-6"
- **FOUNDATION:** BASEMENT, CRAWLSPACE

SEARCH ONLINE @ EPLANS.COM

FIRST FLOOR

SECOND FLOOR

FIRST FLOOR

plan# HPT900221

- **STYLE:** COLONIAL
- **FIRST FLOOR:** 1,561 SQ. FT.
- **SECOND FLOOR:** 634 SQ. FT.
- **TOTAL:** 2,195 SQ. FT.
- **BEDROOMS:** 4
- **BATHROOMS:** 2½
- **WIDTH:** 50'-0"
- **DEPTH:** 50'-10"
- **FOUNDATION:** BASEMENT, CRAWLSPACE

SEARCH ONLINE @ EPLANS.COM

Southern plantation elegance on a generous scale for everyday living. The side-loading two-car garage, home office, screened porch and sun deck are all bonuses in this refined design. The foyer opens to the living area that shares a double-sided fireplace with the breakfast/keeping room. The adjoining kitchen accesses the garage and the utility room. The master suite enjoys a tray-ceilinged bedroom and a lavish private bath. Two family bedrooms share a full bath nearby. The living room and master bedroom open to the sun deck while the breakfast area leads to the screened porch.

plan# HPT900222

- **STYLE:** TRADITIONAL
- **SQUARE FOOTAGE:** 2,788
- **BEDROOMS:** 3
- **BATHROOMS:** 2½
- **WIDTH:** 83'-2"
- **DEPTH:** 60'-5"
- **FOUNDATION:** BASEMENT

SEARCH ONLINE @ EPLANS.COM

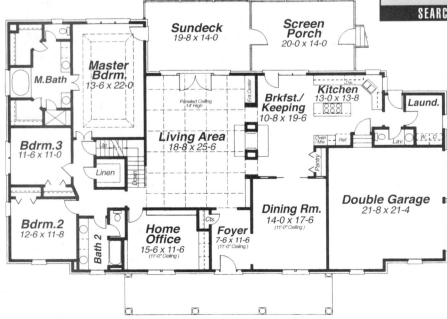

© 2002 Donald A. Gardner, Inc.

plan# HPT900223

- **STYLE:** CRAFTSMAN
- **SQUARE FOOTAGE:** 2,017
- **BONUS SPACE:** 319 SQ. FT.
- **BEDROOMS:** 3
- **BATHROOMS:** 2½
- **WIDTH:** 54'-0"
- **DEPTH:** 74'-0"

SEARCH ONLINE @ EPLANS.COM

This beautiful Arts and Crafts cottage combines stone and siding to create stunning curb appeal. A pair of columns and an arch make a dramatic entrance to an open floor plan. A tray ceiling crowns the great room that features built-in cabinetry, French-door access to the rear porch, a fireplace and a convenient pass-through to the kitchen. The dining room and breakfast nook are surrounded by windows and open space for an airy feeling. The master suite, located in a quiet wing, includes a sitting area, porch access, twin walk-ins and a master bath. Note the optional study/bedroom and flexible bonus room.

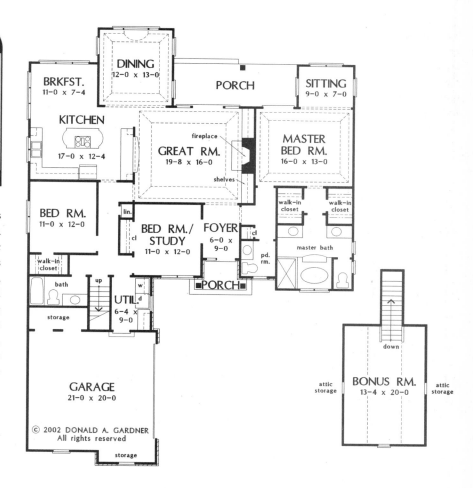

plan# HPT900224

- STYLE: SOUTHERN COLONIAL
- FIRST FLOOR: 1,645 SQ. FT.
- SECOND FLOOR: 563 SQ. FT.
- TOTAL: 2,208 SQ. FT.
- BONUS SPACE: 255 SQ. FT.
- BEDROOMS: 3
- BATHROOMS: 2½
- WIDTH: 50'-0"
- DEPTH: 54'-0"
- FOUNDATION: BASEMENT, CRAWLSPACE

SEARCH ONLINE @ EPLANS.COM

This Southern country home will charm you from the curb, but don't stop there! Inside, a wonderful floor plan offers natural light, spacious rooms, and options to expand. The two-story foyer opens on the right to an elegant dining room. Continue past an art niche to the vaulted family room, lit by radius windows that frame a fireplace. The island kitchen is conveniently located near the breakfast nook and large laundry room. A keeping room offers a cozy place to relax. The master suite claims the entire left side of the home, with a lavish spa bath and abundant closet space. Two bedrooms on the second floor share a full bath and access optional bonus space.

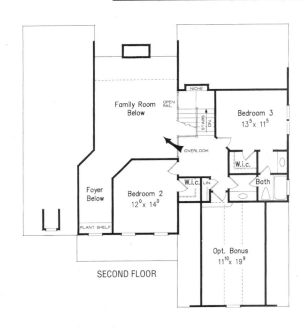

TO ORDER BLUEPRINTS CALL TOLL FREE 1-800-521-6797

Open To Family Rm.

Bth.2

Bdrm.3
11^4 x 10^4

Bdrm.2
10^0 x 11^6

Open To Foyer

Bdrm.4
11^4 x 10^4

M.Bdrm.
13^6 x 14^6
Tray Ceil.

M.Bath

SECOND FLOOR

plan ⊕ HPT900226

- STYLE: TRADITIONAL
- FIRST FLOOR: 890 SQ. FT.
- SECOND FLOOR: 986 SQ. FT.
- TOTAL: 1,876 SQ. FT.
- BEDROOMS: 4
- BATHROOMS: 2½
- WIDTH: 40'-4"
- DEPTH: 42'-0"
- FOUNDATION: BASEMENT

SEARCH ONLINE @ EPLANS.COM

Sundeck

Family Rm.
17^4 x 13^4

Brkfst.
10^0 x 9^4

Kit.
10^0 x 9^4

Foyer
6^0 x 11^8

Dining
11^4 x 10^0

Lav.

Double Garage
19^4 x 20^8

Living
11^4 x 10^0

FIRST FLOOR

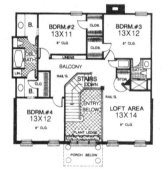

B.

BDRM.#2
13X11
8' CLG.

BDRM.#3
13X12
8' CLG.

DBL. BATH

LINENS

BALCONY

STAIRS DOWN

BDRM.#4
13X12
8' CLG.

LOFT AREA
13X14
8' CLG.

ENTRY BELOW

PLANT LEDGE

PORCH BELOW

SECOND FLOOR

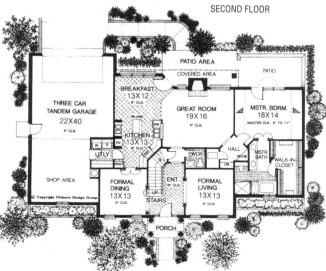

PATIO AREA

COVERED AREA

PATIO

THREE CAR TANDEM GARAGE
22X40
9' CLG.

BREAKFAST
13X12
8' CLG.

GREAT ROOM
19X16
9' CLG.

MSTR. BDRM.
18X14
VAULTED CLG. 9' TO 11'

KITCHEN
13X13

HALL

MSTR. BATH

WALK-IN CLOSET

SHOP AREA

UTLY.

PWDR.

FORMAL DINING
13X13
9' CLG.

ENT.

FORMAL LIVING
13X13
9' CLG.

STAIRS

PORCH

© Copyright Fillmore Design Group

FIRST FLOOR

plan ⊕ HPT900225

- STYLE: GEORGIAN
- FIRST FLOOR: 1,848 SQ. FT.
- SECOND FLOOR: 1,111 SQ. FT.
- TOTAL: 2,959 SQ. FT.
- BEDROOMS: 4
- BATHROOMS: 3½
- WIDTH: 73'-4"
- DEPTH: 44'-1"
- FOUNDATION: BASEMENT, CRAWLSPACE, SLAB

SEARCH ONLINE @ EPLANS.COM

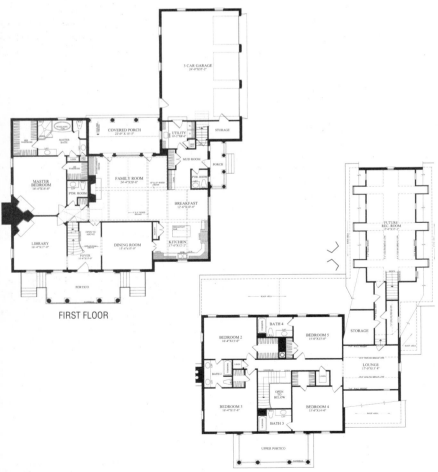

FIRST FLOOR

SECOND FLOOR

plan# HPT900227

- STYLE: SOUTHERN COLONIAL
- FIRST FLOOR: 2,670 SQ. FT.
- SECOND FLOOR: 1,795 SQ. FT.
- TOTAL: 4,465 SQ. FT.
- BONUS SPACE: 744 SQ. FT.
- BEDROOMS: 5
- BATHROOMS: 4½ + ½
- WIDTH: 74'-8"
- DEPTH: 93'-10"
- FOUNDATION: BASEMENT, CRAWLSPACE

SEARCH ONLINE @ EPLANS.COM

A stately brick plantation home, this plan presents all the luxuries that are so desired by today's homeowner. Enter past the columned portico to the formal two-story foyer. To the left is a library with a corner fireplace; to the right, the dining room flows into an enormous kitchen, outfitted with an island serving bar. Exposed wood-beam ceilings in the kitchen, breakfast area and family room add a vintage element. The master suite is a romantic hideaway, with a corner fireplace, whirlpool tub and seated shower. Upstairs, four well-appointed bedrooms join a lounge area to finish the plan. Future space above the three-car garage is limited only by your imagination.

plan # HPT900228

- **STYLE:** NEOCLASSIC
- **FIRST FLOOR:** 2,635 SQ. FT.
- **SECOND FLOOR:** 1,682 SQ. FT.
- **TOTAL:** 4,317 SQ. FT.
- **BEDROOMS:** 4
- **BATHROOMS:** 4½
- **WIDTH:** 79'-0"
- **DEPTH:** 74'-5"
- **FOUNDATION:** BASEMENT, CRAWLSPACE

SEARCH ONLINE @ EPLANS.COM

This home's dramatic pillared entry complements the elegant living space within. The two-story foyer showcases a spiral staircase and opens to an enormous family room, which flows into an island kitchen and hearth-warmed keeping room. The deluxe master suite takes up the right wing of the first floor. Upstairs, three bedrooms each have their own bath.

FIRST FLOOR

SECOND FLOOR

SECOND FLOOR

plan# HPT900230

- **STYLE:** SOUTHERN COLONIAL
- **FIRST FLOOR:** 2,798 SQ. FT.
- **SECOND FLOOR:** 1,496 SQ. FT.
- **TOTAL:** 4,294 SQ. FT.
- **BONUS SPACE:** 515 SQ. FT.
- **BEDROOMS:** 4
- **BATHROOMS:** 3½
- **WIDTH:** 91'-10"
- **DEPTH:** 57'-2"
- **FOUNDATION:** BASEMENT, CRAWLSPACE

SEARCH ONLINE @ EPLANS.COM

FIRST FLOOR

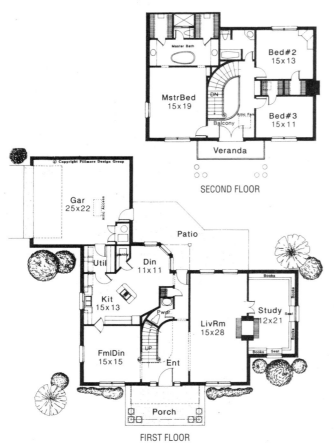

SECOND FLOOR

FIRST FLOOR

plan# HPT900229

- **STYLE:** GEORGIAN
- **FIRST FLOOR:** 1,651 SQ. FT.
- **SECOND FLOOR:** 1,174 SQ. FT.
- **TOTAL:** 2,825 SQ. FT.
- **BEDROOMS:** 3½
- **BATHROOMS:** 2½
- **WIDTH:** 67'-4"
- **DEPTH:** 57'-4"
- **FOUNDATION:** SLAB

SEARCH ONLINE @ EPLANS.COM

plan# HPT900231

- **STYLE:** SOUTHERN COLONIAL
- **FIRST FLOOR:** 3,064 SQ. FT.
- **SECOND FLOOR:** 1,726 SQ. FT.
- **TOTAL:** 4,790 SQ. FT.
- **BONUS SPACE:** 793 SQ. FT.
- **BEDROOMS:** 4
- **BATHROOMS:** 4½ + ½
- **WIDTH:** 94'-2"
- **DEPTH:** 92'-2"
- **FOUNDATION:** CRAWLSPACE

SEARCH ONLINE @ EPLANS.COM

SECOND FLOOR

FIRST FLOOR

This gorgeous estate home's facade is amplified by soaring columns and classic symmetry. Inside, the foyer showcases a spectacular spiral staircase. Flanking the foyer are the formal living and dining rooms—both have fireplaces. Just beyond is the two-story family room, featuring a double-sided fireplace that also warms the master bedroom. To the left of the family room is the spacious C-shaped kitchen, opening to a sunny breakfast area that accesses the rear porch. A half-bath and very roomy laundry area are also convenient to this space. The master suite takes up the right wing of the plan, boasting a walk-in closet that is a room unto itself! The second floor is home to three more bedrooms—each has its own bath—and a sitting room that leads down a hallway to future recreation space.

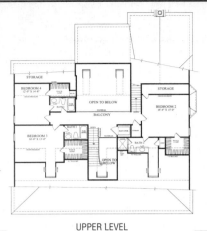

UPPER LEVEL

plan# HPT900232

- **STYLE: SOUTHERN COLONIAL**
- **MAIN LEVEL: 2,945 SQ. FT.**
- **UPPER LEVEL: 1,353 SQ. FT.**
- **LOWER LEVEL: 1,293 SQ. FT.**
- **TOTAL: 5,591 SQ. FT.**
- **BEDROOMS: 5**
- **BATHROOMS: 5½ + ½**
- **WIDTH: 61'-4"**
- **DEPTH: 72'-2"**
- **FOUNDATION: BASEMENT**

SEARCH ONLINE @ EPLANS.COM

LOWER LEVEL

MAIN LEVEL

SECOND FLOOR

FIRST FLOOR

plan# HPT900233

- **STYLE: SOUTHERN COLONIAL**
- **FIRST FLOOR: 2,998 SQ. FT.**
- **SECOND FLOOR: 1,556 SQ. FT.**
- **TOTAL: 4,554 SQ. FT.**
- **BONUS SPACE: 741 SQ. FT.**
- **BEDROOMS: 4**
- **BATHROOMS: 4½**
- **WIDTH: 75'-6"**
- **DEPTH: 91'-2"**
- **FOUNDATION: CRAWLSPACE**

SEARCH ONLINE @ EPLANS.COM

plan# HPT900234

- STYLE: PLANTATION
- FIRST FLOOR: 2,064 SQ. FT.
- SECOND FLOOR: 1,521 SQ. FT.
- TOTAL: 3,585 SQ. FT.
- BONUS SPACE: 427 SQ. FT.
- BEDROOMS: 4
- BATHROOMS: 3
- WIDTH: 84'-8"
- DEPTH: 65'-0"
- FOUNDATION: CRAWLSPACE

SEARCH ONLINE @ EPLANS.COM

This stunning plantation estate home showcases the best of Southern architecture. The round, columned porch, pedimented gable and decorative cupola are understated accents that enhance curb appeal. Enter from the portico to the two-story foyer, flanked by a library/bedroom on one side and a formal living room on the other. The hearth-warmed family room accesses the side piazza and is adjacent to the vaulted sun room. This space opens to the roomy kitchen, which features a breakfast-bar island and a pantry closet. The formal dining room views the front living room through columns. Sleeping quarters reside upstairs, featuring an elegant master suite that accesses the second level of the piazza. Two additional bedrooms share a full bath and a balcony overlook. A future recreation room awaits expansion above the carriage house garage.

SECOND FLOOR

FIRST FLOOR

SECOND FLOOR

plan# HPT900235

- STYLE: SOUTHERN COLONIAL
- FIRST FLOOR: 2,603 SQ. FT.
- SECOND FLOOR: 1,660 SQ. FT.
- TOTAL: 4,263 SQ. FT.
- BONUS SPACE: 434 SQ. FT.
- BEDROOMS: 5
- BATHROOMS: 5½ + ½
- WIDTH: 98'-0"
- DEPTH: 56'-8"
- FOUNDATION: BASEMENT

SEARCH ONLINE @ EPLANS.COM

FIRST FLOOR

SECOND FLOOR

FIRST FLOOR

plan# HPT900236

- STYLE: SOUTHERN COLONIAL
- FIRST FLOOR: 1,887 SQ. FT.
- SECOND FLOOR: 1,133 SQ. FT.
- TOTAL: 3,020 SQ. FT.
- BONUS SPACE: 444 SQ. FT.
- BEDROOMS: 4
- BATHROOMS: 4½
- WIDTH: 63'-4"
- DEPTH: 82'-2"
- FOUNDATION: BASEMENT, CRAWLSPACE

SEARCH ONLINE @ EPLANS.COM

plan# HPT900237

- **STYLE: GEORGIAN**
- **FIRST FLOOR: 3,027 SQ. FT.**
- **SECOND FLOOR: 1,509 SQ. FT.**
- **TOTAL: 4,536 SQ. FT.**
- **BEDROOMS: 5**
- **BATHROOMS: 4½**
- **WIDTH: 85'-0"**
- **DEPTH: 82'-6"**
- **FOUNDATION: BASEMENT, CRAWLSPACE**

SEARCH ONLINE @ EPLANS.COM

This grand home is sure to be the crowning glory of the neighborhood. Shutters and columns accent the stucco facade. Inside, formal rooms flank the foyer. Home life will have the perfect backdrop in the hearth-warmed family room, which opens into the breakfast area and kitchen. The roomy kitchen features ample pantry space and is adjacent to the laundry area. On the opposite side of the plan, a library boasts extra closet space and access to a powder room. The master suite is graced with a bay-windowed tub and an enormous walk-in closet. Upstairs, four bedrooms share three full baths and plenty of storage space.

SECOND FLOOR

FIRST FLOOR

plan# HPT900239

- **STYLE: SOUTHERN COLONIAL**
- **FIRST FLOOR: 2,320 SQ. FT.**
- **SECOND FLOOR: 1,009 SQ. FT.**
- **TOTAL: 3,329 SQ. FT.**
- **BONUS SPACE: 521 SQ. FT.**
- **BEDROOMS: 4**
- **BATHROOMS: 3½**
- **WIDTH: 80'-4"**
- **DEPTH: 58'-0"**
- **FOUNDATION: CRAWLSPACE**

SEARCH ONLINE @ EPLANS.COM

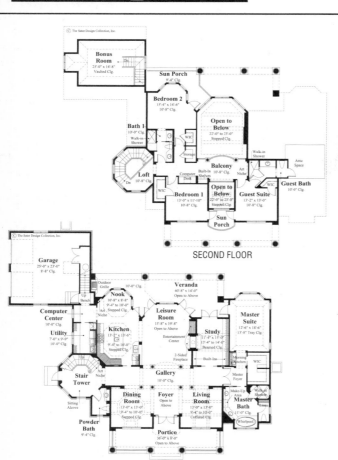

SECOND FLOOR

FIRST FLOOR

© The Sater Design Collection, Inc.

plan# HPT900238

- **STYLE: SOUTHERN COLONIAL**
- **FIRST FLOOR: 2,484 SQ. FT.**
- **SECOND FLOOR: 1,127 SQ. FT.**
- **TOTAL: 3,611 SQ. FT.**
- **BONUS SPACE: 332 SQ. FT.**
- **BEDROOMS: 4**
- **BATHROOMS: 3½**
- **WIDTH: 83'-0"**
- **DEPTH: 71'-8"**
- **FOUNDATION: SLAB**

SEARCH ONLINE @ EPLANS.COM

plan# HPT900240

- STYLE: GREEK REVIVAL
- FIRST FLOOR: 1,944 SQ. FT.
- SECOND FLOOR: 1,427 SQ. FT.
- TOTAL: 3,371 SQ. FT.
- BEDROOMS: 4
- BATHROOMS: 3½
- WIDTH: 52'-0"
- DEPTH: 84'-0"
- FOUNDATION: BASEMENT, CRAWLSPACE, SLAB

SEARCH ONLINE @ EPLANS.COM

The dazzling exterior of this Southern estate is true to form with six magnificent columns creating an awe-inspiring facade. The foyer leads to the living room with its fifteen-foot ceiling and paired window walls. Access to both the rear covered porch and the side courtyard is gained from the living room. The angled kitchen is flanked by the sunny eating bay and the convenient utility room. The side-loading, two-car garage at the rear contains an expansive storage area. The second floor holds the game room, an ancillary kitchen and three bedrooms while the master suite finds seclusion on the first floor. Note that Bedroom 4 includes a dressing area, a private bath and access to the balcony.

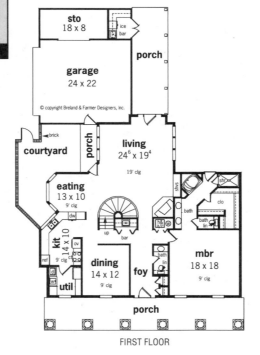

FIRST FLOOR

SECOND FLOOR

This tasteful chateau delights with an ornate dormer, delicate multi-pane windows and a false balcony that will inspire Shakespearean soliloquies. Inside, formal dining and living rooms reside at the front of the home, while casual living takes over the rear. The hearth-warmed family room accesses the back porch and opens to the sunny breakfast area. The kitchen features a snack-bar serving counter and a pantry closet. Secluded to the left, behind the mudroom and utility area, is the luxurious master suite. A huge walk-in closet and elegant bath with a windowed tub offer the utmost in comfort. Upstairs, yet another master suite resides, along with two additional bedrooms sharing a bath. Storage space and a future recreation room round out the second floor.

plan# HPT900241

- STYLE: FRENCH
- FIRST FLOOR: 2,216 SQ. FT.
- SECOND FLOOR: 1,192 SQ. FT.
- TOTAL: 3,408 SQ. FT.
- BONUS SPACE: 458 SQ. FT.
- BEDROOMS: 4
- BATHROOMS: 3½
- WIDTH: 67'-10"
- DEPTH: 56'-10"
- FOUNDATION: CRAWLSPACE

SEARCH ONLINE @ EPLANS.COM

FIRST FLOOR

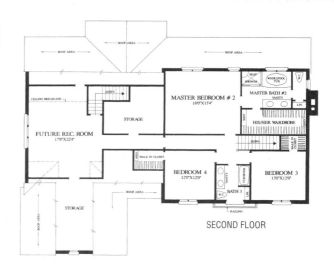

SECOND FLOOR

plan# HPT900242

- **STYLE: FRENCH COUNTRY**
- **FIRST FLOOR: 2,526 SQ. FT.**
- **SECOND FLOOR: 1,215 SQ. FT.**
- **TOTAL: 3,741 SQ. FT.**
- **BONUS SPACE: 547 SQ. FT.**
- **BEDROOMS: 4**
- **BATHROOMS: 4½ + ½**
- **WIDTH: 88'-6"**
- **DEPTH: 53'-6"**
- **FOUNDATION: CRAWLSPACE**

SEARCH ONLINE @ EPLANS.COM

This enchanting manor looks so natural, as if it grew right up from the ground. Stone, stucco and soft, hipped rooflines combine with shutters and multi-pane windows for a European facade. Inside, formal rooms flank the foyer, while casual space reigns at the rear. The fireplace-warmed family room juts out to the rear property, enjoying gorgeous window views. To the left, the large breakfast area flows right into the island kitchen, both beneath a hearty beamed ceiling. An adjacent mudroom accesses both the garage and the spacious utility area. The master suite takes up the right wing of the home with its elegant bath and double walk-in closets. The second floor is home to three bedrooms sharing two full baths and a future recreation room, as well as a balcony overlook.

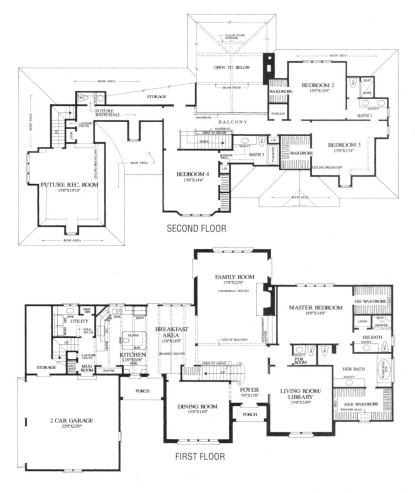

SECOND FLOOR

FIRST FLOOR

This elegant French Country estate features a plush world of luxury within. A beautiful curved staircase cascades into the welcoming foyer, which is flanked by a formal living room and the dining room with a fireplace. A butler's pantry leads to the island kitchen, which is efficiently enhanced by a walk-in storage pantry. The kitchen easily serves the breakfast room. The covered rear porch is accessed from the media/family room and the great room warmed by a fireplace. The master suite is a sumptuous retreat highlighted by its lavish bath and two huge walk-in closets. Next door, double doors open to a large study. All family bedrooms feature walk-in closets. Bedrooms 2 and 3 share a bath. Upstairs, Bedrooms 4 and 5 share another hall bath. A home office is located above the three-car garage.

plan# HPT900243

- ■ STYLE: FRENCH COUNTRY
- ■ FIRST FLOOR: 5,394 SQ. FT.
- ■ SECOND FLOOR: 1,305 SQ. FT.
- ■ TOTAL: 6,699 SQ. FT.
- ■ BEDROOMS: 5
- ■ BATHROOMS: 3½ + ½
- ■ WIDTH: 124'-10"
- ■ DEPTH: 83'-2"
- ■ FOUNDATION: CRAWLSPACE

SEARCH ONLINE @ EPLANS.COM

FIRST FLOOR

SECOND FLOOR

plan # HPT900244

- STYLE: CHATEAU
- FIRST FLOOR: 2,237 SQ. FT.
- SECOND FLOOR: 931 SQ. FT.
- TOTAL: 3,168 SQ. FT.
- BONUS SPACE: 304 SQ. FT.
- BEDROOMS: 4
- BATHROOMS: 3½
- WIDTH: 68'-0"
- DEPTH: 55'-6"
- FOUNDATION: SLAB

SEARCH ONLINE @ EPLANS.COM

This majestic estate has palatial inspiration, with a plan any modern family will love. A hardwood entry leads to brick flooring in the kitchen and breakfast nook, for vintage appeal. The family room and vaulted living room warm heart and soul with extended-hearth fireplaces. For a quiet retreat, the study opens with French doors from the hall, and leads out to the walled lanai courtyard through another set of French doors. The vaulted master suite is impressive, with a bay window, a sumptuous bath and His and Hers walk-in closets. Upstairs, three ample bedrooms will access the future playroom.

SECOND FLOOR

FIRST FLOOR

plan# HPT900245

- **STYLE:** EUROPEAN COTTAGE
- **SQUARE FOOTAGE:** 3,942
- **BEDROOMS:** 4
- **BATHROOMS:** 3½
- **WIDTH:** 97'-0"
- **DEPTH:** 82'-0"
- **FOUNDATION:** BASEMENT, SLAB

SEARCH ONLINE @ EPLANS.COM

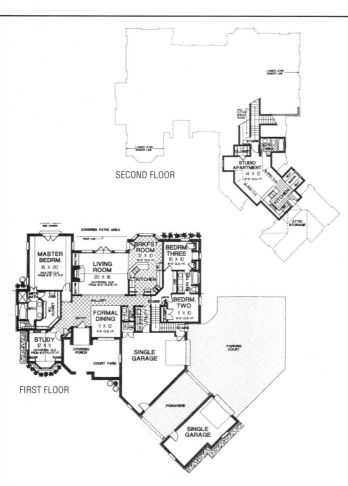

plan# HPT900246

- **STYLE:** EUROPEAN COTTAGE
- **FIRST FLOOR:** 2,387 SQ. FT.
- **SECOND FLOOR:** 509 SQ. FT.
- **TOTAL:** 2,896 SQ. FT.
- **BEDROOMS:** 3
- **BATHROOMS:** 2½
- **WIDTH:** 82'-3"
- **DEPTH:** 86'-6"
- **FOUNDATION:** SLAB

SEARCH ONLINE @ EPLANS.COM

plan# HPT900247

- STYLE: FRENCH COUNTRY
- FIRST FLOOR: 3,168 SQ. FT.
- SECOND FLOOR: 998 SQ. FT.
- TOTAL: 4,166 SQ. FT.
- BONUS SPACE: 210 SQ. FT.
- BEDROOMS: 4
- BATHROOMS: 3½
- WIDTH: 90'-0"
- DEPTH: 63'-5"
- FOUNDATION: BASEMENT, CRAWLSPACE, SLAB

SEARCH ONLINE @ EPLANS.COM

Stucco corner quoins, multiple gables and graceful columns all combine to give this European manor plenty of appeal. Inside, a gallery entry presents a formal dining room on the right, defined by elegant columns, while the formal living room awaits just ahead. The highly efficient kitchen features a worktop island, pantry and a serving bar to the nearby octagonal breakfast area. The family room offers a built-in entertainment center, a fireplace and its own covered patio. The left side of the first floor is dedicated to the master suite. Here, the homeowner is pampered with an octagonal study, huge walk-in closet, lavish bath and a very convenient nursery. The second floor contains two family bedrooms, each with a walk-in closet, and a media area with built-in bookshelves.

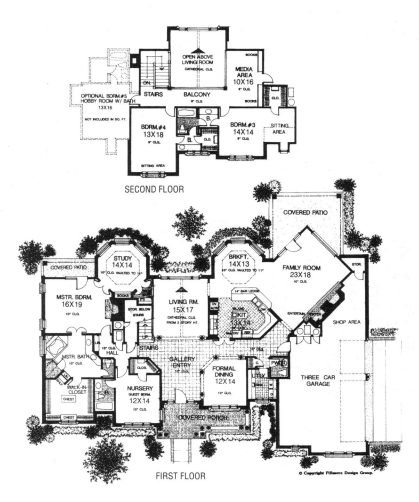

SECOND FLOOR

FIRST FLOOR

© Copyright Fillmore Design Group.

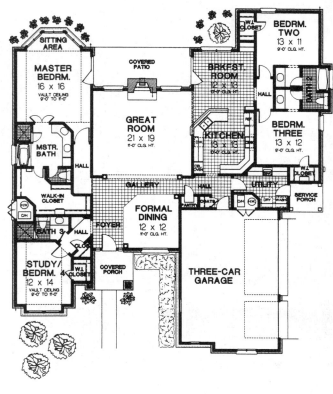

plan# HPT900248

- STYLE: FRENCH COUNTRY
- SQUARE FOOTAGE: 2,744
- BEDROOMS: 4
- BATHROOMS: 3
- WIDTH: 66'-6"
- DEPTH: 74'-6"
- FOUNDATION: SLAB

SEARCH ONLINE @ EPLANS.COM

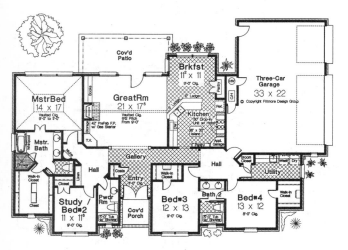

plan# HPT900249

- STYLE: EUROPEAN COTTAGE
- SQUARE FOOTAGE: 2,352
- BEDROOMS: 4
- BATHROOMS: 3
- WIDTH: 77'-6"
- DEPTH: 53'-2"
- FOUNDATION: CRAWLSPACE, SLAB

SEARCH ONLINE @ EPLANS.COM

© 2002 Donald A. Gardner, Inc.

plan# HPT900250

- STYLE: CHATEAU
- FIRST FLOOR: 2,062 SQ. FT.
- SECOND FLOOR: 1,279 SQ. FT.
- TOTAL: 3,341 SQ. FT.
- BONUS SPACE: 386 SQ. FT.
- BEDROOMS: 5
- BATHROOMS: 4½
- WIDTH: 73'-8"
- DEPTH: 50'-0"

SEARCH ONLINE @ EPLANS.COM

Surround yourself with European charm in this Chateau-style beauty. Arched windows and hipped rooflines complement a stone-and-stucco exterior for an elegant facade. Enter from the front columned porch to the two-story foyer, which showcases a gorgeous spiral staircase. The hub of the home is the central two-story great room, with its fireplace and access to the rear porch. The island kitchen and sunny bayed breakfast nook will make cooking and informal dining a delight. A formal dining room is at the front. The right wing is taken up entirely by the deluxe master suite, enjoying two walk-in closets and a spacious private bath. Upstairs, four bedrooms share three full baths and loft space that overlooks the great room and foyer below. A bonus room to the left awaits expansion.

FIRST FLOOR

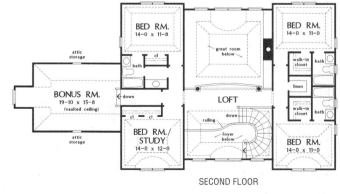

SECOND FLOOR

With sturdy brick detailing, sweeping rooflines and a turret that settles seamlessly into the facade, this fine five-bedroom home will be a winner in any neighborhood. Inside, the two-story foyer leads directly to the spacious great room. A study hides to the right of the foyer, offering privacy. The formal dining room is graced with a ten-foot ceiling, a pass-through to the kitchen and direct access to the backyard. The C-shaped kitchen features a six-burner stove, work island, large walk-in pantry and a nearby octagonal nook. An option for two lavish master suites is available, one on the first floor and one replacing Bedrooms 4 and 5 on the second floor. Each suite includes a decadent bath; the second-floor master bedroom has a romantic fireplace.

plan# HPT900251

- STYLE: EUROPEAN COTTAGE
- FIRST FLOOR: 2,356 SQ. FT.
- SECOND FLOOR: 1,450 SQ. FT.
- TOTAL: 3,806 SQ. FT.
- BONUS SPACE: 261 SQ. FT.
- BEDROOMS: 5
- BATHROOMS: 4
- WIDTH: 67'-0"
- DEPTH: 82'-0"
- FOUNDATION: CRAWLSPACE

SEARCH ONLINE @ EPLANS.COM

FIRST FLOOR

SECOND FLOOR

OPTIONAL LAYOUT

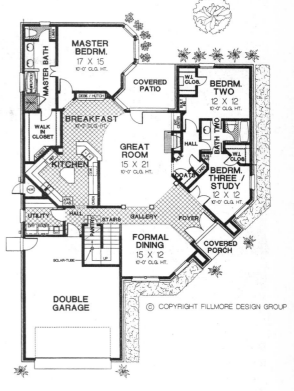

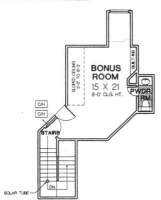

BONUS
ROOM
15 X 21
8'-0" CLG. HT.

© COPYRIGHT FILLMORE DESIGN GROUP

plan# HPT900253

- ■ STYLE: FRENCH COUNTRY
- ■ SQUARE FOOTAGE: 2,192
- ■ BONUS SPACE: 403 SQ. FT.
- ■ BEDROOMS: 3
- ■ BATHROOMS: 2
- ■ WIDTH: 49'-10"
- ■ DEPTH: 75'-11"
- ■ FOUNDATION: SLAB

SEARCH ONLINE @ EPLANS.COM

SECOND FLOOR

FIRST FLOOR

plan# HPT900252

- ■ STYLE: FRENCH
- ■ FIRST FLOOR: 1,818 SQ. FT.
- ■ SECOND FLOOR: 818 SQ. FT.
- ■ TOTAL: 2,636 SQ. FT.
- ■ BONUS SPACE: 270 SQ. FT.
- ■ BEDROOMS: 4
- ■ BATHROOMS: 3½
- ■ WIDTH: 57'-0"
- ■ DEPTH: 56'-7"
- ■ FOUNDATION: SLAB

SEARCH ONLINE @ EPLANS.COM

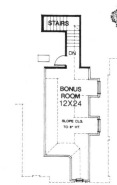

plan# HPT900254

- **STYLE:** EUROPEAN COTTAGE
- **SQUARE FOOTAGE:** 2,624
- **BONUS SPACE:** 352 SQ. FT.
- **BEDROOMS:** 4
- **BATHROOMS:** 3½
- **WIDTH:** 65'-0"
- **DEPTH:** 72'-7"
- **FOUNDATION:** SLAB

SEARCH ONLINE @ EPLANS.COM

plan# HPT900255

- **STYLE:** EUROPEAN COTTAGE
- **SQUARE FOOTAGE:** 2,689
- **BEDROOMS:** 4
- **BATHROOMS:** 3
- **WIDTH:** 65'-0"
- **DEPTH:** 69'-4"
- **FOUNDATION:** SLAB

SEARCH ONLINE @ EPLANS.COM

plan # HPT900256

- STYLE: EUROPEAN COTTAGE
- SQUARE FOOTAGE: 2,293
- BONUS SPACE: 509 SQ. FT.
- BEDROOMS: 3
- BATHROOMS: 2
- WIDTH: 51'-0"
- DEPTH: 79'-4"
- FOUNDATION: SLAB

SEARCH ONLINE @ EPLANS.COM

Multiple rooflines, shutters and a charming vaulted entry lend interest and depth to the exterior of this well-designed three-bedroom home. Inside, double doors to the left open to a cozy den. The dining room, open to the family room and foyer, features a stunning ceiling design. A fireplace and patio access and view adorn the family room. Two family bedrooms share a double-sink bathroom to the right, while the master bedroom resides to the left. Note the private patio access, two walk-in closets and luxurious bath that ensure a restful retreat for the homeowner.

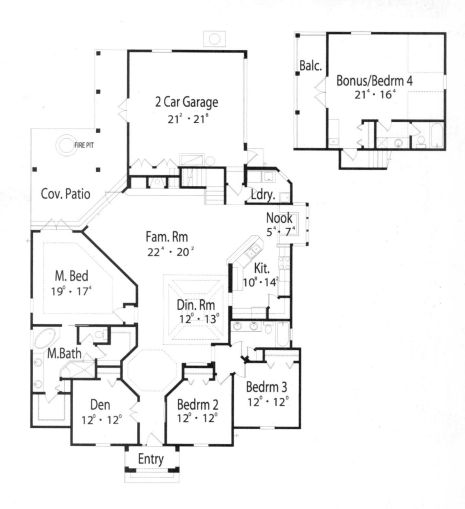

plan# HPT900258

- **STYLE:** FRENCH COUNTRY
- **SQUARE FOOTAGE:** 1,745
- **BEDROOMS:** 4
- **BATHROOMS:** 3
- **WIDTH:** 54'-0"
- **DEPTH:** 50'-0"
- **FOUNDATION:** BASEMENT, CRAWLSPACE

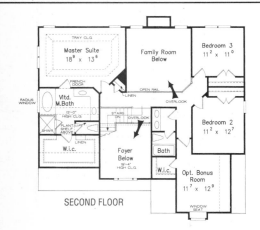

SECOND FLOOR

FIRST FLOOR

plan# HPT900257

- **STYLE:** FRENCH COUNTRY
- **FIRST FLOOR:** 1,278 SQ. FT.
- **SECOND FLOOR:** 1,018 SQ. FT.
- **TOTAL:** 2,296 SQ. FT.
- **BONUS SPACE:** 214 SQ. FT.
- **BEDROOMS:** 4
- **BATHROOMS:** 3
- **WIDTH:** 45'-0"
- **DEPTH:** 44'-4"
- **FOUNDATION:** BASEMENT, CRAWLSPACE, SLAB

plan# HPT900259

- **STYLE: FRENCH COUNTRY**
- **FIRST FLOOR: 1,191 SQ. FT.**
- **SECOND FLOOR: 824 SQ. FT.**
- **TOTAL: 2,015 SQ. FT.**
- **BONUS SPACE: 199 SQ. FT.**
- **BEDROOMS: 3**
- **BATHROOMS: 3**
- **WIDTH: 41'-6"**
- **DEPTH: 55'-0"**
- **FOUNDATION: BASEMENT, CRAWLSPACE**

SEARCH ONLINE @ EPLANS.COM

With a stucco facade and stone accents, this gorgeous French-influenced cottage will look great in any neighborhood. A side-loading garage makes this home perfect for a corner lot—the dormer window above holds a window seat in the bonus room. Inside, the grand foyer opens to the right to an elegant dining room with a box-bay window. Ahead, an open kitchen flows into the bayed breakfast nook with ease. Radius windows brighten the two-story family room, welcoming with a warming fireplace. An adjacent bedroom/study makes a perfect guest room or home office. Upstairs, a bedroom shares a bath with the bonus room (or make it another bedroom). The master suite is a lovely retreat, with a bayed sitting area, French doors, a vaulted bath, and His and Hers walk-in closets.

FIRST FLOOR

SECOND FLOOR

Stone and stucco blend gracefully with sloping roof lines and gables to create the sense of a French chateau. This epitome of an open floor plan is defined only by a center island that houses an angled fireplace, a coat closet and the kitchen pantry. On the upper level, four bedrooms—including a master suite with an intimate sitting area—complete the plan.

plan # HPT900260

- STYLE: EUROPEAN COTTAGE
- FIRST FLOOR: 881 SQ. FT.
- SECOND FLOOR: 1,146 SQ. FT.
- TOTAL: 2,027 SQ. FT.
- BEDROOMS: 4
- BATHROOMS: 2½
- WIDTH: 51'-0"
- DEPTH: 35'-6"
- FOUNDATION: BASEMENT, CRAWLSPACE

SEARCH ONLINE @ EPLANS.COM

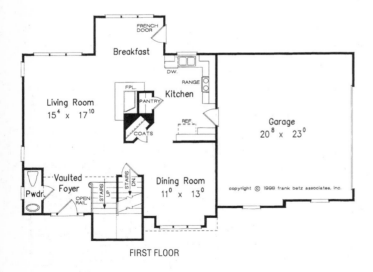

FIRST FLOOR

SECOND FLOOR

plan# HPT900261

- **STYLE: EUROPEAN COTTAGE**
- **FIRST FLOOR: 2,654 SQ. FT.**
- **SECOND FLOOR: 1,013 SQ. FT.**
- **TOTAL: 3,667 SQ. FT.**
- **BONUS SPACE: 192 SQ. FT.**
- **BEDROOMS: 4**
- **BATHROOMS: 3½**
- **WIDTH: 75'-4"**
- **DEPTH: 74'-2"**
- **FOUNDATION: BASEMENT, CRAWLSPACE, SLAB**

SEARCH ONLINE @ EPLANS.COM

European accents shape the exterior of this striking family home. Inside, the foyer is open to the dining room on the right and the living room straight ahead. Here, two sets of double doors open to the rear covered porch. Casual areas of the home include a family room warmed by a fireplace and an island kitchen opening to a bayed breakfast room. The first-floor master retreat is a luxurious perk, which offers a bayed sitting area, a whirlpool bath and large His and Hers walk-in closets. Bedroom 2—with its close proximity to the master suite—is perfect for a nursery or home office. Upstairs, Bedrooms 3 and 4 boast walk-in closets and share a bath. Future space is available just off the game room.

SECOND FLOOR

FIRST FLOOR

SECOND FLOOR

plan# HPT900263

- **STYLE: EUROPEAN COTTAGE**
- **FIRST FLOOR: 1,998 SQ. FT.**
- **SECOND FLOOR: 1,898 SQ. FT.**
- **TOTAL: 3,896 SQ. FT.**
- **BEDROOMS: 4**
- **BATHROOMS: 2½**
- **WIDTH: 60'-0"**
- **DEPTH: 56'-4"**
- **FOUNDATION: CRAWLSPACE**

SEARCH ONLINE @ EPLANS.COM

FIRST FLOOR

SECOND FLOOR

FIRST FLOOR

plan# HPT900262

- **STYLE: CRAFTSMAN**
- **FIRST FLOOR: 1,608 SQ. FT.**
- **SECOND FLOOR: 581 SQ. FT.**
- **TOTAL: 2,189 SQ. FT.**
- **BEDROOMS: 3**
- **BATHROOMS: 2½**
- **WIDTH: 46'-0"**
- **DEPTH: 63'-0"**

SEARCH ONLINE @ EPLANS.COM

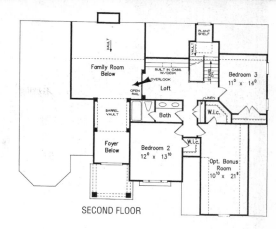

SECOND FLOOR

FIRST FLOOR

plan# HPT900264

- STYLE: FRENCH
- FIRST FLOOR: 1,866 SQ. FT.
- SECOND FLOOR: 640 SQ. FT.
- TOTAL: 2,506 SQ. FT.
- BONUS SPACE: 280 SQ. FT.
- BEDROOMS: 4
- BATHROOMS: 3½
- WIDTH: 58'-0"
- DEPTH: 48'-4"
- FOUNDATION: BASEMENT, CRAWLSPACE

SEARCH ONLINE @ EPLANS.COM

plan# HPT900265

- STYLE: FRENCH COUNTRY
- SQUARE FOOTAGE: 1,464
- BEDROOMS: 3
- BATHROOMS: 2
- WIDTH: 56'-2"
- DEPTH: 45'-2"
- FOUNDATION: CRAWLSPACE, SLAB

SEARCH ONLINE @ EPLANS.COM

This elegant design brings back the sophistication and elegance of days gone by, yet its modern layout creates a natural traffic flow to enhance easy living. Columns partition space without enclosing it, while built-ins in the great room and counter space in the utility/mudroom add convenience. The family efficient floor plan can be witnessed in the kitchen's handy pass-through, and the kitchen has porch access to the rear porch for outdoor entertaining. Cathedral ceilings highlight the master bedroom and bedroom/study, while vaulted ceilings top the breakfast area and loft/study. The bonus room can be used as a home theatre, playroom, or gym, and its position allows it to keep recreational noise away from the house proper.

plan# HPT900266

- STYLE: CHATEAU
- FIRST FLOOR: 2,477 SQ. FT.
- SECOND FLOOR: 742 SQ. FT.
- TOTAL: 3,219 SQ. FT.
- BONUS SPACE: 419 SQ. FT.
- BEDROOMS: 4
- BATHROOMS: 4
- WIDTH: 99'-10"
- DEPTH: 66'-2"

SEARCH ONLINE @ EPLANS.COM

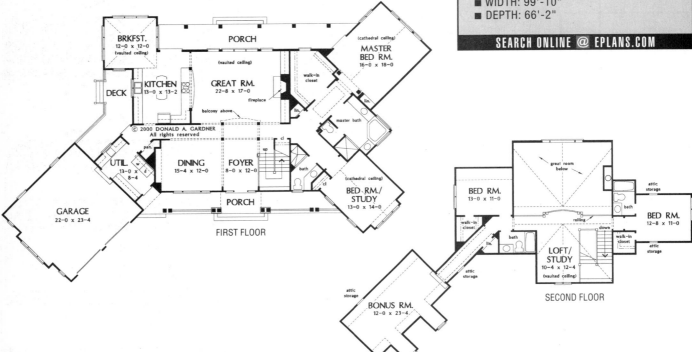

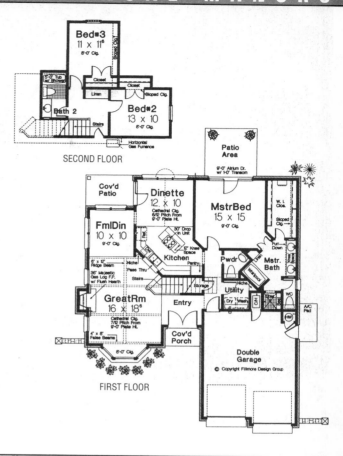

SECOND FLOOR

FIRST FLOOR

plan # HPT900268

- **STYLE: COUNTRY COTTAGE**
- **FIRST FLOOR: 1,375 SQ. FT.**
- **SECOND FLOOR: 446 SQ. FT.**
- **TOTAL: 1,821 SQ. FT.**
- **BEDROOMS: 3**
- **BATHROOMS: 2½**
- **WIDTH: 44'-10"**
- **DEPTH: 52'-11"**
- **FOUNDATION: SLAB**

SEARCH ONLINE @ EPLANS.COM

plan # HPT900267

- **STYLE: FRENCH**
- **SQUARE FOOTAGE: 2,585**
- **BEDROOMS: 4**
- **BATHROOMS: 3½**
- **WIDTH: 73'-6"**
- **DEPTH: 64'-7"**
- **FOUNDATION: SLAB**

SEARCH ONLINE @ EPLANS.COM

plan# HPT900269

- STYLE: FRENCH COUNTRY
- SQUARE FOOTAGE: 2,483
- BEDROOMS: 4
- BATHROOMS: 3½
- WIDTH: 71'-0"
- DEPTH: 66'-1"
- FOUNDATION: SLAB

SEARCH ONLINE @ EPLANS.COM

With a turret-style bay window, flower boxes and beautiful stone accents, this French country home is sure to delight. Upon entering, the great room is presented with a cathedral ceiling and extended-hearth fireplace. To the left, the formal dining room, defined by decorative columns, rests in the turret. The expertly planned kitchen flows into the bayed breakfast nook effortlessly. The vaulted master suite enjoys a lovely bath. On the far right, three family bedrooms, each with ample closets, complete the plan.

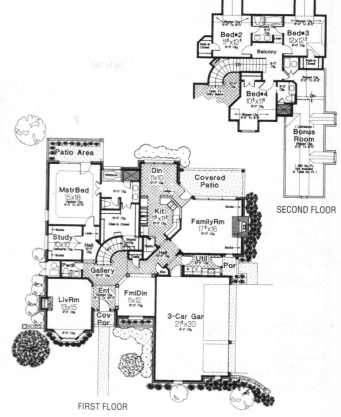

SECOND FLOOR

FIRST FLOOR

plan# HPT900270

- STYLE: FRENCH COUNTRY
- FIRST FLOOR: 2,039 SQ. FT.
- SECOND FLOOR: 772 SQ. FT.
- TOTAL: 2,811 SQ. FT.
- BONUS SPACE: 480 SQ. FT.
- BEDROOMS: 4
- BATHROOMS: 3½
- WIDTH: 56'-0"
- DEPTH: 63'-6"
- FOUNDATION: SLAB

SEARCH ONLINE @ EPLANS.COM

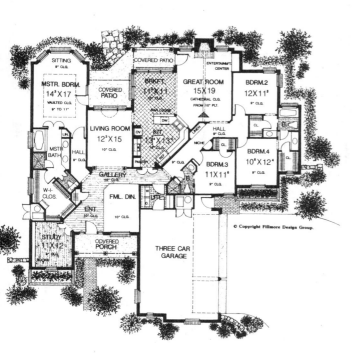

© Copyright Fillmore Design Group.

plan# HPT900271

- STYLE: EUROPEAN COTTAGE
- SQUARE FOOTAGE: 2,631
- BEDROOMS: 4
- BATHROOMS: 3
- WIDTH: 70'-0"
- DEPTH: 70'-4"
- FOUNDATION: SLAB

SEARCH ONLINE @ EPLANS.COM

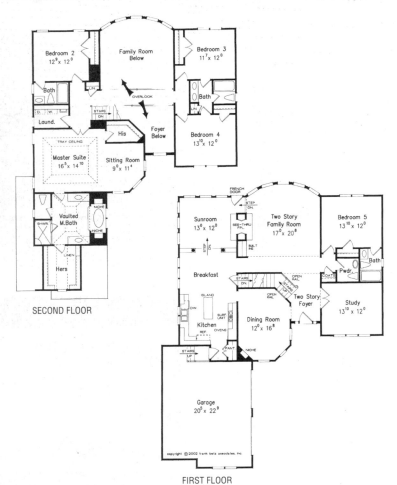

SECOND FLOOR

FIRST FLOOR

copyright © 2002 frank betz associates, inc.

plan# HPT900272

- **STYLE: FRENCH**
- **FIRST FLOOR: 1,685 SQ. FT.**
- **SECOND FLOOR: 1,596 SQ. FT.**
- **TOTAL: 3,281 SQ. FT.**
- **BEDROOMS: 5**
- **BATHROOMS: 4½**
- **WIDTH: 51'-0"**
- **DEPTH: 66'-10"**
- **FOUNDATION: BASEMENT, CRAWLSPACE**

SEARCH ONLINE @ EPLANS.COM

Strong lines lead the eye upwards toward this home's varied roof line. The formal dining room enjoys views from the two-story turret. The breakfast room opens to a glorious sun room that accesses the rear property. The two-story family room enjoys a curved wall of windows and a double-sided fireplace. At the right of the plan, a study and powder room share space with a comfortable guest suite. Upstairs, three family bedrooms with ample closet space share two baths. The sumptuous master suite boasts a sitting room, vaulted bath and His-and-Hers walk-in closets.

SECOND FLOOR

FIRST FLOOR

plan # HPT900273

- **STYLE: EUROPEAN COTTAGE**
- **FIRST FLOOR: 2,055 SQ. FT.**
- **SECOND FLOOR: 935 SQ. FT.**
- **TOTAL: 2,990 SQ. FT.**
- **BEDROOMS: 3**
- **BATHROOMS: 4**
- **WIDTH: 65'-5"**
- **DEPTH: 55'-10"**
- **FOUNDATION: CRAWLSPACE**

SEARCH ONLINE @ EPLANS.COM

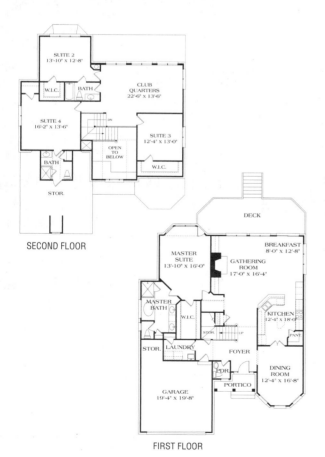

SECOND FLOOR

FIRST FLOOR

plan # HPT900274

- **STYLE: EUROPEAN COTTAGE**
- **FIRST FLOOR: 1,725 SQ. FT.**
- **SECOND FLOOR: 1,239 SQ. FT.**
- **TOTAL: 2,964 SQ. FT.**
- **BEDROOMS: 4**
- **BATHROOMS: 3½**
- **WIDTH: 45'-10"**
- **DEPTH: 59'-2"**
- **FOUNDATION: CRAWLSPACE**

SEARCH ONLINE @ EPLANS.COM

SECOND FLOOR

plan # HPT900275

- **STYLE: FRENCH COUNTRY**
- **FIRST FLOOR: 2,317 SQ. FT.**
- **SECOND FLOOR: 1,302 SQ. FT.**
- **TOTAL: 3,619 SQ. FT.**
- **BEDROOMS: 4**
- **BATHROOMS: 3½**
- **WIDTH: 74'-0"**
- **DEPTH: 56'-4"**
- **FOUNDATION: SLAB**

SEARCH ONLINE @ EPLANS.COM

FIRST FLOOR

SECOND FLOOR

FIRST FLOOR

plan # HPT900276

- **STYLE: FRENCH**
- **FIRST FLOOR: 2,223 SQ. FT.**
- **SECOND FLOOR: 1,163 SQ. FT.**
- **TOTAL: 3,386 SQ. FT.**
- **BEDROOMS: 4**
- **BATHROOMS: 3½**
- **WIDTH: 68'-10"**
- **DEPTH: 58'-1"**
- **FOUNDATION: CRAWLSPACE, SLAB**

SEARCH ONLINE @ EPLANS.COM

plan# HPT900277

- **STYLE:** FRENCH COUNTRY
- **FIRST FLOOR:** 2,451 SQ. FT.
- **SECOND FLOOR:** 1,762 SQ. FT.
- **TOTAL:** 4,213 SQ. FT.
- **BONUS SPACE:** 353 SQ. FT.
- **BEDROOMS:** 4
- **BATHROOMS:** 3½
- **WIDTH:** 92'-6"
- **DEPTH:** 46'-0"
- **FOUNDATION:** CRAWLSPACE

SEARCH ONLINE @ EPLANS.COM

Shingles, stone and shutters all combine to give this attractive manor a warm and welcoming feel. The two-story foyer presents the formal living room on the right—complete with a fireplace. The spacious family room also features a fireplace, along with a built-in media center, a wall of windows and a ten-foot ceiling. Open to the family room, the efficient kitchen provides plenty of cabinet and counter space, as well as a nearby bayed nook. A study is available, with built-in bookshelves. Upstairs, the master suite is sure to please. It includes a large walk-in closet, a pampering bath with dual vanities and a tub set in a bay, a ten-foot ceiling and a corner fireplace. Bedrooms 3 and 4 share a bath, while Bedroom 2 offers privacy. A bonus room is available for future expansion.

SECOND FLOOR

FIRST FLOOR

SECOND FLOOR

FIRST FLOOR

plan# HPT900279

- STYLE: CHATEAU
- FIRST FLOOR: 2,246 SQ. FT.
- SECOND FLOOR: 966 SQ. FT.
- TOTAL: 3,212 SQ. FT.
- BONUS SPACE: 250 SQ. FT.
- BEDROOMS: 4
- BATHROOMS: 3½
- WIDTH: 68'-10"
- DEPTH: 60'-1"
- FOUNDATION: BASEMENT, SLAB

SEARCH ONLINE @ EPLANS.COM

SECOND FLOOR

plan# HPT900278

- STYLE: FRENCH COUNTRY
- FIRST FLOOR: 3,538 SQ. FT.
- SECOND FLOOR: 1,432 SQ. FT.
- TOTAL: 4,970 SQ. FT.
- BEDROOMS: 5
- BATHROOMS: 4½
- WIDTH: 102'-10"
- DEPTH: 77'-10"
- FOUNDATION: SLAB

SEARCH ONLINE @ EPLANS.COM

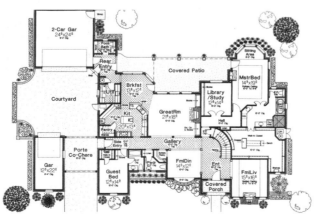

FIRST FLOOR

© The Sater Design Collection, Inc.

plan# HPT900280

- **STYLE:** EUROPEAN COTTAGE
- **SQUARE FOOTAGE:** 3,351
- **BEDROOMS:** 3
- **BATHROOMS:** 2½ + ½
- **WIDTH:** 84'-0"
- **DEPTH:** 92'-0"
- **FOUNDATION:** SLAB

SEARCH ONLINE @ EPLANS.COM

This stately European stucco manor is accented with brick, quoins and fanlight windows for a majestic facade. The striking entry and foyer present a living room/dining room, revered for its infinite interior design possibilities. Here, a vintage exposed-beam ceiling, warming fireplace and French doors to the veranda welcome family and guests. To the right, a wonderful country kitchen prepares gourmet meals with ease, courtesy of expansive workspace and cabinetry. The bayed nook could serve as a breakfast nook or sitting area. In the leisure room, a built-in entertainment center and veranda access (don't miss the outdoor grill!) are sure to make this room a family favorite. Two bedrooms share a full bath and hall storage on the far right. The left wing houses the master suite, separated for privacy and brimming with luxurious amenities.

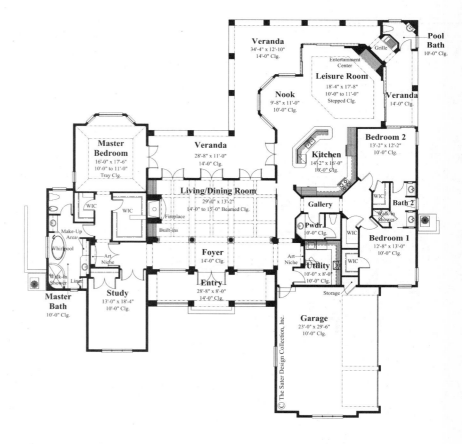

© The Sater Design Collection, Inc.

This chateau estate will be the envy of neighbors, friends and passers-by. Inside, stylish tile flooring runs throughout the home, from the entry to the kitchen and bayed breakfast nook. The living room entertains with a fireplace and natural light; the family room is a showpiece, with an exposed-beam cathedral ceiling, access to the rear patio and an extended-hearth fireplace. The master suite revels in a tiled bath with a whirlpool tub and an enormous walk-in closet. Three upstairs bedrooms all have private baths and share a sitting area and future space.

plan# HPT900281

- **STYLE: CHATEAU**
- **FIRST FLOOR: 2,907 SQ. FT.**
- **SECOND FLOOR: 1,148 SQ. FT.**
- **TOTAL: 4,055 SQ. FT.**
- **BONUS SPACE: 543 SQ. FT.**
- **BEDROOMS: 4**
- **BATHROOMS: 4½**
- **WIDTH: 79'-11"**
- **DEPTH: 79'-1"**
- **FOUNDATION: SLAB**

SEARCH ONLINE @ EPLANS.COM

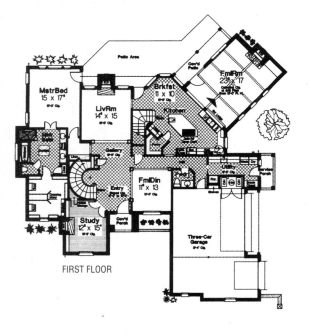

FIRST FLOOR

SECOND FLOOR

plan # HPT900282

- **STYLE: CHATEAU**
- **FIRST FLOOR: 3,617 SQ. FT.**
- **SECOND FLOOR: 1,542 SQ. FT.**
- **TOTAL: 5,159 SQ. FT.**
- **BONUS SPACE: 450 SQ. FT.**
- **BEDROOMS: 4**
- **BATHROOMS: 3½ + ½**
- **WIDTH: 108'-11"**
- **DEPTH: 88'-7"**
- **FOUNDATION: SLAB**

SEARCH ONLINE @ EPLANS.COM

This sprawling chateau estate encompasses over 5,000 square feet, yet the delicate touches and handsome details lend a lived-in, personal quality. Stretching throughout the entry, gallery, island kitchen, bayed breakfast nook and utility areas, tile flooring is both elegant and easy to maintain. The formal dining room and the living room, with its extended stone fireplace, are graced with hardwood floors. From the living room, the trellis patio transforms to wrap around the entire right side of the home. The left wing is devoted to the master suite, grand with a Pullman ceiling, entertainment center, dual walk-in closets, fabulous bath and private exercise room. Upstairs, three large bedrooms, a recreation room and a future bonus room allow plenty of room for family and friends.

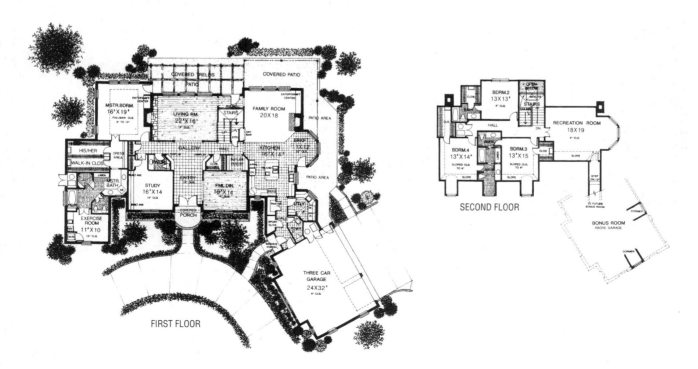

FIRST FLOOR

SECOND FLOOR

BONUS ROOM
ABOVE GARAGE

© The Sater Design Collection, Inc.

SECOND FLOOR

Opt. Bedroom
15'-11" x 14'-2"
10'-0" Clg.

FIRST FLOOR

plan# HPT900284

- STYLE: EUROPEAN COTTAGE
- FIRST FLOOR: 3,023 SQ. FT.
- SECOND FLOOR: 1,623 SQ. FT.
- TOTAL: 4,646 SQ. FT.
- BONUS SPACE: 294 SQ. FT.
- BEDROOMS: 4
- BATHROOMS: 4½
- WIDTH: 70'-0"
- DEPTH: 100'-0"
- FOUNDATION: SLAB

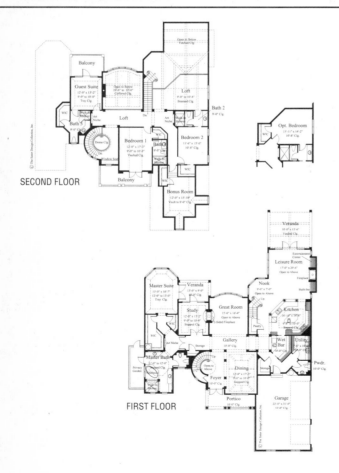

SECOND FLOOR

Opt. Bedroom
15'-11" x 14'-2"
10'-0" Clg.

FIRST FLOOR

© Sater Design Collection, Inc.

plan# HPT900283

- STYLE: FRENCH COUNTRY
- FIRST FLOOR: 3,018 SQ. FT.
- SECOND FLOOR: 1,646 SQ. FT.
- TOTAL: 4,664 SQ. FT.
- BONUS SPACE: 294 SQ. FT.
- BEDROOMS: 4
- BATHROOMS: 4½
- WIDTH: 70'-0"
- DEPTH: 100'-0"
- FOUNDATION: SLAB

© The Sater Design Collection, Inc.

plan # HPT900285

- **STYLE:** FRENCH COUNTRY
- **FIRST FLOOR:** 1,996 SQ. FT.
- **SECOND FLOOR:** 2,171 SQ. FT.
- **TOTAL:** 4,167 SQ. FT.
- **BEDROOMS:** 5
- **BATHROOMS:** 5½
- **WIDTH:** 58'-0"
- **DEPTH:** 65'-0"
- **FOUNDATION:** SLAB

SEARCH ONLINE @ EPLANS.COM

Striking on the outside, extraordinary on the inside, this French country manor is no cookie-cutter home! Sloping rooflines, a flower-box window and a two-story turret encased in multi-pane glass give great curb appeal; step inside to voluminous ten-foot ceilings and a stylish floorplan designed for family living. A living room/dining room combination allows endless possibilities in interior design. Here, the two-sided fireplace shares its warmth with the library/study. The kitchen invites gourmet cooking with space for a six-burner range and tons of preparation area (including an over-size island). The second-floor master retreat is anything but ordinary; a unique quadrilateral shape highlights the expansive rear windows. Private porch access and a soothing spa bath are engaging. Three additional bedrooms enjoy two sun porches and great views.

FIRST FLOOR

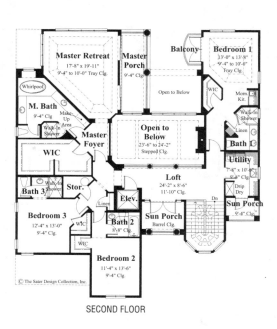

SECOND FLOOR

© The Sater Design Collection, Inc.

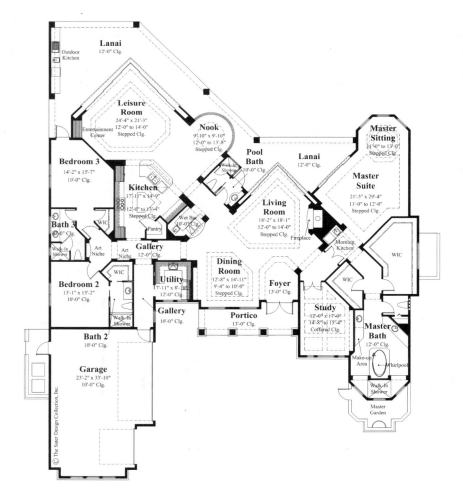

plan# **HPT900286**

- **STYLE: EUROPEAN COTTAGE**
- **SQUARE FOOTAGE: 3,942**
- **BEDROOMS: 3**
- **BATHROOMS: 4**
- **WIDTH: 83'-10"**
- **DEPTH: 106'-0"**
- **FOUNDATION: SLAB**

SEARCH ONLINE @ EPLANS.COM

Welcome home to a country manor with Renaissance flair. Full-length, squint-style windows and brick accents bring Old World charm to a modern plan. Designed for flexibility, the open foyer, living room and dining room have infinite decor options. Down a gallery (with art niches) two bedroom suites enjoy private baths. The bon-vivant island kitchen is introduced with a wet bar and pool bath. In the leisure room, family and friends will revel in expansive views of the rear property. An outdoor kitchen on the lanai invites alfresco dining. Separated for ultimate privacy, the master suite is an exercise in luxurious living. Past the morning kitchen and into the grand bedroom, an octagonal sitting area is bathed in light. The bath is gracefully set in the turret, with a whirlpool tub and views of the master garden.

© The Sater Design Collection, Inc.

plan# HPT900287

- STYLE: FRENCH
- FIRST FLOOR: 2,163 SQ. FT.
- SECOND FLOOR: 2,302 SQ. FT.
- TOTAL: 4,465 SQ. FT.
- BEDROOMS: 5
- BATHROOMS: 5½
- WIDTH: 58'-0"
- DEPTH: 65'-0"
- FOUNDATION: SLAB

SEARCH ONLINE @ EPLANS.COM

In true Williamsburg style, this stunning brick and stucco manor combines elegance and functionality for a perfect family home. Double doors open to reveal a foyer encircled by formal living areas. To the left, a library/study and formal dining room enjoy vintage beamed ceilings. Ahead, the living room, defined by decorative columns, displays expansive views of the rear property. A full guest suite is great for frequent visitors. The country kitchen lies to the far right; here, an island and a bayed nook create a charming and efficient workspace. The leisure room is sure to be a family favorite. Not to be missed: the wine cellar, located behind the staircase. Upstairs, the master suite enjoys privacy and luxury. Three additional suites have private baths. All four generous bedrooms access porches and balconies.

FIRST FLOOR

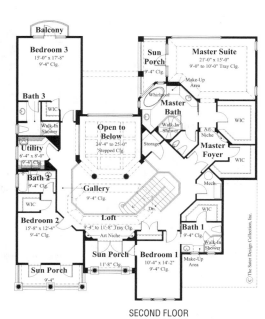

SECOND FLOOR

Share the intriguing floorplan of this brick Bayou home with family and friends—there's room for everyone! The front porch is lovely with balcony-style apertures framing two sets of French doors, and a paneled front door framed by sidelights and a sunburst. Inside, the dining room is set off from the foyer by decorative columns. The great room enjoys a fireplace and a snack bar pass-through to the island kitchen. Two bedrooms, one with porch access, share a full bath. The master suite is tucked away with a spa bath and twin walk-in closets. Upstairs, a fourth bedroom, media room and game room share a full bath.

plan ⊕ HPT900288

- **STYLE: TRADITIONAL**
- **FIRST FLOOR: 2,082 SQ. FT.**
- **SECOND FLOOR: 1,013 SQ. FT.**
- **TOTAL: 3,095 SQ. FT.**
- **BEDROOMS: 4**
- **BATHROOMS: 3½**
- **WIDTH: 70'-6"**
- **DEPTH: 57'-10"**
- **FOUNDATION: BASEMENT, CRAWLSPACE, SLAB**

SEARCH ONLINE @ EPLANS.COM

FIRST FLOOR

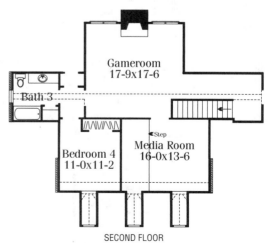

SECOND FLOOR

plan# HPT900289

- STYLE: FRENCH
- FIRST FLOOR: 1,973 SQ. FT.
- SECOND FLOOR: 1,062 SQ. FT.
- TOTAL: 3,035 SQ. FT.
- BONUS SPACE: 384 SQ. FT.
- BEDROOMS: 4
- BATHROOMS: 3½
- WIDTH: 57'-2"
- DEPTH: 60'-2"
- FOUNDATION: BASEMENT, CRAWLSPACE

SEARCH ONLINE @ EPLANS.COM

Bring the beauty of Provence home with this understated manor. Stucco and rounded accents soften the facade for a cozy, lived-in feel. Inside, the foyer opens to a living room on the left and dining room on the right. Straight ahead, beyond the staircase, is the hearth-warmed two-story family room, which leads to the breakfast area and kitchen on the right. The kitchen enjoys a roomy pantry and access to the laundry area. Secluded behind the garage is the master suite, with double walk-in closets and an elegant bath. Upstairs, three bedrooms share two full baths and a balcony overlook. Future recreation space awaits expansion.

SECOND FLOOR

FIRST FLOOR

Exterior details are only the beginning. This breathtaking European cottage packs abundant living space in less than 2,000 square feet. Enter through the covered front porch; the formal dining room and study are on either side of the foyer. Continue to the family room, featuring an extended-hearth fireplace and built-ins, and out to the patio—perfect for summer barbecues. The master suite includes a separate tub and shower and dual vanities. Two upstairs bedrooms are lit by flower-box windows and share a full bath.

plan# HPT900290

- STYLE: EUROPEAN COTTAGE
- FIRST FLOOR: 1,836 SQ. FT.
- SECOND FLOOR: 775 SQ. FT.
- TOTAL: 2,611 SQ. FT.
- BEDROOMS: 3
- BATHROOMS: 2½
- WIDTH: 54'-10"
- DEPTH: 56'-7"
- FOUNDATION: CRAWLSPACE

SEARCH ONLINE @ EPLANS.COM

FIRST FLOOR

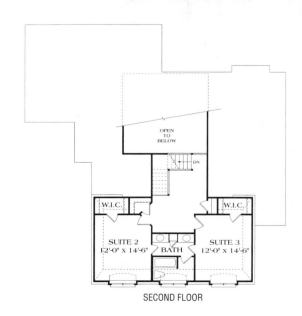

SECOND FLOOR

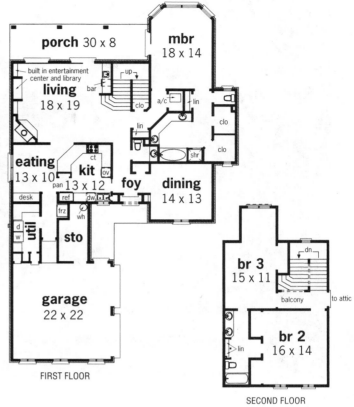

porch 30 x 8

mbr
18 x 14

built in entertainment
center and library

living
18 x 19

bar

up

clo

a/c

lin

lin

clo

eating
13 x 10

kit
13 x 12

ct

ov

lin

clo

clo

shr

pan

foy

dining
14 x 13

desk

ref

dw

frz

wh

d w

util

sto

garage
22 x 22

FIRST FLOOR

br 3
15 x 11

dn

balcony

to attic

lin

br 2
16 x 14

SECOND FLOOR

plan⊕ HPT900291

- STYLE: EUROPEAN COTTAGE
- FIRST FLOOR: 1,802 SQ. FT.
- SECOND FLOOR: 670 SQ. FT.
- TOTAL: 2,472 SQ. FT.
- BEDROOMS: 3
- BATHROOMS: 2½
- WIDTH: 49'-0"
- DEPTH: 79'-0"
- FOUNDATION: CRAWLSPACE

SEARCH ONLINE @ EPLANS.COM

mbr
18 x 17

shr

study/
br 4
16 x 13

bar

books

4-way vault clg

living
22 x 18

books

porch
18 x 10

br 3
13 x 12

den/
eating
15 x 12

bar

ov

pan

step clg

4-way vault clg

foy

lin

4-way vault clg

wh

a/c

br 2
13 x 12

porch 18 x 7

sto

sto

util

snk

ct

kit
17x12

ref

dw

dining
14x12

desk

d w

sto

sto
11x8

garage
22 x 22

plan⊕ HPT900292

- STYLE: EUROPEAN COTTAGE
- SQUARE FOOTAGE: 2,713
- BEDROOMS: 3
- BATHROOMS: 2½
- WIDTH: 94'-0"
- DEPTH: 62'-0"
- FOUNDATION: SLAB

SEARCH ONLINE @ EPLANS.COM

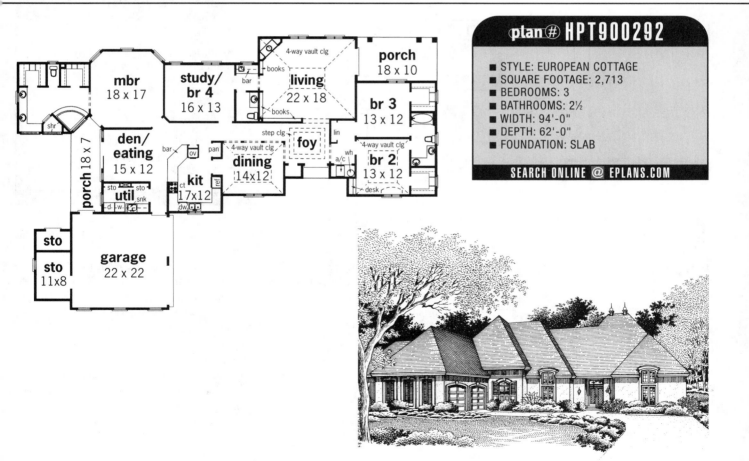

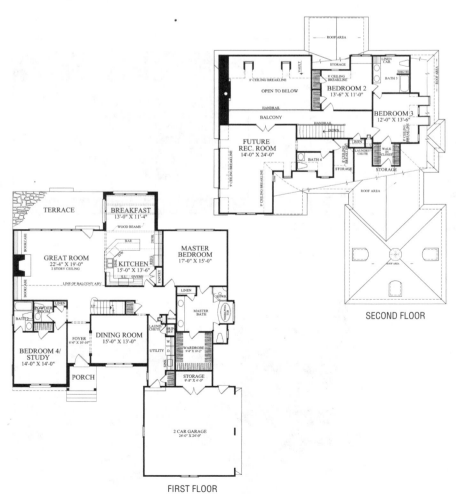

SECOND FLOOR

FIRST FLOOR

plan# HPT900293

- **STYLE:** FRENCH COUNTRY
- **FIRST FLOOR:** 2,433 SQ. FT.
- **SECOND FLOOR:** 774 SQ. FT.
- **TOTAL:** 3,207 SQ. FT.
- **BONUS SPACE:** 540 SQ. FT.
- **BEDROOMS:** 4
- **BATHROOMS:** 3½ + ½
- **WIDTH:** 59'-8"
- **DEPTH:** 77'-7"
- **FOUNDATION:** BASEMENT, CRAWLSPACE

SEARCH ONLINE @ EPLANS.COM

French Country elegance with a touch of Tudor, this home will bring grand European style to the neighborhood. The foyer opens to a formal dining room on the right and looks straight ahead to the hearth-warmed great room. A guest suite sits to the front right of the home, as does a convenient powder room. The kitchen and breakfast room are adjacent to the great room and enjoy plenty of light and views of the rear terrace. The master suite features a huge wardrobe and deluxe bath. The remaining sleeping quarters reside upstairs. Two bedrooms share a roomy bath and access to the future recreation room.

Start marking off your wish list—this beautiful European home has it all! The study and dining room, on either side of the two-story foyer, open to the gallery. Columns define the family room, featuring a built-in entertainment center and library that frame the fireplace, sweeping views and deck access. A wet bar joins the family room with the den. A fireplace here shares its warmth with the angled kitchen. The master suite is truly a haven, with a built-in entertainment center, fireplace and elongated bath. Here, a separate shower and tub, individual vanities and two compartmented toilets (one with a bidet) will pamper you. Upstairs, twin bedroom suites enjoy a library and built-in desks.

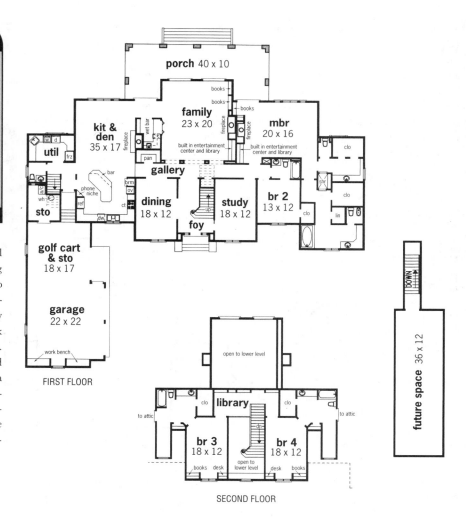

COPYRIGHT LARRY E. BELK

This majestic storybook cottage, from the magical setting of rural Europe, provides the perfect home for any large family with a wealth of modern comforts within. A graceful staircase cascades from the two-story foyer. To the left, a sophisticated study offers a wall of built-ins. To the right, a formal dining room is easily served from the island kitchen. The breakfast room accesses the rear screened porch. Fireplaces warm the great room and keeping room. Two sets of double doors open from the great room to the rear covered porch. The master bedroom features private porch access, a sitting area, lavish bath and two walk-in closets. Upstairs, three additional family bedrooms offer walk-in closet space galore! The game room is great entertainment for both family and friends. A three-car garage with golf-cart storage completes the plan.

plan # HPT900295

- **STYLE:** EUROPEAN COTTAGE
- **FIRST FLOOR:** 3,033 SQ. FT.
- **SECOND FLOOR:** 1,545 SQ. FT.
- **TOTAL:** 4,578 SQ. FT.
- **BEDROOMS:** 4
- **BATHROOMS:** 3½ + ½
- **WIDTH:** 91'-6"
- **DEPTH:** 63'-8"
- **FOUNDATION:** BASEMENT, CRAWLSPACE, SLAB

SEARCH ONLINE @ EPLANS.COM

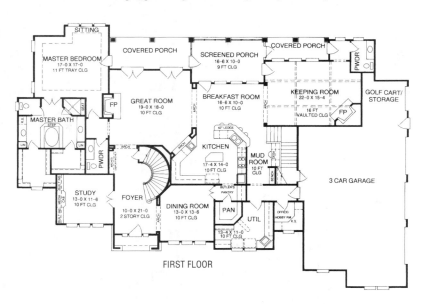

FIRST FLOOR

SECOND FLOOR

plan # HPT900296

- **STYLE: CONTEMPORARY**
- **FIRST FLOOR: 3,478 SQ. FT.**
- **SECOND FLOOR: 1,037 SQ. FT.**
- **TOTAL: 4,515 SQ. FT.**
- **BONUS SPACE: 314 SQ. FT.**
- **BEDROOMS: 4**
- **BATHROOMS: 4½**
- **WIDTH: 86'-8"**
- **DEPTH: 84'-4"**
- **FOUNDATION: SLAB**

SEARCH ONLINE @ EPLANS.COM

Live it up in stunning Southwestern style! This stucco beauty is accented by arched windows and a traditional Spanish tiled roof. Inside, the living space goes on and on. The formal dining room flows into the center living room, where a double-sided fireplace also warms the kitchen and breakfast nook to the left. The island kitchen opens to the spacious hearth-warmed family room. A bedroom with a private patio is tucked to the left rear, convenient to a full bath and the laundry room. A hallway here accesses the three-car garage. On the opposite side of the plan, past the den/study, is the spectacular master suite. This suite pushes the limits of luxury with double walk-in closets, bay window and enormous bath with a corner windowed tub and separate vanities. The second floor is home to two more bedrooms—each with its own bath—and a loft that opens to a balcony. Bonus space on this floor awaits expansion.

FIRST FLOOR

SECOND FLOOR

© The Sater Design Collection, Inc.

plan# HPT900297

- **STYLE: MEDITERRANEAN**
- **SQUARE FOOTAGE: 2,191**
- **BEDROOMS: 3**
- **BATHROOMS: 2½**
- **WIDTH: 62'-10"**
- **DEPTH: 73'-6"**
- **FOUNDATION: SLAB**

SEARCH ONLINE @ EPLANS.COM

Perfect for a corner lot, this Mediterranean villa is a beautiful addition to any neighborhood. Low and unassuming on the outside, this plan brings modern amenities and classic stylings together for a great family home. The study and two-story dining room border the foyer; an elongated gallery introduces the great room. Here, a rustic beamed ceiling, fireplace and art niche are thoughtful touches. The step-saving U-shaped kitchen flows into a sunny bayed breakfast nook. To the far right, two bedrooms share a full bath. The master suite is separated for privacy, situated to the far left. French door access to the veranda and a sumptuous bath make this a pleasurable retreat.

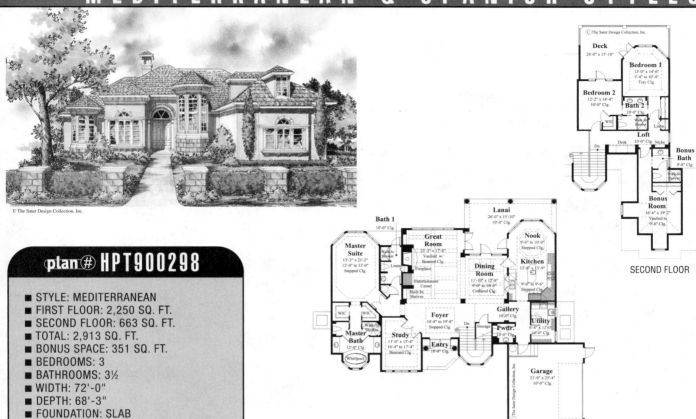

© The Sater Design Collection, Inc.

SECOND FLOOR

- Deck
  26'-0" x 15'-10"
- Bedroom 1
  13'-0" x 14'-6"
  9'-4" to 10'-4"
  Tray Clg.
- Bedroom 2
  12'-2" x 14'-4"
  10'-0" Clg.
- Bath 2
  10'-0" Clg.
- WIC
- Loft
  10'-0" Clg. Niche
- Desk
- Dn.
- Bonus Bath
  9'-8" Clg.
- Bonus Room
  16'-6" x 19'-2"
  Vaulted w/
  9'-8" Clg.

FIRST FLOOR

- Bath 1
  10'-0" Clg.
- Master Suite
  13'-2" x 21'-2"
  12'-0" to 13'-0"
  Stepped Clg.
- Great Room
  21'-3" x 17'-8"
  Vaulted w/
  Beamed Clg.
  Fireplace
- Lanai
  26'-0" x 15'-10"
  10'-0" Clg.
- Nook
  9'-0" x 10'-0"
  Stepped Clg.
- Dining Room
  11'-10" x 12'-8"
  9'-0" to 10'-0"
  Coffered Clg.
- Kitchen
  13'-0" x 13'-9"
  9'-0" to 9'-6"
  Stepped Clg.
- Entertainment Center
- Built-In Shelves
- WIC
- Walk-In Shower
- Master Bath
  12'-0" Clg.
- Whirlpool
- Study
  15'-0" x 15'-4"
  16'-4" to 17'-4"
  Beamed Clg.
- Foyer
  18'-8" x 19'-8"
  Stepped Clg.
- Dn.
- Storage
- Entry
  18'-8" Clg.
- Gallery
  10'-0" Clg.
- Pwdr.
- Utility
  6'-8" x 12'-0"
  10'-0" Clg.
- Garage
  21'-0" x 25'-4"
  10'-0" Clg.

© The Sater Design Collection, Inc.

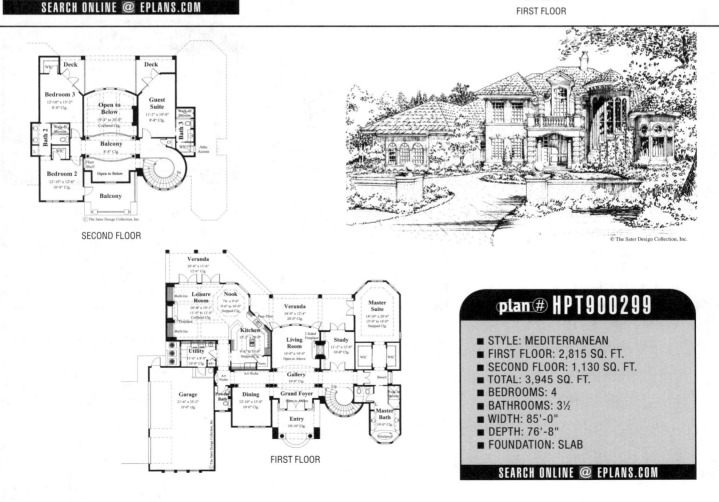

SECOND FLOOR

- Deck
- Bedroom 3
  12'-10" x 15'-2"
  8'-8" Clg.
- Bath 2
- Walk-In Shower
- WIC
- Open to Below
  19'-4" to 20'-0"
  Coffered Clg.
- Balcony
  8'-8" Clg.
- Deck
- Guest Suite
  11'-2" x 19'-8"
  8'-8" Clg.
- Walk-In Shower
- Bath 3
- WIC
- Attic Access
- Plant Shelf
- Open to Below
- Bedroom 2
  12'-10" x 12'-6"
  10'-8" Clg.
- Dn.
- Balcony

© The Sater Design Collection, Inc.

FIRST FLOOR

- Veranda
  28'-0" x 11'-6"
  12'-6" Clg.
- Built-Ins
- Leisure Room
  20'-8" x 19'-1"
  11'-0" to 12'-0"
  Coffered Clg.
- Built-Ins
- Nook
  7'-6" x 9'-0"
  9'-6" to 10'-0"
  Stepped Clg.
- Kitchen
  15'-2" x 13'-0"
- Pass-Thru
- Veranda
  34'-9" x 12'-4"
  20'-0" Clg.
- Master Suite
  14'-10" x 20'-6"
  15'-0" to 16'-0"
  Stepped Clg.
- Utility
  11'-6" x 8'-8"
  10'-0" Clg.
- Living Room
  16'-0" x 14'-4"
  Open to Above
- 2 Sided Fireplace
- Study
  11'-2" x 12'-8"
  10'-0" Clg.
- WIC
- WIC
- Art Niche
- Art Niche
- Pantry
- Gallery
  10'-0" Clg.
- Bench
- Walk-In Shower
- Garage
  21'-0" x 35'-2"
  10'-0" Clg.
- Powder Bath
- Dining
  12'-10" x 13'-0"
  10'-0" Clg.
- Grand Foyer
  Open to Above
- Up
- Entry
  10'-0" Clg.
- Master Bath
  10'-0" Clg.
- Whirlpool

© The Sater Design Collection, Inc.

© The Sater Design Collection, Inc.

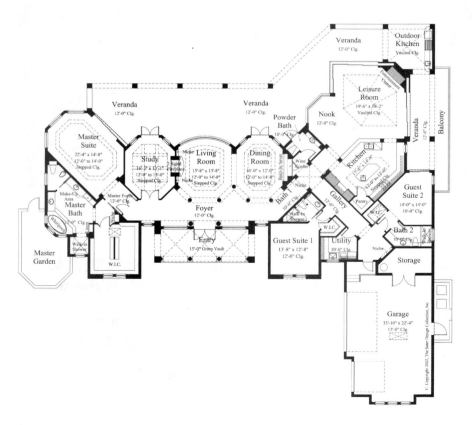

plan# HPT900300

- **STYLE: MEDITERRANEAN**
- **SQUARE FOOTAGE: 3,640**
- **BEDROOMS: 3**
- **BATHROOMS: 3½**
- **WIDTH: 106'-4"**
- **DEPTH: 102'-4"**
- **FOUNDATION: SLAB**

SEARCH ONLINE @ EPLANS.COM

Come home to luxurious living—all on one level—with this striking Mediterranean plan. Unique ceiling treatments highlight the living areas—the living and dining rooms, as well as the study, feature stepped ceilings, while the leisure room includes a vaulted ceiling. The gourmet kitchen includes a spacious center island; another kitchen, this one outdoors, can be accessed from the leisure room. The master suite boasts plenty of amenities: a large, skylit walk-in closet, a bath with a whirlpool tub and walk-in shower, and private access to a charming garden area. Two suites, both with private baths, sit to the right of the plan.

© The Sater Design Collection, Inc.

plan# HPT900301

- **STYLE:** MEDITERRANEAN
- **SQUARE FOOTAGE:** 3,942
- **BEDROOMS:** 3
- **BATHROOMS:** 4
- **WIDTH:** 83'-10"
- **DEPTH:** 106'-0"
- **FOUNDATION:** SLAB

SEARCH ONLINE @ EPLANS.COM

Italian Renaissance flair sets the tone for this majestic Old World estate. An impressive entrance reveals an open floor plan; the foyer, living room and dining room are all defined by distinctive ceiling treatments for endless interior design possibilities. A wet bar and pool bath announce the gourmet kitchen with a pentagonal island and lots of counter space. Past a half-moon nook, the leisure room will be a family favorite. On the lanai, an outdoor kitchen is an easy way to cook up all-weather fun. To the far right, the master suite will amaze; an octagonal sitting area and morning kitchen are only the beginning. Two enormous walk-in closets beckon with built-in shelving and room for even the biggest clotheshorses' collections. The master bath, set in a turret, will soothe and pamper with a central whirlpool tub, walk-in shower and views to the garden.

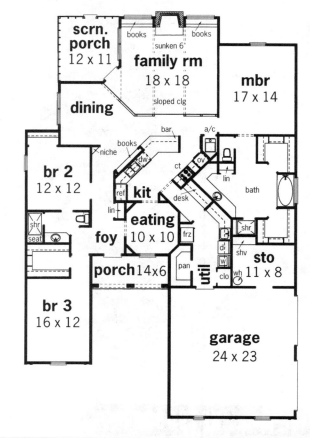

plan# HPT900303

- STYLE: MEDITERRANEAN
- SQUARE FOOTAGE: 2,111
- BEDROOMS: 3
- BATHROOMS: 2
- WIDTH: 49'-0"
- DEPTH: 74'-0"
- FOUNDATION: CRAWLSPACE, SLAB

SEARCH ONLINE @ EPLANS.COM

plan# HPT900302

- STYLE: MEDITERRANEAN
- SQUARE FOOTAGE: 2,349
- BEDROOMS: 3
- BATHROOMS: 2
- WIDTH: 63'-0"
- DEPTH: 74'-0"
- FOUNDATION: CRAWLSPACE, SLAB

SEARCH ONLINE @ EPLANS.COM

plan# HPT900304

- STYLE: TRADITIONAL
- SQUARE FOOTAGE: 2,715
- BEDROOMS: 3
- BATHROOMS: 2½
- WIDTH: 72'-0"
- DEPTH: 64'-8"

SEARCH ONLINE @ EPLANS.COM

This exquisite Sun Country villa features stunning Mediterranean accents that combine Old-World style with modern convenience. Three arches welcome you to a covered front porch, which opens into a spacious tiled foyer. Enchanting arches frame the great room and formal dining room. The computer alcove is a modern touch. The island snack-bar kitchen opens to a casual gathering room warmed by a fireplace. At the rear, a covered courtyard is a relaxing retreat, featuring a serene built-in fountain. The luxurious master wing offers a private covered terrace with a spa, a kitchenette, a whirlpool bath and two huge walk-in closets—one with built-in dressers.

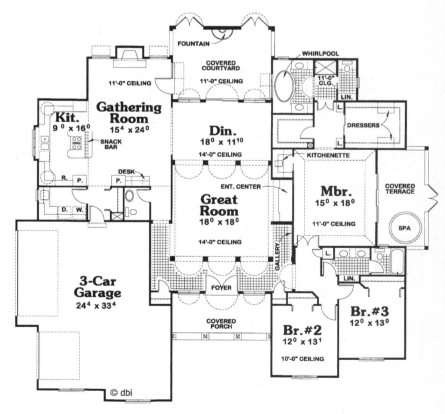

© design basics inc.

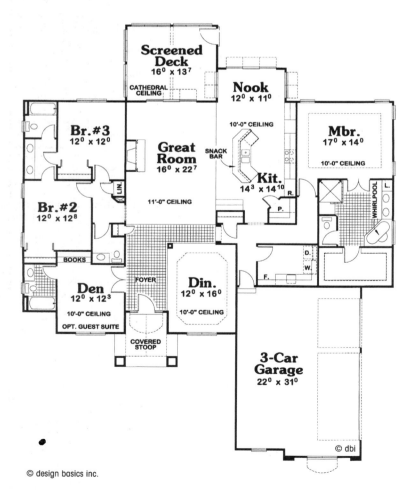

Screened Deck
16⁰ x 13⁷
CATHEDRAL CEILING

Nook
12⁰ x 11⁰
10'-0" CEILING

Mbr.
17⁰ x 14⁰
10'-0" CEILING

Br. #3
12⁰ x 12⁰

Great Room
16⁰ x 22⁷
11'-0" CEILING

SNACK BAR

Kit.
14³ x 14¹⁰

Br. #2
12⁰ x 12⁸

WHIRLPOOL

BOOKS

Den
12⁰ x 12³
10'-0" CEILING
OPT. GUEST SUITE

FOYER

Din.
12⁰ x 16⁰
10'-0" CEILING

COVERED STOOP

3-Car Garage
22⁰ x 31⁰

© dbi

© design basics inc.

plan # HPT900305

- STYLE: TRADITIONAL
- SQUARE FOOTAGE: 2,647
- BEDROOMS: 3
- BATHROOMS: 2½
- WIDTH: 66'-8"
- DEPTH: 79'-8"

SEARCH ONLINE @ EPLANS.COM

A convenient one-story floor plan is provided for this attractive Sun Country home. A covered front porch welcomes you inside to a foyer flanked on either side by a den and a formal dining room. A fireplace in the great room warms family and friends. The kitchen opens to a breakfast nook. The rear screened porch is enhanced by a cathedral ceiling. The master suite features a luxurious bath and huge walk-in closet. Bedrooms 2 and 3 share a full bath. A laundry room is placed just outside of the three-car garage.

TO ORDER BLUEPRINTS CALL TOLL FREE 1-800-521-6797

© The Sater Design Collection, Inc.

plan# HPT900306

- **STYLE:** ITALIAN RENAISSANCE
- **SQUARE FOOTAGE:** 3,743
- **BEDROOMS:** 3
- **BATHROOMS:** 3½
- **WIDTH:** 80'-0"
- **DEPTH:** 103'-8"
- **FOUNDATION:** SLAB

SEARCH ONLINE @ EPLANS.COM

With California style and Mediterranean good looks, this striking stucco manor is sure to delight. The portico and foyer open to reveal a smart plan with convenience and flexibility in mind. The columned living room has a warming fireplace and access to the rear property. In the gourmet kitchen, an open design with an island and walk-in pantry will please any chef. From here, the elegant dining room and sunny nook are easily served. The leisure room is separated from the game room by a built-in entertainment center. The game area can also be finished off as a bedroom. To the rear, a guest room is perfect for frequent visitors or as an in-law suite. The master suite features a bright sitting area, oversized walk-in closets and a pampering bath with a whirlpool tub. Extra features not to be missed: the outdoor grill, game-room storage and gallery window seat.

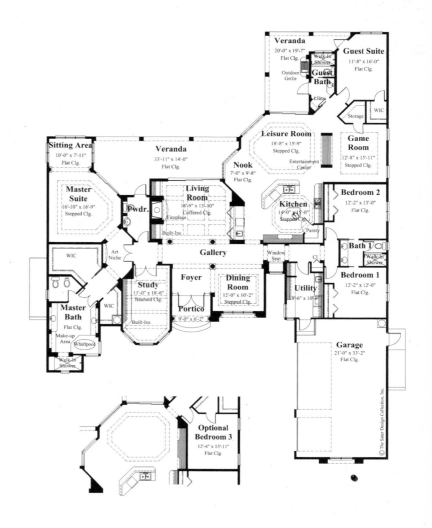

© The Sater Design Collection, Inc.

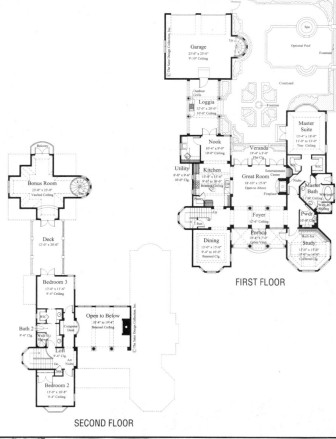

Balcony

Bonus Room
23'-0" x 23'-0"
Vaulted Ceiling

Deck
12'-0" x 20'-0"

Bedroom 3
13'-0" x 11'-6"
9'-4" Ceiling

Bath 2
9'-4" Clg.

Open to Below
18'-4" x 19'-4"
Beamed Ceiling

Loft
9'-4" Clg.

Bedroom 2
13'-0" x 10'-8"
9'-4" Ceiling

© The Sater Design Collection, Inc.

SECOND FLOOR

Garage
23'-0" x 23'-0"
9'-10" Ceiling

Up

Spa

Optional Pool

Fountain

Courtyard

Fountain

Loggia
23'-6" x 20'-0"
10'-0" Ceiling

Nook
10'-4" x 9'-0"
10'-0" Ceiling

Veranda
19'-4" x 8'-0"
Flat Clg.

Master Suite
13'-4" x 18'-0"
11'-0" x 13'-0"
Tray Ceiling

Utility
6'-8" x 9'-6"
10'-0" Clg.

Kitchen
13'-0" x 15'-6"
9'-6" x 15'-0"
Beamed Ceiling

Great Room
19'-10" x 15'-9"
Open to Above

Entertainment Centre

Fireplace

WIC

Master Bath

Pwdr.

Foyer
12'-6" Ceiling

Dining
13'-0" x 15'-0"
9'-4" x 10'-0"
Beamed Clg.

Portico
19'-4" x 7'-0"
Groin Vault

Study
13'-0" x 15'-0"
13'-6" to 15'-0"
Coffered Clg.

FIRST FLOOR

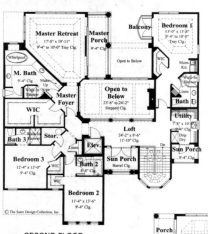

Master Retreat
17'-8" x 19'-11"
9'-4" to 10'-0" Tray Clg.

Master Porch
9'-4" Clg.

Balcony

Bedroom 1
13'-0" x 13'-8"
9'-4" to 10'-0" Tray Clg.

Whirlpool

M. Bath
9'-4" Clg.

Mom's Kit.

Open to Below

WIC

Walk-In Shower

Bath

Master Foyer

Open to Below
23'-6" to 24'-2"
Stepped Clg.

Linen

Utility
7'-8" x 10'-4"
9'-4" Clg.

WIC

Bath 3

Stor.

Elev.

Loft
24'-2" x 8'-6"
11'-10" Clg.

Drip Dry

Bedroom 3
12'-4" x 13'-0"
9'-4" Clg.

WIC

Bath 2
8'-8" Clg.

Sun Porch
Barrel Clg.

Dn

Sun Porch
9'-4" Clg.

Bedroom 2
11'-4" x 13'-6"
9'-4" Clg.

© The Sater Design Collection, Inc.

SECOND FLOOR

© The Sater Design Collection, Inc.

Porch
10'-0" Clg.

Leisure Room
17'-8" x 19'-11"
9'-4" to 10'-0"
Stepped Clg.

Entertainment Center

Cabana/Guest Suite
13'-0" x 13'-4"
10'-0" Clg.

Nook
9'-0" x 9'-8"
9'-4" Clg.

Veranda
26'-6" x 10'-2"
Open to Above

Outdoor Grille

Bath 1

Walk-In Shower

Kitchen
17'-4" x 13'-6"
10'-0" to 10'-0"
Stepped Clg.

Living/Dining Room
21'-11" x 11'-9"
Open to Above

Two Sided Fireplace

Library / Study
13'-3" x 15'-0"
9'-4" to 10'-0"
Stepped Clg.

Pantry

Pwdr.

Stor.

Elev.

Foyer
10'-0" Clg.

Up

Built-Ins

Porch
Clg.

Garage
29'-0" x 23'-8"
10'-0" Clg.

Stor.

Entry
10'-0" Clg.

© The Sater Design Collection, Inc.

FIRST FLOOR

TO ORDER BLUEPRINTS CALL TOLL FREE 1-800-521-6797

© The Sater Design Collection, Inc.

plan # HPT900309

- **STYLE:** SPANISH COLONIAL
- **FIRST FLOOR:** 3,025 SQ. FT.
- **SECOND FLOOR:** 1,639 SQ. FT.
- **TOTAL:** 4,664 SQ. FT.
- **BONUS SPACE:** 294 SQ. FT.
- **BEDROOMS:** 4
- **BATHROOMS:** 4½
- **WIDTH:** 70'-0"
- **DEPTH:** 100'-0"
- **FOUNDATION:** SLAB

SEARCH ONLINE @ EPLANS.COM

A Spanish Colonial masterpiece, this family-oriented design is ideal for entertaining. Double doors reveal a foyer, with a columned dining room to the right and a spiral staircase enclosed in a turret to the left. Ahead, the great room opens above to a soaring coffered ceiling. Here, a bowed window wall and a two-sided fireplace (shared with the study) make an elegant impression. The country-style kitchen is a host's dream, with an adjacent wet bar, preparation island and space for a six-burner cooktop. Near the leisure room, a bayed nook could serve as a breakfast or reading area. The master suite is a pampering sanctuary, with no rooms directly above and personal touches you will surely appreciate. Upstairs, two bedrooms, one with a window seat, and a guest suite with a balcony, all enjoy private baths and walk-in closets.

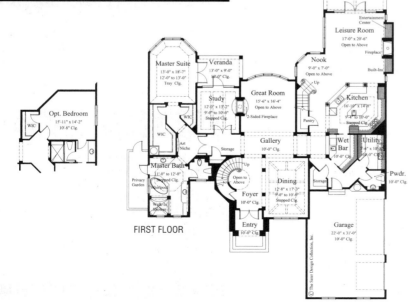

FIRST FLOOR

SECOND FLOOR

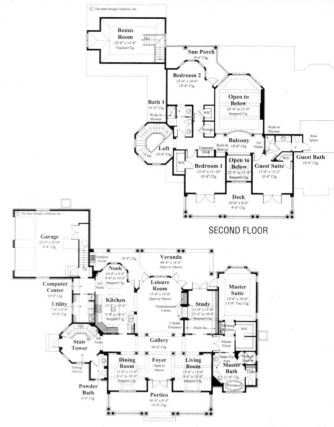

SECOND FLOOR

FIRST FLOOR

plan # HPT900310

- **STYLE:** ITALIAN RENAISSANCE
- **FIRST FLOOR:** 2,481 SQ. FT.
- **SECOND FLOOR:** 1,132 SQ. FT.
- **TOTAL:** 3,613 SQ. FT.
- **BONUS SPACE:** 332 SQ. FT.
- **BEDROOMS:** 4
- **BATHROOMS:** 3½
- **WIDTH:** 83'-0"
- **DEPTH:** 71'-8"
- **FOUNDATION:** SLAB

SEARCH ONLINE @ EPLANS.COM

SECOND FLOOR

FIRST FLOOR

plan # HPT900311

- **STYLE:** MEDITERRANEAN
- **FIRST FLOOR:** 1,996 SQ. FT.
- **SECOND FLOOR:** 2,171 SQ. FT.
- **TOTAL:** 4,167 SQ. FT.
- **BEDROOMS:** 5
- **BATHROOMS:** 5½
- **WIDTH:** 58'-0"
- **DEPTH:** 65'-0"
- **FOUNDATION:** SLAB

SEARCH ONLINE @ EPLANS.COM

plan# HPT900312

- **STYLE: TRADITIONAL**
- **FIRST FLOOR: 1,707 SQ. FT.**
- **SECOND FLOOR: 1,036 SQ. FT.**
- **TOTAL: 2,743 SQ. FT.**
- **BONUS SPACE: 843 SQ. FT.**
- **BEDROOMS: 4**
- **BATHROOMS: 3½**
- **WIDTH: 67'-0"**
- **DEPTH: 64'-0"**
- **FOUNDATION: CRAWLSPACE, SLAB**

SEARCH ONLINE @ EPLANS.COM

This stucco home with multi-pane windows and an intriguing floor plan will look great from coast to coast. A grand facade introduces a design made for family living. An expansive den includes a piano niche and an extended-hearth fireplace framed by bookshelves. The living room is separated by accordion doors for privacy. The bayed dining room welcomes guests; through the gourmet kitchen, a breakfast nook is perfect for casual meals. The first-floor master suite features a vaulted bath with an angled, bumped-out tub. Upstairs, three bedrooms offer individual amenities and share access to future space.

FIRST FLOOR

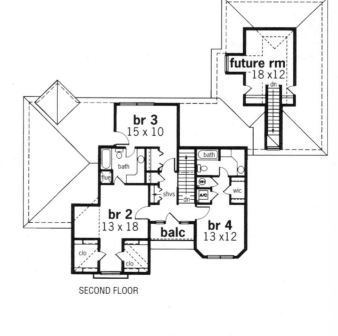

SECOND FLOOR

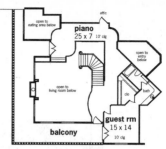

SECOND FLOOR

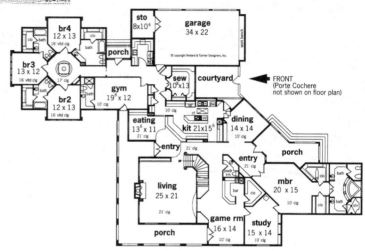

FIRST FLOOR

plan# HPT900313

- STYLE: MEDITERRANEAN
- FIRST FLOOR: 5,120 SQ. FT.
- SECOND FLOOR: 880 SQ. FT.
- TOTAL: 6,000 SQ. FT.
- BEDROOMS: 5
- BATHROOMS: 6½
- WIDTH: 91'-0"
- DEPTH: 132'-0"
- FOUNDATION: CRAWLSPACE

SEARCH ONLINE @ EPLANS.COM

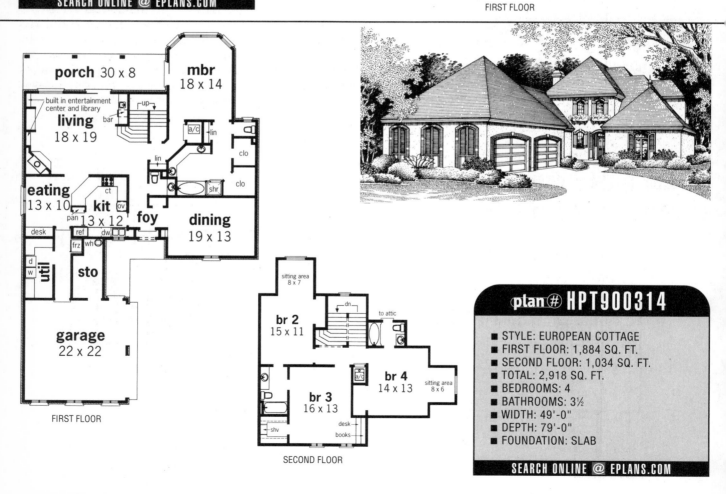

FIRST FLOOR

SECOND FLOOR

plan# HPT900314

- STYLE: EUROPEAN COTTAGE
- FIRST FLOOR: 1,884 SQ. FT.
- SECOND FLOOR: 1,034 SQ. FT.
- TOTAL: 2,918 SQ. FT.
- BEDROOMS: 4
- BATHROOMS: 3½
- WIDTH: 49'-0"
- DEPTH: 79'-0"
- FOUNDATION: SLAB

SEARCH ONLINE @ EPLANS.COM

plan# HPT900315

- **STYLE: TRADITIONAL**
- **FIRST FLOOR: 2,111 SQ. FT.**
- **SECOND FLOOR: 985 SQ. FT.**
- **TOTAL: 3,096 SQ. FT.**
- **BEDROOMS: 4**
- **BATHROOMS: 4½**
- **WIDTH: 70'-0"**
- **DEPTH: 78'-0"**
- **FOUNDATION: BASEMENT, CRAWLSPACE, SLAB**

SEARCH ONLINE @ EPLANS.COM

Straight from a New Orleans scene, this romantic modern design is enhanced by a creative array of Southern and European details. Mediterranean-style arches grace the formal entrance. The entry hall leads to the formal dining room. The contemporary layout includes a snack-bar kitchen with a walk-in pantry nearby. Classic columns separate the breakfast room from the formal living room. A buffet table serves the breakfast room, while an angled fireplace warms family gatherings nearby. The deluxe media room includes built-ins for a TV and books, a wet bar and an equipment room for storage. The first-floor master suite boasts a private bath and walk-in closet. This level is completed by a rear porch, two-car garage and shop. A balcony from the second floor views the living and breakfast rooms. All three secondary bedrooms include their own walk-in closets and private baths.

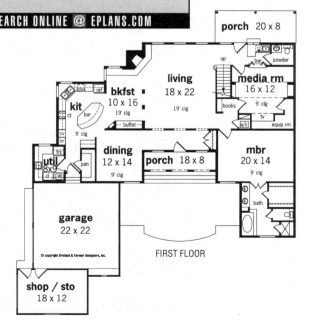

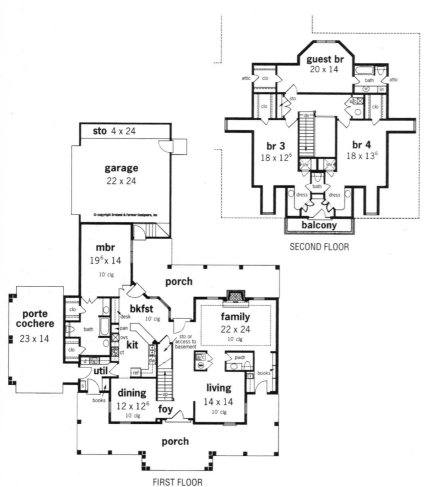

SECOND FLOOR

FIRST FLOOR

plan# HPT900316

- STYLE: MEDITERRANEAN
- FIRST FLOOR: 1,892 SQ. FT.
- SECOND FLOOR: 1,400 SQ. FT.
- TOTAL: 3,292 SQ. FT.
- BEDROOMS: 4
- BATHROOMS: 3½
- WIDTH: 70'-0"
- DEPTH: 90'-0"
- FOUNDATION: BASEMENT, CRAWLSPACE, SLAB

SEARCH ONLINE @ EPLANS.COM

This exquisite design offers a contemporary spin on Southern and French architectural elements. Perfect for a waterfront estate, the elegant wraparound porch encourages outdoor livability and provides breathtaking vistas of the front property. An abundance of tall windows welcomes the outdoors in. Just inside, formal living and dining rooms flank the foyer. The family room is warmed by a fireplace, while a wall of built-in bookshelves leads to a side-porch access. The kitchen/breakfast area is brightened by a bay and features a handy built-in desk. The first-floor master suite includes a pampering bath with two walk-in closets. The rear garage and porte cochere offer shelter for family cars. Upstairs, Bedrooms 3 and 4 share a romantic front-facing balcony. The guest bedroom provides a private bath.

plan# HPT900317

- STYLE: TRADITIONAL
- FIRST FLOOR: 3,465 SQ. FT.
- SECOND FLOOR: 975 SQ. FT.
- TOTAL: 4,440 SQ. FT.
- BONUS SPACE: 440 SQ. FT.
- BEDROOMS: 4
- BATHROOMS: 5½
- WIDTH: 94'-0"
- DEPTH: 92'-0"
- FOUNDATION: CRAWLSPACE, SLAB

SEARCH ONLINE @ EPLANS.COM

Stucco and brick combine with quoins, capped roofs and multi-pane windows for a fairy tale home that is sure to please. From the garage with a designated space for the golf cart to the luxurious master suite, this floor plan is designed with you in mind. The two-story foyer is bordered by a dining room and study; from here, the gallery opens to a family room with a soaring ceiling and a warming fireplace. The den shares a wet bar with the family room and the warmth of its fireplace with the gourmet kitchen. The master suite has rear-property access and a romantic fireplace. The pampering private bath will delight with two walk-in closets and a spa tub. An adjacent bedroom with a bath makes a great guest room or nursery. Up the dramatic staircase, twin bedroom suites share a library area. Future space is limited only by your imagination.

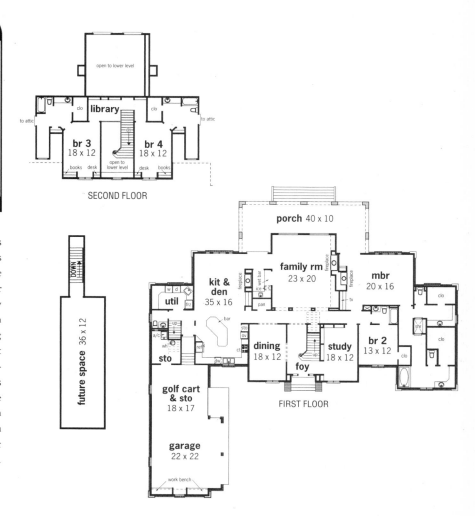

SECOND FLOOR

FIRST FLOOR

Why settle for a cookie-cutter home when you could build a unique ranch house that is perfect for a small family, retired couple or vacation home. From the entry, you are immediately greeted by the living room and its warming fireplace. To the right, a bright dining room and utility area are joined by the L-shaped kitchen with an island cooktop and a breakfast area, lit by an arched window. Across the courtyard, the master suite includes a private bath with a corner step-up tub and a walk-in closet. A second bedroom enjoys a pampering private bath and walk-in closet as well.

plan # HPT900318

- **STYLE: TRADITIONAL**
- **SQUARE FOOTAGE: 2,142**
- **BEDROOMS: 2**
- **BATHROOMS: 2½**
- **WIDTH: 55'-0"**
- **DEPTH: 84'-0"**
- **FOUNDATION: SLAB**

SEARCH ONLINE @ EPLANS.COM

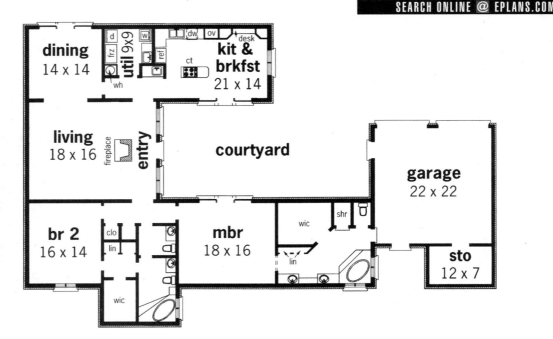

plan # HPT900319

- STYLE: MEDITERRANEAN
- FIRST FLOOR: 3,097 SQ. FT.
- SECOND FLOOR: 873 SQ. FT.
- TOTAL: 3,970 SQ. FT.
- BEDROOMS: 3
- BATHROOMS: 4
- WIDTH: 78'-0"
- DEPTH: 75'-4"
- FOUNDATION: SLAB

SEARCH ONLINE @ EPLANS.COM

Dentils accent the hipped roof, while white double columns outline the entry of this lovely three-bedroom home. Formal entertaining will be enjoyed at the front of the plan, in either the dining room or den. Tucked out of sight from the living room, yet close to the dining area, the island kitchen features acres of counter space and a convenient utility room. The breakfast nook sits open to the family room, sharing the spacious views and warming fireplace of this relaxing informal zone. A wonderful master suite fills the right side of the plan with luxury elements, such as a sitting room, large walk-in closet and soaking tub. Two family bedrooms to the left of the plan share a full bath.

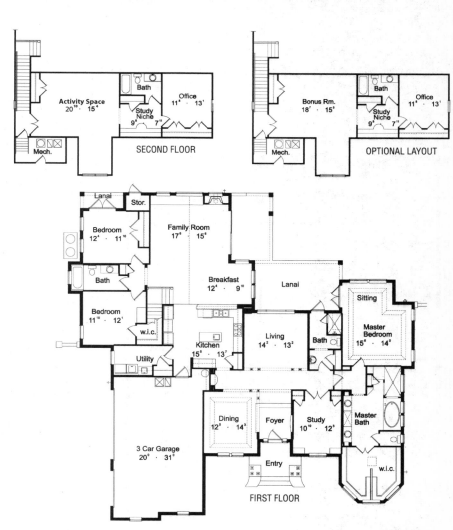

2743-A-35

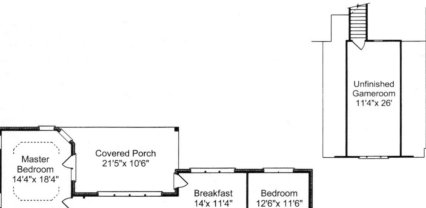

Master Bedroom 14'4" x 18'4"

Covered Porch 21'5" x 10'6"

Walk-In Closet

Walk-In Closet

Master Bath

Breakfast 14' x 11'4"

Bedroom 12'6" x 11'6"

Living 21'6" x 23'

Kitchen 14' x 13'

Bath

Dressing

Bath

Foyer

Dining 14'5" x 14'

Utility

Bedroom 12' x 12'

Bedroom 11'10" x 13'

Porch

Two Car Garage 21'2" x 26'

Unfinished Gameroom 11'4" x 26'

plan# HPT900320

- STYLE: MEDITERRANEAN
- SQUARE FOOTAGE: 2,781
- BONUS SPACE: 319 SQ. FT.
- BEDROOMS: 4
- BATHROOMS: 3
- WIDTH: 64'-10"
- DEPTH: 76'-9"
- FOUNDATION: SLAB

SEARCH ONLINE @ EPLANS.COM

A multi-faceted facade and classic arches blend with an intricate hipped roof design, dressing this home with a sheer sense of elegance. The dining and living rooms meld with the breakfast nook creating an expansive common area that spills out onto the rear covered porch. The four bedrooms are split with two on each side of the plan—the master suite on the left boasts a lavish master bath and twin walk-in closets. The unfinished game room easily converts to a home office or attic storage.

plan # HPT900321

- STYLE: TRADITIONAL
- SQUARE FOOTAGE: 3,190
- BONUS SPACE: 769 SQ. FT.
- BEDROOMS: 3
- BATHROOMS: 2½
- WIDTH: 91'-0"
- DEPTH: 83'-0"
- FOUNDATION: SLAB

SEARCH ONLINE @ EPLANS.COM

Plentiful amenities abound in this charming design. Family bedrooms and a dining room flank the foyer. A fireplace warms the formal living area, which features a wall of double doors opening to the rear pool and patio. The kitchen features an island workstation and is open to the breakfast room. Courtyards to the left and right of the plan encourage outdoor enjoyment. The master suite offers an exquisite private bath and roomy walk-in closet. The two-car garage and recreation room are appealing additions to the floor plan. Optional space above the garage is reserved for future use.

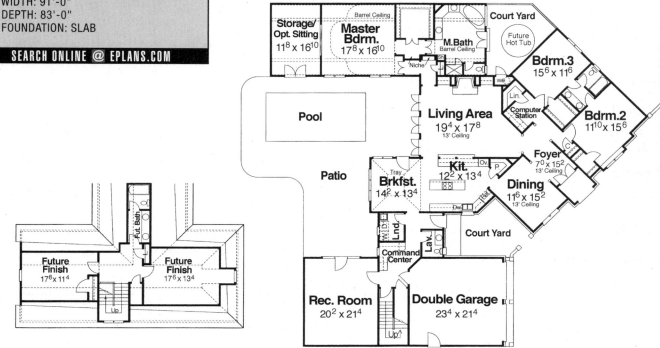

This traditional country home has steep-sloped rooflines, three dormers and an inviting front porch for great curb appeal. Raised ceilings throughout the home increase the sense of spaciousness. Three sets of French doors open to the living room, with an extended-hearth fireplace and rear porch access. The eating area and U-shaped kitchen are bathed in light and offer views of the deck. Down a hallway, past the powder and utility rooms, the master suite revels in a quiet retreat. A vaulted bath with a spa tub and an oversize walk-in closet are sure to please. Upstairs, two bedrooms have walk-in closets, private vanities and a shared bath. A sitting area overlooks the living room and kitchen below.

plan# HPT900322

- STYLE: TRADITIONAL
- FIRST FLOOR: 2,045 SQ. FT.
- SECOND FLOOR: 1,456 SQ. FT.
- TOTAL: 3,501 SQ. FT.
- BEDROOMS: 3
- BATHROOMS: 2½
- WIDTH: 70'-0"
- DEPTH: 64'-0"
- FOUNDATION: BASEMENT, CRAWLSPACE, SLAB

SEARCH ONLINE @ EPLANS.COM

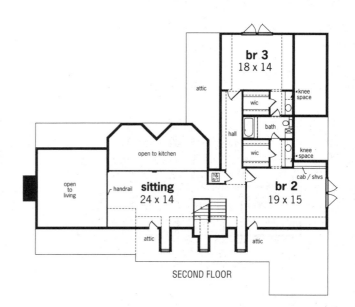

© 2002 Donald A. Gardner, Inc.

plan# HPT900323

- **STYLE:** SANTA FE
- **SQUARE FOOTAGE:** 3,061
- **BEDROOMS:** 3
- **BATHROOMS:** 3½
- **WIDTH:** 86'-1"
- **DEPTH:** 84'-8"

SEARCH ONLINE @ EPLANS.COM

Meanwhile, back at the ranch...an updated hacienda was offering the utmost in livability. Round up the horses—or the family cars—in the front motor court. Enter through a rugged stone lanai to an elegant gallery hall, which accesses the combined great room/dining area. A double-sided fireplace warms this space as well as the courtyard to the right. The adjacent master suite features a curved wall of windows and a deluxe bath with a huge walk-in closet. On the opposite side of the plan, the kitchen's serving-bar island looks into the bay-windowed breakfast nook. A roomy pantry will delight the family cook. A utility room and half-bath are convenient to both the kitchen and the two-car garage. Opening from the other side of the kitchen is a hearth-warmed family room that accesses the rear lanai. At the right front of the plan reside two additional bedrooms—each with its own bath.

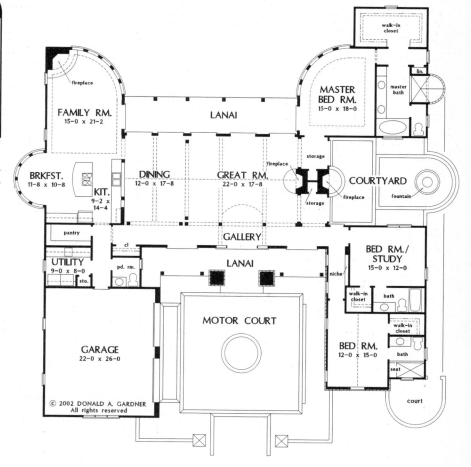

© 2002 Donald A. Gardner, Inc.

© 2002 DONALD A. GARDNER
All rights reserved

plan# HPT900324

- STYLE: SANTA FE
- SQUARE FOOTAGE: 1,895
- BEDROOMS: 3
- BATHROOMS: 2
- WIDTH: 65'-10"
- DEPTH: 59'-9"

SEARCH ONLINE @ EPLANS.COM

Giddyup! Santa Fe style at its best brings you back to the days of open skies and covered wagons. Rich with history on the outside, this plan's interior has all the up-to-date amenities that today's families require. The arched loggia entry opens to a soaring foyer, flanked on the right by a formal dining room. To the left is a bedroom that could easily become a study. Straight ahead, the hearth-warmed great room enjoys sliding glass door access to the rear loggia. Another bedroom is tucked in the back left corner, convenient to a full hall bath. On the other side of the great room, a roomy kitchen opens to a breakfast nook with a curved wall of windows. Secluded to the back is the luxurious master suite, featuring a ten-foot ceiling and spectacular private bath. The two-car garage opens to a utility room with a handy linen closet.

plan# HPT900325

- **STYLE:** SANTA FE
- **SQUARE FOOTAGE:** 1,883
- **BEDROOMS:** 3
- **BATHROOMS:** 2
- **WIDTH:** 66'-2"
- **DEPTH:** 59'-8"

SEARCH ONLINE @ EPLANS.COM

Home on the range—where luxury and livability go hand-in-hand. Rustic details like heavy shutters and beams accent the facade of this Santa Fe classic. Enter the front covered porch to the spacious foyer, which opens at a unique angle to the windowed formal dining room to the right. At the center of the home is the hearth-warmed great room, which flows right into the island serving-bar kitchen and bayed breakfast nook—both feature eleven-foot ceilings. The left wing of the plan is taken up by the sleeping quarters, including two family bedrooms—each with its own walk-in closet—and a deluxe master suite. The suite boasts another curved wall of windows, a walk-in closet, twin-vanity bath and rear-porch access.

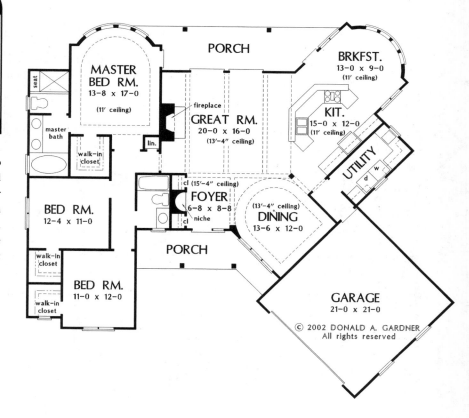

MASTER BED RM.
13-8 x 17-0
(11' ceiling)

master bath

seat

walk-in closet

BED RM.
12-4 x 11-0

walk-in closet

BED RM.
11-0 x 12-0

walk-in closet

PORCH

fireplace

GREAT RM.
20-0 x 16-0
(13'-4" ceiling)

lin.

BRKFST.
13-0 x 9-0
(11' ceiling)

KIT.
15-0 x 12-0
(11' ceiling)

UTILITY

cl

FOYER
6-8 x 8-8
(15'-4" ceiling)

niche

cl

DINING
13-6 x 12-0
(13'-4" ceiling)

PORCH

GARAGE
21-0 x 21-0

COPYRIGHT DOS & DON'TS

Blueprints for residential construction (or working drawings, as they are often called in the industry) are copyrighted intellectual property, protected under the terms of United States Copyright Law and, therefore, cannot be copied legally for use in building. However, we've made it easy for you to get what you need to build your home, without violating copyright law. Following are some guidelines to help you obtain the right number of copies for your chosen blueprint design.

COPYRIGHT DO

■ Do purchase enough copies of the blueprints to satisfy building requirements. As a rule for a home or project plan, you will need a set for yourself, two or three for your builder and subcontractors, two for the local building department, and one to three for your mortgage lender. You may want to check with your local building department or your builder to see how many they need before you purchase. You may need to buy eight to 10 sets; note that some areas of the country require purchase of vellums (also called reproducibles) instead of blueprints. Vellums can be written on and changed more easily than blueprints. Also, remember, plans are only good for one-time construction.

■ Do consider reverse blueprints if you want to flop the plan. Lettering and numbering will appear backward, but the reversed sets will help you and your builder better visualize the design.

■ Do take advantage of multiple-set discounts at the time you place your order. Usually, purchasing additional sets after you receive your initial order is not as cost-effective.

■ Do take advantage of vellums. Though they are a little more expensive, they can be changed, copied, and used for one-time construction of a home. You will receive a copyright release letter with your vellums that will allow you to have them copied.

■ Do talk with one of our professional service representatives before placing your order. They can give you great advice about what packages are available for your chosen design and what will work best for your particular situation.

COPYRIGHT DON'T

■ Don't think you should purchase only one set of blueprints for a building project. One is fine if you want to study the plan closely, but will not be enough for actual building.

■ Don't expect your builder or a copy center to make copies of standard blueprints. They cannot legally—most copy centers are aware of this.

■ Don't purchase standard blueprints if you know you'll want to make changes to the plans; vellums are a better value.

■ Don't use blueprints or vellums more than one time. Additional fees apply if you want to build more than one time from a set of drawings. ■

LET US SHOW YOU OUR HOME BLUEPRINT PACKAGE.

BUILDING A HOME? PLANNING A HOME?

OUR BLUEPRINT PACKAGE HAS NEARLY EVERYTHING YOU NEED TO GET THE JOB DONE RIGHT,

whether you're working on your own or with help from an architect, designer, builder or subcontractors. Each Blueprint Package is the result of many hours of work by licensed architects or professional designers.

QUALITY

Hundreds of hours of painstaking effort have gone into the development of your blueprint plan. Each home has been quality-checked by professionals to insure accuracy and buildability.

VALUE

Because we sell in volume, you can buy professional quality blueprints at a fraction of their development cost. With our plans, your dream home design costs substantially less than the fees charged by architects.

SERVICE

Once you've chosen your favorite home plan, you'll receive fast, efficient service whether you choose to mail or fax your order to us or call us toll free at 1-800-521-6797. After you have received your order, call for customer service toll free 1-888-690-1116.

SATISFACTION

Over 50 years of service to satisfied home plan buyers provide us unparalleled experience and knowledge in producing quality blueprints.

ORDER TOLL FREE 1-800-521-6797

After you've looked over our Blueprint Package and Important Extras, call toll free on our Blueprint Hotline: 1-800-521-6797, for current pricing and availability prior to mailing the order form on page 253. We're ready and eager to serve you. After you have received your order, call for customer service toll free 1-888-690-1116.

Each set of blueprints is an interrelated collection of detail sheets which includes components such as floor plans, interior and exterior elevations, dimensions, cross-sections, diagrams and notations. These sheets show exactly how your house is to be built.

SETS MAY INCLUDE:

FRONTAL SHEET

This artist's sketch of the exterior of the house gives you an idea of how the house will look when built and landscaped. Large floor plans show all levels of the house and provide an overview of your new home's livability, as well as a handy reference for deciding on furniture placement.

FOUNDATION PLANS

This sheet shows the foundation layout including support walls, excavated and unexcavated areas, if any, and foundation notes. If slab construction rather than basement, the plan shows footings and details for a monolithic slab. This page, or another in the set, may include a sample plot plan for locating your house on a building site.

DETAILED FLOOR PLANS

These plans show the layout of each floor of the house. Rooms and interior spaces are carefully dimensioned and keys are given for cross-section details provided later in the plans. The positions of electrical outlets and switches are shown.

HOUSE CROSS-SECTIONS

Large-scale views show sections or cut-aways of the foundation, interior walls, exterior walls, floors, stairways and roof details. Additional cross-sections may show important changes in floor, ceiling or roof heights or the relationship of one level to another. Extremely valuable for construction, these sections show exactly how the various parts of the house fit together.

INTERIOR ELEVATIONS

Many of our drawings show the design and placement of kitchen and bathroom cabinets, laundry areas, fireplaces, bookcases and other built-ins. Little "extras," such as mantelpiece and wainscoting drawings, plus molding sections, provide details that give your home that custom touch.

EXTERIOR ELEVATIONS

These drawings show the front, rear and sides of your house and give necessary notes on exterior materials and finishes. Particular attention is given to cornice detail, brick and stone accents or other finish items that make your home unique.

INTRODUCING IMPORTANT PLANNING AND CONSTRUCTION
AIDS DEVELOPED BY OUR PROFESSIONALS TO HELP YOU
SUCCEED IN YOUR HOME-BUILDING PROJECT

MATERIALS LIST

(Note: Because of the diversity of local building codes, our Materials List does not include mechanical materials.)

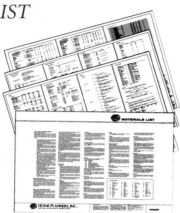

For many of the designs in our portfolio, we offer a customized materials take-off that is invaluable in planning and estimating the cost of your new home. This Materials List outlines the quantity, type and size of materials needed to build your house (with the exception of mechanical system items). Included are framing lumber, windows and doors, kitchen and bath cabinetry, rough and finish hardware, and much more. This handy list helps you or your builder cost out materials and serves as a reference sheet when you're compiling bids. Some Materials Lists may be ordered before blueprints are ordered, call for information.

SPECIFICATION OUTLINE

This valuable 16-page document is critical to building your house correctly. Designed to be filled in by you or your builder, this book lists 166 stages or items crucial to the building process. It provides a comprehensive review of the construction process and helps in choosing materials. When combined with the blueprints, a signed contract, and a schedule, it becomes a legal document and record for the building of your home.

QUOTE ONE®

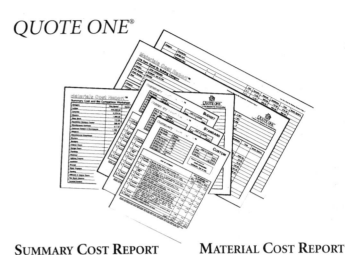

SUMMARY COST REPORT   **MATERIAL COST REPORT**

A product for estimating the cost of building select designs, the Quote One® system is available in two separate stages: The Summary Cost Report and the Material Cost Report.

The **Summary Cost Report** is the first stage in the package and shows the total cost per square foot for your chosen home in your zip-code area and then breaks that cost down into various categories showing the costs for building materials, labor and installation. The report includes three grades: Budget, Standard and Custom. These reports allow you to evaluate your building budget and compare the costs of building a variety of homes in your area.

Make even more informed decisions about your home-building project with the second phase of our package, our **Material Cost Report.** This tool is invaluable in planning and estimating the cost of your new home. The material and installation (labor and equipment) cost is shown for each of over 1,000 line items provided in the Materials List (Standard grade), which is included when you purchase this estimating tool. It allows you to determine building costs for your specific zip-code area and for your chosen home design. Space is allowed for additional estimates from contractors and subcontractors, such as for mechanical materials, which are not included in our packages. This invaluable tool includes a Materials List. A Material Cost Report cannot be ordered before blueprints are ordered. Call for details. In addition, ask about our Home Planners Estimating Package.

If you are interested in a plan that is not indicated as Quote One®, please call and ask our sales reps. They will be happy to verify the status for you. To order these invaluable reports, use the order form.

CONSTRUCTION INFORMATION

If you want to know more about techniques— and deal more confidently with subcontractors — we offer these useful sheets. Each set is an excellent tool that will add to your understanding of these technical subjects. These helpful details provide general construction information and are not specific to any single plan.

PLUMBING

The Blueprint Package includes locations for all the plumbing fixtures, including sinks, lavatories, tubs, showers, toilets, laundry trays and water heaters. However, if you want to know more about the complete plumbing system, these Plumbing Details will prove very useful. Prepared to meet requirements of the National Plumbing Code, these fact-filled sheets give general information on pipe schedules, fittings, sump-pump details, water-softener hookups, septic system details and much more. Sheets also include a glossary of terms.

ELECTRICAL

The locations for every electrical switch, plug and outlet are shown in your Blueprint Package. However, these Electrical Details go further to take the mystery out of household electrical systems. Prepared to meet requirements of the National Electrical Code, these comprehensive drawings come packed with helpful information, including wire sizing, switch-installation schematics, cable-routing details, appliance wattage, doorbell hook-ups, typical service panel circuitry and much more. A glossary of terms is also included.

CONSTRUCTION

The Blueprint Package contains information an experienced builder needs to construct a particular house. However, it doesn't show all the ways that houses can be built, nor does it explain alternate construction methods. To help you understand how your house will be built—and offer additional techniques—this set of Construction Details depicts the materials and methods used to build foundations, fireplaces, walls, floors and roofs. Where appropriate, the drawings show acceptable alternatives.

MECHANICAL

These Mechanical Details contain fundamental principles and useful data that will help you make informed decisions and communicate with subcontractors about heating and cooling systems. Drawings contain instructions and samples that allow you to make simple load calculations, and preliminary sizing and costing analysis. Covered are the most commonly used systems from heat pumps to solar fuel systems. The package is filled with illustrations and diagrams to help you visualize components and how they relate to one another.

THE HANDS-ON HOME FURNITURE PLANNER

Effectively plan the space in your home using The **Hands-On Home Furniture Planner**. It's fun and easy—no more moving heavy pieces of furniture to see how the room will go together. And you can try different layouts, moving furniture at a whim.

The kit includes reusable peel and stick furniture templates that fit onto a 12" x 18" laminated layout board—space enough to layout every room in your home.

Also included in the package are a number of helpful planning tools. You'll receive:

✓ Helpful hints and solutions for difficult situations.
✓ Furniture planning basics to get you started.
✓ Furniture planning secrets that let you in on some of the tricks of professional designers.

The **Hands-On Home Furniture Planner** is the one tool that no new homeowner or home remodeler should be without. It's also a perfect housewarming gift!

To Order, Call Toll Free
1-800-521-6797

After you've looked over our Blueprint Package and Important Extras on these pages, call for current pricing and availability prior to mailing the order form. We're ready and eager to serve you. After you have received your order, call for customer service toll free 1-888-690-1116.

THE DECK BLUEPRINT PACKAGE

Many of the homes in this book can be enhanced with a professionally designed Home Planners Deck Plan. Those homes marked with a **D** have a complementary Deck Plan, sold separately, which includes a Deck Plan Frontal Sheet, Deck Framing and Floor Plans, Deck Elevations and a Deck Materials List. A Standard Deck Details Package, also available, provides all the how-to information necessary for building *any* deck. Our Complete Deck Building Package contains one set of Custom Deck Plans of your choice, plus one set of Standard Deck Building Details, all for one low price. Our plans and details are carefully prepared in an easy-to-understand format that will guide you through every stage of your deck-building project. This page shows a sample Deck layout to match your favorite house. See Blueprint Price Schedule for ordering information.

THE LANDSCAPE BLUEPRINT PACKAGE

For the homes marked with an **L** in this book, Home Planners has created a front-yard Landscape Plan that is complementary in design to the house plan. These comprehensive blueprint packages include a Frontal Sheet, Plan View, Regionalized Plant & Materials List, a sheet on Planting and Maintaining Your Landscape, Zone Maps and Plant Size and Description Guide. These plans will help you achieve professional results, adding value and enjoyment to your property for years to come. Each set of blueprints is a full 18" x 24" in size with clear, complete instructions and easy-to-read type. A sample Landscape Plan is shown below. See Blueprint Price Schedule for ordering information.

CONTEMPORARY LEISURE DECK
Deck ODA021

CAPE COD COTTAGE
Landscape OLA003

REGIONAL ORDER MAP

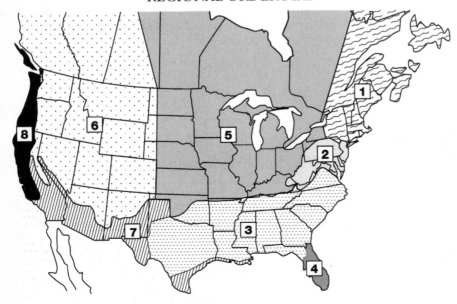

Most Landscape Plans are available with a Plant & Materials List adapted by horticultural experts to 8 different regions of the country. Please specify the Geographic Region when ordering your plan. See Blueprint Price Schedule for ordering information and regional availability.

Region	1	Northeast
Region	2	Mid-Atlantic
Region	3	Deep South
Region	4	Florida & Gulf Coast
Region	5	Midwest
Region	6	Rocky Mountains
Region	7	Southern California & Desert Southwest
Region	8	Northern California & Pacific Northwest

BLUEPRINT PRICE SCHEDULE

Prices guaranteed through December 31, 2003

TIERS	1-SET STUDY PACKAGE	4-SET BUILDING PACKAGE	8-SET BUILDING PACKAGE	1-SET REPRODUCIBLE*
P1	$20	$50	$90	$140
P2	$40	$70	$110	$160
P3	$70	$100	$140	$190
P4	$100	$130	$170	$220
P5	$140	$170	$210	$270
P6	$180	$210	$250	$310
A1	$440	$480	$520	$660
A2	$480	$520	$560	$720
A3	$530	$575	$615	$800
A4	$575	$620	$660	$870
C1	$620	$665	$710	$935
C2	$670	$715	$760	$1000
C3	$715	$760	$805	$1075
C4	$765	$810	$855	$1150
L1	$870	$925	$975	$1300
L2	$945	$1000	$1050	$1420
L3	$1050	$1105	$1155	$1575
L4	$1155	$1210	$1260	$1735
SQ1				.35/sq. ft.

* Requires a fax number

OPTIONS FOR PLANS IN TIERS A1–L4

Additional Identical Blueprints
in same order for "A1–L4" price plans ....$50 per set
Reverse Blueprints (mirror image)
with 4- or 8-set order for "A1–L4" plans ....$50 fee per order
Specification Outlines ....$10 each
Materials Lists for "A1–C3" plans ....$60 each
Materials Lists for "C4–SQ1" plans ....$70 each

IMPORTANT NOTES

- SQ one-set building package includes one set of reproducible vellum construction drawings plus one set of study blueprints.
- The 1-set study package is marked "not for construction."
- Prices for 4- or 8-set Building Packages honored only at time of original order.
- Some foundations carry a $225 surcharge.
- Right-reading reverse blueprints, if available, will incur a $165 surcharge.
- Additional identical blueprints may be purchased within 60 days of original order.

TO USE THE INDEX,

refer to the design number listed in numerical order (a helpful page reference is also given). Note the price tier and refer to the Blueprint Price Schedule above for the cost of one, four or eight sets of blueprints or the cost of a reproducible drawing. Additional prices are shown for identical and reverse blueprint sets, as well as a very useful Materials List for some of the plans. Also note in the Plan Index those plans that have Deck Plans or Landscape Plans. Refer to the schedules above for prices of these plans. The letter "Y" identifies plans that are part of our Quote One® estimating service and those that offer Materials Lists.

TO ORDER,

Call toll free 1-800-521-6797 for current pricing and availability prior to mailing the order form. FAX: 1-800-224-6699 or 520-544-3086.

OPTIONS FOR PLANS IN TIERS P1–P6

Additional Identical Blueprints
in same order for "P1–P6" price plans ....$10 per set
Reverse Blueprints (mirror image) for "P1–P6" price plans ....$10 fee per order
1 Set of Deck Construction Details...$14.95 each
Deck Construction Package ....**add $10 to Building Package price**
(includes 1 set of "P1–P6" plans, plus
1 set Standard Deck Construction Details)

PLAN INDEX

DESIGN	PRICE	PAGE	MATERIALS LIST	QUOTE ONE*	DECK	DECK PRICE	LANDSCAPE	LANDSCAPE PRICE	REGIONS
HPT900001	L1	5							
HPT900002	C1	6		Y					
HPT900003	C2	7							
HPT900004	A4	8							
HPT900005	SQ1	9							
HPT900006	SQ1	10							
HPT900007	A3	11							
HPT900008	A4	12							
HPT900009	C1	17							
HPT900010	C1	13							
HPT900011	C2	20							
HPT900012	C4	15							
HPT900013	C3	121		Y					
HPT900014	C3	14							
HPT900015	A2	19		Y					
HPT900016	L1	16							
HPT900017	C1	21		Y					
HPT900018	A4	18							
HPT900019	C1	22							
HPT900020	A4	23							
HPT900021	A4	24		Y					
HPT900022	A3	25		Y					

PLAN INDEX

DESIGN	PRICE	PAGE	MATERIALS LIST	QUOTE ONE®	DECK	DECK PRICE	LANDSCAPE	LANDSCAPE PRICE	REGIONS
HPT900023	A4	25							
HPT900024	A4	26	Y						
HPT900025	C1	27							
HPT900026	C1	28							
HPT900027	C1	28							
HPT900028	A4	29	Y						
HPT900029	C1	29	Y						
HPT900030	C3	30							
HPT900031	C1	30	Y						
HPT900033	C2	31	Y						
HPT900034	A4	32	Y						
HPT900035	C1	33							
HPT900036	C4	34							
HPT900037	C3	34							
HPT900038	C2	35							
HPT900039	C2	35							
HPT900040	C1	36							
HPT900041	C2	36							
HPT900042	C2	37							
HPT900043	C1	37							
HPT900044	C1	38							
HPT900045	C3	38							
HPT900046	C3	39							
HPT900047	A4	39							
HPT900048	C3	40							
HPT900049	C3	41							
HPT900050	C2	42							
HPT900051	C3	42							
HPT900052	A3	43							
HPT900053	A2	43							
HPT900054	A3	44							
HPT900055	A3	45							
HPT900056	A2	46							
HPT900057	A3	46							
HPT900058	A4	47							
HPT900059	A3	47	Y						
HPT900060	A2	48							
HPT900061	A3	49	Y						
HPT900062	A3	50	Y						
HPT900063	A4	51	Y						
HPT900064	C2	52							
HPT900065	L2	53							
HPT900066	A3	54							
HPT900067	L1	54							
HPT900068	C1	55							
HPT900069	C2	55							
HPT900070	SQ1	56							
HPT900071	C1	57	Y						
HPT900072	A4	58							
HPT900073	C2	59	Y						
HPT900074	A4	59	Y						
HPT900075	A3	60	Y						
HPT900076	A4	60	Y						
HPT900077	A4	61							
HPT900078	C1	62	Y						
HPT900079	C2	63	Y						
HPT900080	A3	64	Y						
HPT900081	SQ1	64							
HPT900082	C1	65							
HPT900083	C1	65	Y						
HPT900084	A2	66							
HPT900085	A2	66	Y						
HPT900086	C1	67							
HPT900087	A3	67							
HPT900088	A2	68							
HPT900089	A2	68							
HPT900090	A2	69							
HPT900091	A2	69							
HPT900092	A3	70							
HPT900093	A1	71	Y						
HPT900094	A2	72	Y						
HPT900095	A2	72							
HPT900096	A2	73	Y						
HPT900097	A3	73							
HPT900098	A3	74	Y						
HPT900099	C1	75	Y						
HPT900100	C1	76	Y						
HPT900101	C3	77							
HPT900102	C2	78	Y						
HPT900103	C3	79	Y						
HPT900104	C3	80							
HPT900105	C3	81							
HPT900106	C1	81	Y						
HPT900107	C1	82	Y						
HPT900108	A3	82							
HPT900109	C2	83							
HPT900110	C1	84							
HPT900111	A4	85							
HPT900112	C3	85							
HPT900113	C1	86	Y						
HPT900114	C4	86							
HPT900115	C2	87	Y						
HPT900116	C3	88							
HPT900117	C4	88							
HPT900118	C1	89							
HPT900119	C1	90							
HPT900120	A3	91	Y						
HPT900121	C1	92	Y						
HPT900122	A4	92	Y						
HPT900123	A4	93	Y						
HPT900124	C1	94							
HPT900125	C2	94							
HPT900126	A3	95							
HPT900127	C2	95							
HPT900128	C3	96	Y						
HPT900129	A3	97							
HPT900130	A4	98	Y						
HPT900131	C1	98	Y						
HPT900132	A4	99	Y						
HPT900133	C1	100	Y						
HPT900134	C1	101							
HPT900135	C1	101							
HPT900136	A4	102							
HPT900137	C1	103							
HPT900138	C2	104							
HPT900139	A3	104							
HPT900140	A4	105							
HPT900141	A4	106							
HPT900142	C1	106							
HPT900143	C1	107	Y						
HPT900144	C1	108	Y						
HPT900145	A4	109	Y						
HPT900146	A4	109	Y						
HPT900147	A2	110	Y						
HPT900148	C1	111	Y						
HPT900149	A3	111							
HPT900150	A2	112	Y						
HPT900151	A2	112	Y						
HPT900152	A2	113	Y						
HPT900153	A3	113	Y						
HPT900154	A3	114							
HPT900155	A3	114							
HPT900156	A2	115							
HPT900157	A2	115							
HPT900158	A2	116							
HPT900159	C2	117							
HPT900160	C1	118							
HPT900161	C2	119							
HPT900162	C1	119							
HPT900163	C3	120							
HPT900164	C4	121							
HPT900165	C1	122							
HPT900166	A4	122	Y						
HPT900167	L1	123							
HPT900168	A4	124	Y						
HPT900169	C2	124	Y						
HPT900170	C1	125	Y						
HPT900171	A4	126							
HPT900172	C1	127	Y						
HPT900173	A4	127							
HPT900174	C2	128							
HPT900175	A4	129							

TO ORDER BLUEPRINTS CALL TOLL FREE 1-800-521-6797

DESIGN	PRICE	PAGE	MATERIALS LIST	QUOTE ONE	DECK	DECK PRICE	LANDSCAPE	LANDSCAPE PRICE	REGIONS
HPT900176	C2	130	Y						
HPT900177	C1	131							
HPT900178	C1	131							
HPT900179	C1	132							
HPT900180	A4	133							
HPT900181	C1	134							
HPT900182	C3	134							
HPT900183	C1	135	Y						
HPT900184	A4	136	Y						
HPT900185	C1	136							
HPT900186	C1	137	Y						
HPT900187	A3	138							
HPT900188	A3	139							
HPT900189	A3	139							
HPT900190	A4	140	Y						
HPT900191	A4	141	Y						
HPT900192	A3	142							
HPT900193	AE	142							
HPT900194	A3	143	Y						
HPT900195	A3	143	Y						
HPT900196	A4	144	Y						
HPT900197	A4	145	Y						
HPT900198	C1	146							
HPT900199	C1	146							
HPT900200	C3	147							
HPT900201	A3	148	Y						
HPT900202	A4	149							
HPT900203	A4	150							
HPT900204	C2	151							
HPT900205	C3	152							
HPT900206	C2	153	Y						
HPT900207	C3	154							
HPT900208	A2	154							
HPT900209	A4	155							
HPT900210	C2	156							
HPT900211	C2	157							
HPT900212	C2	157							
HPT900213	C2	158							
HPT900214	C2	159							
HPT900215	C2	159							
HPT900216	C3	160							
HPT900217	C3	160							
HPT900218	C3	161							
HPT900219	C1	162							
HPT900220	C3	163							
HPT900221	C2	163							
HPT900222	C1	164							
HPT900223	C1	165	Y						
HPT900224	C2	166							
HPT900225	C2	167							
HPT900226	A3	167							
HPT900227	L2	168							
HPT900228	L2	169							
HPT900229	C1	170							
HPT900230	L2	170							
HPT900231	L2	171							
HPT900232	L2	172							
HPT900233	L2	172							
HPT900234	C3	173							
HPT900235	L2	174							
HPT900236	C3	174							
HPT900237	L2	175							
HPT900238	L1	176							
HPT900239	C2	176							
HPT900240	C2	177	Y						
HPT900241	C2	178							
HPT900242	C3	179							
HPT900243	L3	180							
HPT900244	C2	181							
HPT900245	C4	182							
HPT900246	C1	182							
HPT900247	C4	183							
HPT900248	C1	184							
HPT900249	A4	184							
HPT900250	C3	185							
HPT900251	C3	186							
HPT900252	C1	187							
HPT900253	C1	187							
HPT900254	C1	188							
HPT900255	C1	188							
HPT900256	C1	189							
HPT900257	C2	190							
HPT900258	C1	190							
HPT900259	C1	191							
HPT900260	C2	192							
HPT900261	SQ1	193							
HPT900262	C1	194	Y						
HPT900263	C3	194							
HPT900264	C2	195							
HPT900265	A2	195							
HPT900266	C3	196	Y						
HPT900267	C1	197							
HPT900268	A3	197							
HPT900269	A4	198							
HPT900270	C1	199							
HPT900271	C1	199							
HPT900272	C4	200							
HPT900273	C1	201							
HPT900274	C2	201							
HPT900275	C3	202							
HPT900276	C2	202							
HPT900277	SQ1	203							
HPT900278	C4	204							
HPT900279	C2	204							
HPT900280	C4	205							
HPT900281	C4	206							
HPT900282	L1	207							
HPT900283	L2	208							
HPT900284	L2	208							
HPT900285	L2	209							
HPT900286	L1	210							
HPT900287	L2	211							
HPT900288	C2	212							
HPT900289	C2	213							
HPT900290	C1	214							
HPT900291	C1	215	Y						
HPT900292	C1	215	Y						
HPT900293	C2	216							
HPT900294	C4	217	Y						
HPT900295	C4	218							
HPT900296	SQ1	219							
HPT900297	C2	220							
HPT900298	C3	221							
HPT900299	L1	221							
HPT900300	L1	222							
HPT900301	L1	223							
HPT900302	A4	224							
HPT900303	A4	224							
HPT900304	C3	225							
HPT900305	C3	226							
HPT900306	L1	227							
HPT900307	C3	228							
HPT900308	L2	228							
HPT900309	L2	229							
HPT900310	L1	230							
HPT900311	L2	230							
HPT900312	C1	231	Y						
HPT900313	L2	232	Y						
HPT900314	C1	232	Y						
HPT900315	C2	233	Y						
HPT900316	C2	234	Y						
HPT900317	C4	235	Y						
HPT900318	A4	236							
HPT900319	SQ1	237							
HPT900320	C1	238							
HPT900321	C2	239							
HPT900322	C3	240	Y						
HPT900323	C3	241	Y						
HPT900324	A4	242	Y						
HPT900325	A4	243							

BEFORE FILLING OUT THE ORDER FORM, PLEASE CALL US ON OUR TOLL-FREE BLUEPRINT HOTLINE 1-800-521-6797. YOU MAY WANT TO LEARN MORE ABOUT OUR SERVICES AND PRODUCTS. HERE'S SOME INFORMATION YOU WILL FIND HELPFUL.

OUR EXCHANGE POLICY

With the exception of reproducible plan orders, we will exchange your entire first order for an equal or greater number of blueprints within our plan collection within 90 days of the original order. The entire content of your original order must be returned before an exchange will be processed. Please call our customer service department for your return authorization number and shipping instructions. If the returned blueprints look used, redlined or copied, we will not honor your exchange. Fees for exchanging your blueprints are as follows: 20% of the amount of the original order...plus the difference in cost if exchanging for a design in a higher price bracket or less the difference in cost if exchanging for a design in a lower price bracket. (**Reproducible blueprints are not exchangeable or refundable.**) Please call for current postage and handling prices. Shipping and handling charges are not refundable.

ABOUT REPRODUCIBLES

When purchasing a reproducible you may be required to furnish a fax number. The designer will fax documents that you must sign and return to them before shipping will take place.

ABOUT REVERSE BLUEPRINTS

Although lettering and dimensions will appear backward, reverses will be a useful aid if you decide to flop the plan. See Price Schedule and Plans Index for pricing.

REVISING, MODIFYING AND CUSTOMIZING PLANS

Like many homeowners who buy these plans, you and your builder, architect or engineer may want to make changes to them. We recommend purchase of a reproducible plan for any changes made by your builder, licensed architect or engineer. As set forth below, we cannot assume any responsibility for blueprints which have been changed, whether by you, your builder or by professionals selected by you or referred to you by us, because such individuals are outside our supervision and control.

ARCHITECTURAL AND ENGINEERING SEALS

Some cities and states are now requiring that a licensed architect or engineer review and "seal" a blueprint, or officially approve it, prior to construction due to concerns over energy costs, safety and other factors. Prior to application for a building permit or the start of actual construction, we strongly advise that you consult your local building official who can tell you if such a review is required.

ABOUT THE DESIGNS

The architects and designers whose work appears in this publication are among America's leading residential designers. Each plan was designed to meet the requirements of a nationally recognized model building code in effect at the time and place the plan was drawn. Because national building codes change from time to time, plans may not comply with any such code at the time they are sold to a customer. In addition, building officials may not accept these plans as final construction documents of record as the plans may need to be modified and additional drawings and details added to suit local conditions and requirements. We strongly advise that purchasers consult a licensed architect or engineer, and their local building official, before starting any construction related to these plans.

LOCAL BUILDING CODES AND ZONING REQUIREMENTS

At the time of creation, our plans are drawn to specifications published by the Building Officials and Code Administrators (BOCA) International, Inc.; the Southern Building Code Congress (SBCCI) International, Inc.; the International Conference of Building Officials (ICBO); or the Council of American Building Officials (CABO). Our plans are designed to meet or exceed national building standards. Because of the great differences in geography and climate throughout the United States and Canada, each state, county and municipality has its own building codes, zone requirements, ordinances and building regulations. Your plan may need to be modified to comply with local requirements regarding snow loads, energy codes, soil and seismic conditions and a wide range of other matters. In addition, you may need to obtain permits or inspections from local governments before and in the course of construction. Prior to using blueprints ordered from us, we strongly advise that you consult a licensed architect or engineer—and speak with your local building official—before applying for any permit or beginning construction. We authorize the use of our blueprints on the express condition that you strictly comply with all local building codes, zoning requirements and other applicable laws, regulations, ordinances and requirements. Notice: Plans for homes to be built in Nevada must be re-drawn by a Nevada-registered professional. Consult your building official for more information on this subject.

TOLL FREE 1-800-521-6797

REGULAR OFFICE HOURS:
8:00 a.m.-9:00 p.m. EST, Monday-Friday

If we receive your order by 3:00 p.m. EST, Monday-Friday, we'll process it and ship within **two business days**. When ordering by phone, please have your credit card or check information ready. We'll also ask you for the Order Form Key Number at the bottom of the order form.

By FAX: Copy the Order Form on the next page and send it on our FAX line: 1-800-224-6699 or 520-544-3086.

**Canadian Customers
Order Toll Free 1-877-223-6389**

DISCLAIMER

The designers we work with have put substantial care and effort into the creation of their blueprints. However, because they cannot provide on-site consultation, supervision and control over actual construction, and because of the great variance in local building requirements, building practices and soil, seismic, weather and other conditions, WE CANNOT MAKE ANY WARRANTY, EXPRESS OR IMPLIED, WITH RESPECT TO THE CONTENT OR USE OF THE BLUEPRINTS, INCLUDING BUT NOT LIMITED TO ANY WARRANTY OF MERCHANTABILITY OR OF FITNESS FOR A PARTICULAR PURPOSE. **ITEMS, PRICES, TERMS AND CONDITIONS ARE SUBJECT TO CHANGE WITHOUT NOTICE. REPRODUCIBLE PLAN ORDERS MAY REQUIRE A CUSTOMER'S SIGNED RELEASE BEFORE SHIPPING.**

TERMS AND CONDITIONS

These designs are protected under the terms of United States Copyright Law and may not be copied or reproduced in any way, by any means, unless you have purchased Reproducibles which clearly indicate your right to copy or reproduce. We authorize the use of your chosen design as an aid in the construction of one single family home only. You may not use this design to build a second or multiple dwellings without purchasing another blueprint or blueprints or paying additional design fees.

HOW MANY BLUEPRINTS DO YOU NEED?

Although a standard building package may satisfy many states, cities and counties, some plans may require certain changes. For your convenience, we have developed a Reproducible plan which allows a local professional to modify and make up to 10 copies of your revised plan. As our plans are all copyright protected, with your purchase of the Reproducible, we will supply you with a Copyright release letter. The number of copies you may need: 1 for owner; 3 for builder; 2 for local building department and 1-3 sets for your mortgage lender.

ORDER TOLL FREE!

**For information about
any of our services
or to order call
1-800-521-6797**

**Browse our website:
www.eplans.com**

**BLUEPRINTS ARE
NOT REFUNDABLE
EXCHANGES ONLY**

**For Customer Service,
call toll free
1-888-690-1116.**

HOME PLANNERS, LLC wholly owned by Hanley-Wood, LLC
3275 WEST INA ROAD, SUITE 220 • TUCSON, ARIZONA • 85741

THE BASIC BLUEPRINT PACKAGE

Rush me the following (please refer to the Plans Index and Price Schedule in this section):

___Set(s) of reproducibles*, plan number(s) _____ $_____
indicate foundation type_____ surcharge (if applicable): $_____
___Set(s) of blueprints, plan number(s) _____ indicate foundation type _____
indicate foundation type_____ surcharge (if applicable): $_____
___Additional identical blueprints (standard or reverse) in same order @ $50 per set $_____
___Reverse blueprints @ $50 fee per order. Right-reading reverse @ $165 surcharge $_____

IMPORTANT EXTRAS

Rush me the following:

___Materials List: $60 (Must be purchased with Blueprint set.) Add $10 for Schedule C4–SQ1 plans $_____
___**Quote One**® Summary Cost Report @ $29.95 for one, $14.95 for each additional,
for plans _____. $_____
Building location: City _____ Zip Code _____
___**Quote One**® Material Cost Report @ $120 Schedules P1–C3; $130 Schedules C4–SQ1,
for plan _____(Must be purchased with Blueprints set.) $_____
Building location: City _____ Zip Code _____
___Specification Outlines @ $10 each $_____
___Detail Sets @ $14.95 each; any two $22.95; any three $29.95; all four for $39.95 (save $19.85) $_____
___❑ Plumbing ❑ Electrical ❑ Construction ❑ Mechanical
___Home Furniture Planner @ $15.95 each $_____

DECK BLUEPRINTS

(Please refer to the Plans Index and Price Schedule in this section)

___Set(s) of Deck Plan _____ $_____
___Additional identical blueprints in same order @ $10 per set. $_____
___Reverse blueprints @ $10 fee per order. $_____
___Set of Standard Deck Details @ $14.95 per set. $_____
___Set of Complete Deck Construction Package (Best Buy!) Add $10 to Building Package.
Includes Custom Deck Plan _____ Plus Standard Deck Details

LANDSCAPE BLUEPRINTS

(Please refer to the Plans Index and Price Schedule in this section.)

___Set(s) of Landscape Plan _____ $_____
___Additional identical blueprints in same order @ $10 per set $_____
___Reverse blueprints @ $10 fee per order $_____
Please indicate appropriate region of the country for Plant & Material List. Region _____

POSTAGE AND HANDLING _SIGNATURE IS REQUIRED FOR ALL DELIVERIES._	1–3 sets	4+ sets
DELIVERY
No CODs (Requires street address—No P.O. Boxes)		
•Regular Service (Allow 7–10 business days delivery)	❑ $20.00	❑ $25.00
•Priority (Allow 4–5 business days delivery)	❑ $25.00	❑ $35.00
•Express (Allow 3 business days delivery)	❑ $35.00	❑ $45.00
OVERSEAS DELIVERY	fax, phone or mail for quote	

Note: All delivery times are from date Blueprint Package is shipped.

POSTAGE (From box above) $_____
SUBTOTAL $_____
SALES TAX (AZ & MI residents, please add appropriate state and local sales tax.) $_____
TOTAL (Subtotal and tax) $_____

YOUR ADDRESS (please print legibly)

Name _____

Street _____

City_____State _____Zip _____

Daytime telephone number (required) (_____) _____

* Fax number (required for reproducible orders) _____
TeleCheck® Checks By Phone℠ available

FOR CREDIT CARD ORDERS ONLY

Credit card number _____ Exp. Date: (M/Y) _____

Check one ❑ Visa ❑ MasterCard ❑ American Express

Order Form Key

HPT90

Signature (required)_____

Please check appropriate box: ❑ Licensed Builder-Contractor ❑ Homeowner

ORDER TOLL FREE!
1-800-521-6797

BY FAX: Copy the order form above and send it on
our FAXLINE: 1-800-224-6699 OR 520-544-3086

1 BIGGEST & BEST

1001 of our best-selling plans in one volume. 1,074 to 7,275 square feet. 704 pgs $12.95 1K1

2 ONE-STORY

450 designs for all lifestyles. 800 to 4,900 square feet. 384 pgs $9.95 OS

3 MORE ONE-STORY

475 superb one-level plans from 800 to 5,000 square feet. 448 pgs $9.95 MO2

4 TWO-STORY

443 designs for one-and-a-half and two stories. 1,500 to 6,000 square feet. 448 pgs $9.95 TS

5 VACATION

430 designs for recreation, retirement and leisure. 448 pgs $9.95 VS3

6 HILLSIDE

208 designs for split-levels, bi-levels, multi-levels and walk-outs. 224 pgs $9.95 HH

7 FARMHOUSE

300 Fresh Designs from Classic to Modern. 320 pgs. $10.95 FCP

8 COUNTRY HOUSES

208 unique home plans that combine traditional style and modern livability. 224 pgs $9.95 CN

9 BUDGET-SMART

200 efficient plans from 7 top designers, that you can really afford to build! 224 pgs $8.95 BS

10 BARRIER-FREE

Over 1,700 products and 51 plans for accessible living. 128 pgs $15.95 UH

11 ENCYCLOPEDIA

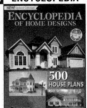

500 exceptional plans for all styles and budgets—the best book of its kind! 528 pgs $9.95 ENC

12 ENCYCLOPEDIA II

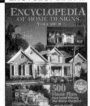

500 completely new plans. Spacious and stylish designs for every budget and taste. 352 pgs $9.95 E2

13 AFFORDABLE

300 Modest plans for savvy homebuyers.256 pgs. $9.95 AH2

14 VICTORIAN

210 striking Victorian and Farmhouse designs from today's top designers. 224 pgs $15.95 VDH2

15 ESTATE

Dream big! Eighteen designers showcase their biggest and best plans. 224 pgs $16.95 EDH3

16 LUXURY

170 lavish designs, over 50% brand-new plans added to a most elegant collection. 192 pgs $12.95 LD3

17 EUROPEAN STYLES

200 homes with a unique flair of the Old World. 224 pgs $15.95 EURO

18 COUNTRY CLASSICS

Donald Gardner's 101 best Country and Traditional home plans. 192 pgs $17.95 DAG

19 COUNTRY

85 Charming Designs from American Home Gallery. 160 pgs. $17.95 CTY

20 TRADITIONAL

85 timeless designs from the Design Traditions Library. 160 pgs $17.95 TRA

21 COTTAGES

245 Delightful retreats from 825 to 3,500 square feet. 256 pgs. $10.95 COOL

22 CABINS TO VILLAS

Enchanting Homes for Mountain Sea or Sun, from the Sater collection. 144 pgs $19.95 CCV

23 CONTEMPORARY

The most complete and imaginative collection of contemporary designs available anywhere. 256 pgs. $10.95 CM2

24 FRENCH COUNTRY

Live every day in the French countryside using these plans, landscapes and interiors. 192 pgs. $14.95 PN

25 SOUTHERN

207 homes rich in Southern styling and comfort. 240 pgs $8.95 SH

26 SOUTHWESTERN

138 designs that capture the spirit of the Southwest. 144 pgs $10.95 SW

27 SHINGLE-STYLE

155 Home plans from Classic Colonials to Breezy Bungalows. 192 pgs. $12.95 SNG

28 NEIGHBORHOOD

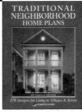

170 designs with the feel of main street America. 192 pgs $12.95 TND

29 CRAFTSMAN

170 Home plans in the Craftsman and Bungalow style. 192 pgs $12.95 CC

30 GRAND VISTAS

200 Homes with a View. 224 pgs. $10.95 GV

31 DUPLEX & TOWNHOMES

115 Duplex, Multiplex &
Townhome Designs. 128 pgs.
$17.95 MFH

32 WATERFRONT

200 designs perfect for your
waterside wonderland.
208 pgs $10.95 WF

33 NATURAL LIGHT

223 Sunny home plans for all
regions. 240 pgs. $8.95 NA

34 NOSTALGIA

100 Time-Honored designs
updated with today's features.
224 pgs. $14.95 NOS

35 STREET OF DREAMS

Over 300 photos showcase
54 prestigious homes.
256 pgs $19.95 SOD

36 NARROW-LOT

250 Designs for houses
17' to 50' wide. 256 pgs.
$9.95 NL2

37 SMALL HOUSES

Innovative plans for
sensible lifestyles.
224 pgs. $8.95 SM2

38 GARDENS & MORE

225 gardens, landscapes,
decks and more to
enhance every home.
320 pgs. $19.95 GLP

39 EASY-CARE

41 special landscapes
designed for beauty and
low maintenance.
160 pgs $14.95 ECL

40 BACKYARDS

40 designs focused solely on
creating your own specially
themed backyard oasis. 160
pgs $14.95 BYL

41 BEDS & BORDERS

40 Professional designs
for do-it-yourselfers
160 pgs. $14.95 BB

42 BUYER'S GUIDE

A comprehensive look at 2700
products for all aspects of
landscaping & gardening.
128 pgs $19.95 LPBG

LANDSCAPE DESIGNS

43 OUTDOOR

74 easy-to-build designs,
lets you create and build
your own backyard oasis.
128 pgs $9.95 YG2

44 GARAGES

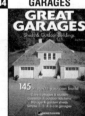

145 exciting projects from
64 to 1,900 square feet.
160 pgs. $9.95 GG2

45 DECKS

A brand new collection
of 120 beautiful and
practical decks. 144 pgs.
$9.95 DP2

46 HOME BUILDING

Everything you need to know
to work with contractors and
subcontractors. 212 pgs
$14.95 HBP

47 RURAL BUILDING

Everything you need to know
to build your home in the
country. 232 pgs.
$14.95 BYC

48 VACATION HOMES

Your complete guide to
building your vacation
home. 224 pgs.
$14.95 BYV

PROJECT GUIDES

Book Order Form

To order your books, just check the box of the book numbered below and complete the coupon. We will process your order and ship it from our office within two business days. Send coupon and check (in U.S. funds).

YES! Please send me the books I've indicated:

❏ 1:1K1.........$12.95	❏ 17:EURO ...$15.95	❏ 33:NA $8.95
❏ 2:OS $9.95	❏ 18:DAG.....$17.95	❏ 34:NOS.....$14.95
❏ 3:MO2 ....$9.95	❏ 19:CTY $17.95	❏ 35:SOD.....$19.95
❏ 4:TS.............$9.95	❏ 20:TRA $17.95	❏ 36:NL2 ....$9.95
❏ 5:VS3............$9.95	❏ 21:COOL...$10.95	❏ 37:SM2 ....$8.95
❏ 6:HH $9.95	❏ 22:CCV $19.95	❏ 38:GLP $19.95
❏ 7:FCP $10.95	❏ 23:CM2 ....$10.95	❏ 39:ECL.....$14.95
❏ 8:CN $9.95	❏ 24:PN $14.95	❏ 40:BYL $14.95
❏ 9:BS $8.95	❏ 25:SH $8.95	❏ 41:BB $14.95
❏ 10:UH $15.95	❏ 26:SW $10.95	❏ 42:LPBG $19.95
❏ 11:ENC $9.95	❏ 27:SNG $12.95	❏ 43:YG2 ....$9.95
❏ 12:E2 ....$9.95	❏ 28:TND $12.95	❏ 44:GG2 ....$9.95
❏ 13:AH2 ....$9.95	❏ 29:CC $12.95	❏ 45:DP2 ....$9.95
❏ 14:VDH2....$15.95	❏ 30:GV $10.95	❏ 46:HBP $14.95
❏ 15:EDH3....$16.95	❏ 31:MFH $17.95	❏ 47:BYC $14.95
❏ 16:LD3 .....$12.95	❏ 32:WF $10.95	❏ 48:BYV $14.95

Books Subtotal	$_____
ADD Postage and Handling (allow 4–6 weeks for delivery)	$ 4.00
Sales Tax: (AZ & MI residents, add state and local sales tax.)	$_____
YOUR TOTAL (Subtotal, Postage/Handling, Tax)	$_____

YOUR ADDRESS (PLEASE PRINT)

Name_____

Street _____

City _____ State_____ Zip _____

Phone (_____) _____ — _____

YOUR PAYMENT

TeleCheck® Checks By Phone℠ available

Check one: ❏ Check ❏ Visa ❏ MasterCard ❏ American Express
Required credit card information:

Credit Card Number_____

Expiration Date (Month/Year) _____ / _____

Signature Required _____

Canadian Customers Order Toll Free 1-877-223-6389

Home Planners, LLC
3275 W. Ina Road, Suite 220, Dept. BK, Tucson, AZ 85741

HPT90

TO ORDER BLUEPRINTS CALL TOLL FREE 1-800-521-6797

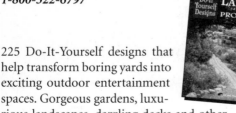